BACHMAN'S BOOK OF FREEDOM QUOTATIONS

Edited by MICHAEL IVENS and REGINALD DUNSTAN

Bachman & Turner
London

Bachman & Turner
5 Plough Place
Fetter Lane
London EC4A 1LD

ISBN 0 85974 068 4

First published 1978

CONTENTS

INTRODUCTION

There will always be a need for a book of Freedom Quotations — though each generation will give it a different emphasis. We have compiled this first book, of what we hope will be many editions, for pleasure, for reflection, for use in speeches and articles, for humour and for glimpses of mankind at its best and worst.

The pursuit of Freedom and its quotations has led the editors across a very wide landscape indeed. Obviously to politics and power, to art, to sex, to religion, to law, property, revolution, resistance and exile. It has inevitably led to philosophy — because how can there be freedom if there is no free will? It has particular implications for women, for men, for children, for minorities, for animals. It has contradictions and conflicts, between licence and liberty, between freedom and peace and — as de Tocqueville had often pointed out — between freedom and equality.

There are sections on its betrayers, its persecutors, and those who fear freedom.

The editors have ranged across time and space in their choice of speakers and writers. They include novelists, politicians and economists, philosophers, wits and worriers, revolutionaries and saints, poets and pedants, commissars and comics.

The book provides many morals — not least that freedom cannot be taken for granted, that it must be argued and worked and, if necessary, fought for.

Reginald Dunstan, that saint and stoic among editors, has borne the brunt of assembling and putting into order the gleaming catches from many strange seas. Josef Josten, that walking symbol of freedom (despite the disclosure by Mr Joseph Frolik, a former Soviet Bloc intelligence agent, that three attempts were planned to put him out of this world), has persuaded many prominent people to suggest some of their own quotations. Among the distinguished contributors is the Duke of Edinburgh. My son Martin, on this occasion demonstrating the virtues of enlightened nepotism, did much of the research en route to St Peter's College, Oxford; and Pam King has typed and assembled the text.

We thank those many publishers who gave their permission to use material; they are recorded at the end of this book.

Michael Ivens

Affirmations

LORD ACTON
Liberty is the delicate fruit of a ripe civilisation.

ANON
From a Parliament that's wild, and a people that's tame.
(*A Free Parliament Litany*)

From Long knives, Long ears, Long Parliaments, and Long Pray'rs
In mercy to this Nation — Deliver us and our heirs.
From Fools and Knaves, in our Parliament free,
Libera nos, Domine!
(*A Free Parliament Litany*)

ARATOR
For ever art thou free.
(*Revised by Alcuin (trans. Helen Waddell; More Latin Lyrics, Virgil to Milton)*)

ARISTOTLE
Liberty appears to flourish in democracies.

JOHN BARBOUR
A! fredome is a noble thing!
Fredome mahse man to haiff liking.
Fredome al solace to man giffs;
He levys at eas that frely levys.
(*The Bruce*)

ERNEST BECKER
The only secure truth men have is that which they themselves create and dramatise; to live is to play at the meaning of life.
(*The Denial of Death*)

The urge to cosmic heroism, then, is sacred and mysterious and not to be neatly ordered and rationalised by science and secularism.
(*The Denial of Death*)

CLIVE BELL

Only reason can convince us of those three fundamental truths without a recognition of which there can be no effective liberty: that what we believe is not necessarily true; that what we like is not necessarily good; and that all questions are open.
(*Civilization*)

ISAIAH BERLIN

Liberty is liberty, not equality or fairness or justice or human happiness or a quiet conscience.
(*Two Concepts of Liberty*)

JOHN BIGGS-DAVISON

We need nothing less than a constitutional counter-revolution of Liberty, Inequality (without the right to be different there is no liberty) and Responsibility — responsibility and wider ownership for individuals. for families and for workers.
(*Address to Paddington CPC, July 19, 1976*)

BILL OF RIGHTS (1791)

Excessive bail shall not be required, nor excessive fines imposed, nor cruel and unusual punishments inflicted.

W. L. BOWLES

The cause of Freedom is the cause of God!
(*Edmund Burke*)

NORMAN O. BROWN

What the great world needs, of course, is a little more Eros and less strife; but the intellectual world needs it just as much.
(*Life Against Death*)

ROBERT BROWNING

But, thanks to wine-lees and democracy,
We've still our stage where truth calls spade a spade!
(*Aristophanes' Apology*)

WILLIAM JENNINGS BRYAN

You shall not press down upon the brow of labour this crown of thorns, you shall not crucify mankind upon a cross of gold.
(*Speech at the National Democratic Convention, Chicago, 1896*)

MARTIN BUBER

If the globe is not to burst asunder, every man must be given what he needs for a really human life.
(*The National Home and Our Policy in Palestine*)

It is important also that there should be a possibility of meditation, of contemplation. There should be enough space around a man so that his individuality can remain intact. If the density does not allow a man to look at his comrade, to have some perspective, he will not be able to acquire any relation to him. And then the fact that they follow the same cause will not be enough to avert a poverty in human bonds.
(*Encounter with Martin Buber, Aubrey Hodes*)

RUDOLF BULTMANN

In fact, philosophy does know of faith, knows it just because it knows of the questionability which is an essential part of its freedom.
(*Faith and Understanding*)

Freedom is promised to the possessor of this faith-knowledge. From what? From the world, from sham ''reality'', from both its seductiveness and its open enmity.
(*The Theology of the New Testament*)

EDMUND BURKE

All government, indeed every human benefit and enjoyment, every virtue and every prudent act, is founded on compromise and barter.
(*Speech on conciliation with America, 1775*)

Abstract liberty, like other mere abstractions, is not to be found.
(*Speech on conciliation with America, 1775*)

LORD BYRON

I wish men to be free
As much from mobs as kings — from you as me.
(*Don Juan*)

ALBERT CAMUS

The only conception of freedom I can have is that of the prisoner or the individual in the midst of the State. The only one I know is freedom of thought and action. Now if the absurd cancels all my chances of eternal freedom, it restores and magnifies on the other my freedom of action. That privation of hope and future means an increase in man's availability.
(*The Myth of Sisyphus*)

JIMMY CARTER
Our nation can be strong abroad only if it is strong at home, and we know that the best way to enhance freedom in the other lands is to demonstrate here that our democratic system is worthy of emulation.
(*Inaugural speech, January 20, 1977*)

HARTLEY COLERIDGE
But what is Freedom? Rightly understood,
A universal licence to be good.
(*Liberty*)

WILLIAM HENRY DAVIES
What is this life if, full of care,
We have no time to stand and stare.
(*Leisure*)

JOHN DONNE
But thinke that Death hath now enfranchis'd thee,
Thou has thy expansion now, and libertie.
(*Of the Progress of the Soul: the Second Anniversaries*)

As thou
Are Jealous, Lord, so I am jealous now,
Thou lov'st not, till from loving more, thou free
My soul: whoever gives, takes liberty . . .
(*Hymn to Christ, at the author's last going into Germany*)

FYODOR DOSTOYEVSKY
People laugh at obedience, prayer, and fasting, and yet it is through them that the way lies to real, true freedom.
(*Father Zossimov in The Brothers Karamazov*)

JOHN S. DUNNE
The fully meaningful life is the unconditionally acceptable life, so that when a man goes in quest of a fully meaningful life he is in quest of unconditional acceptance.
(*A Search for God in Time and Memory*)

It could still be, nevertheless, that it is necessary for the modern man to descend into hell before he can emerge from it.
(*A Search for God in Time and Memory*)

As long as man hopes to escape death, he is enslaved by his fear of it. When he gives up hope, on the other hand, he frees himself from its sovereignty.
(*A Search for God in Time and Memory*)

HAVELOCK ELLIS
On the threshold of the moral world we meet the idea of Freedom, "one of the weightiest conceptions man has ever formed," once a dogma, in course of time a hypothesis, now in the eyes of many a fiction, yet we cannot do without it, even although we may be firmly convinced that our acts are determined by laws that cannot be broken.
(*The Dance of Life*)

BÁRÓ JOSEF EÖTVÖS
The only road that leads to the solution of the nationality question in our homeland must be sought in the absolute safe-guarding of individual freedom.
(*Osszes Munkai*)

MILTON FRIEDMAN
In a free society, a government has no business using the power of the law or the taxpayers' money to propagandize for some views and to prevent the transmission of others . . . Freedom of speech is for the listener as well as the speaker — to enable him to make his own choice among as wide an assortment of views as his fellows are inclined, for whatever reason, to set forth.
(*Newsweek, June 16, 1969*)

There is all the difference in the world between the more fortunate among us giving of our substance in order to establish a minimum standard below which no disadvantaged person or child shall be forced to live, and trying to legislate uniformity of condition. The difference is between freedom and slavery.
(*Homogenized Schools, Newsweek, February 28, 1972*)

JOHN KENNETH GALBRAITH
An angry god may have endowed capitalism with inherent contradictions. But at least as an afterthought he was kind enough to make social reform surprisingly consistent with improved operation of the system.
(*The Great Crash 1929*)

WILLIAM GERHARDIE

We are unhappy because we do not seek how our happiness can end; whereas what we really fail to see is that unhappiness cannot last, since even a continuance of the same conditions will bring about a change of attitude, a change of mood. For the same reason happiness does not last. To live up to this knowledge is given to few; yet to achieve this double victory over disillusion and illusion, which between them prey upon our liberty, no more is asked than a suspension of belief in the impossible.
(*Of Mortal Love*)

PIETER GEYL

The plot of National Socialism had had an ending that we may count as a striking proof of the West's powers of resistance and recovery.
(*Encounters in History*)

JULIAN GREEN

To know everything no longer interests me. To know everything is a young man's dream. What interests me passionately today is to understand, and I no longer wish to know except for the sake of understanding more clearly.
(*Diary 1928-1957*)

JORGE GUILLÉN

Death is no more than the last dictate of life itself.
(*Cántico*)

F. A. HAYEK

Freedom necessarily means that many things will be done which we do not like. Our faith in freedom does not rest on the foreseable results in particular circumstances but in the belief that it will, on balance, release more forces for the good than the bad.
(*Constitution of Liberty*)

There is nothing in the basic principles of liberalism to make it a stationary creed.
(*The Road to Serfdom*)

As for most of us the time we spend at our work is a large part of our whole lives, and as our job usually determines the place where and the people among whom we live, some freedom in choosing our work is, probably, even more important for our happiness than freedom to spend our income during the hours of leisure.
(*The Road to Serfdom*)

HELSINKI — CONFERENCE ON SECURITY & CO-OPERATION IN EUROPE

The participating States will promote and encourage the effective exercise of civil, political, economic, social, cultural and other rights and freedoms all of which derive from the inherent dignity of the human person and are essential for his free and full development.
(*Signatories include the USSR and eastern bloc*)

HERMANN HESSE

Is it a calamity to have been born into fresh, stormy, blustering times? Isn't it your good fortune?
(*Zarathustra's Return: A word to German Youth, 1919; If the War Goes On*)

THOMAS HOBBES

The measure of liberty must be calculated after the well-being of the citizens and of the State.

JOHAN HUIZINGA

The play-concept as such is of a higher order than is seriousness. For seriousness seeks to exclude play, whereas play can very well include seriousness.
(*Homo Ludens*)

JOHN OF SALISBURY

Whoever he be that is willing to suffer for his faith, whether he be little lad or man grown, Jew or Gentile, Christian or Infidel, man or woman, it matters not at all; who dies for justice dies a martyr, a defender of the cause of Christ.
(*Letters*)

SAMUEL JOHNSON

They make a rout about *universal* liberty, without considering that all that is to be valued, or indeed can be enjoyed by individuals, is *private* liberty. Political liberty is good only so far as it produces private liberty.
(*"Sir," said Dr Johnson; arranged by H. C. Biron*)

C. G. JUNG

From the middle of life onwards only he remains vitally alive who is ready to *die with life*. For in the secret hour of life's midday the parabola is reversed, death is born. The second half of life does not signify ascent, unfolding, increase, exuberance, but death, since the end is its goal. The negation of life's fulfilment is synonymous with the refusal to accept its ending. Both mean not wanting to live, and not wanting to live is identical with not wanting to die. Waxing and waning make one curve.
(*The Soul and Death from Collected Works*)

The spiritual adventure of our time is the exposure of human consciousness to the undefined and the indefinable.
(*Psychology and Religion: West and East*)

JUNIUS

The right of election is the very essence of the constitution.
(*Letter 11, 1796*)

IMMANUEL KANT

If there is any science man really needs it is the one I teach, of how to occupy properly that place in creation that is assigned to man, and how to learn from it what one must be in order to be a man.

HANS KELSEN

Democracy by its very nature means freedom.
(*The Pure Theory of Law*)

JOHN F. KENNEDY

In free society art is not a weapon . . . Artists are not engineers of the soul.
(*Address at Dedication of the Robert Frost Library, November 1963*)

JOHN MAYNARD KEYNES

If a partisan or a child wants a silly or harmful thing it may be better to meet him with a silly harmful thing than with explanations he cannot understand. This is the traditional wisdom of statesmen and nursery-maids.

PAVEL KOHOUT

Co-operation and security in Europe can be offered and guaranteed only by those who first offer and guarantee security and co-operation to their own citizens.
(*Prominent Czech writer, persecuted for his adherence to Dubcek's "Communism with a human face", quoted by Religion in Communist Dominated Areas, USA, no. 7/9, 1976*).

VLADIMIR ILYITCH LENIN

Morality is that which serves to destroy the old exploiting society.
(*Speech before the Party Court*)

ANTHONY LESTER

I don't believe that the basic rights and liberties of the citizen are or should be seen as political questions.
(*November 1976*)

FATHER PETER LEVI

What makes a man profound is liberty.
(*Christmas Sermon from Death is a Pulpit*)

LEVITICUS

Proclaim liberty throughout the land unto all the inhabitants thereof.

ABRAHAM LINCOLN

I intend no modification of my oft-expressed personal wish that all men everywhere could be free.
(*Letter, August 22, 1862*)

. . . we here highly resolve that the dead shall not have died in vain, that this nation, under God, shall have a new birth of freedom; and that government of the people, by the people, and for the people, shall not perish from the earth.
(*Address at Dedication of National Cemetery at Gettysburg, November 19, 1863*)

J. LOCKE

The liberty of Man in society is to be under no other legislative power but that established by consent in the commonwealth; nor under the dominion of any rule or restraint of the law, but what the legislative shall enact according to the trust put in it.
(*Two Treatises on Civil Government*)

MARTIN LUTHER

Here I stand. I cannot do otherwise. God help me. Amen.

ROSA LUXEMBURG
Freedom only for the supporters of the Government, only for the members of one party — however numerous thay may be — is no freedom at all. Freedom is always and exclusively freedom for the one who thinks differently.

MAGNA CARTA
No freeman shall be taken or imprisoned or disseised (i.e. deprived of his lands) or in any way destroyed, nor will we go upon him nor put upon him, except by the lawful judgement of his peers or the law of the land.

MAO TSE-TUNG
Letting a hundred flowers blossom and a hundred schools of thought contend is the policy for promoting the progress of the arts and the sciences and a flourishing socialist culture in our land.
(*Broken Promises?*)

HERBERT MARCUSE
Men can die without anxiety if they know what they love is protected from misery and oblivion.
(*Eros and Civilisation*)

MASAS MARUYAMA
The extent to which politics can become the object of free scientific enquiry is a most accurate barometer by which to measure the degree of academic freedom in any country.
(*Thought and Behaviour in Modern Japanese Politics*)

HERMANN MELVILLE
Close! stand close to me, Starbuck; let me look into a human eye; it is better than to gaze into sea or sky; better than to gaze upon God. By the green land; by the bright hearthstone! this is the magic glass, man; I see my wife and my child in thine eye.
(*Moby Dick*)

JOHN STUART MILL
If we would know whether or not it is desirable that a proposition should be believed, is it possible to exclude the consideration of whether or not it is true?
(*On Liberty*)

All free communities have both been more exempt from social injustice and crime, and have attained more brilliant prosperity, than any others, or than they themselves after they have lost their freedom.
(*Representative Government*)

Liberty, of conscience, which above all things ought to be to all men most dearest and most precious, no government more inclinable not to favour only, but to protect than a free commonwealth.
(*To Establish a Free Commonwealth*)

BASIL MITCHELL
The liberal wants the initial position to be that the balance is already tilted in favour of freedom, so that whoever would intervene must produce on his side of the balance a heavier weight. It is not enough just to produce any weight however small.
(*Law, Morality and Religion*)

ROBERT OWEN
I will die an Englishman in exile, or an Englishman in England free.

BORIS PASTERNAK
It is not revolutions and upheavals
That clear the road to new and better days,
But revelations, lavishness and torments
Of someone's soul, inspired and ablaze.
(*After the Storm; trans. Lydia Pasternak Slater; from Fifty Poems*)

Nothing is more spurious than outer freedom if one lacks inner freedom.

JOHN PEYTON
It is time that those who believe in a free society proclaimed its merits to others, who not being familiar with the grey horrors of a Soviet system, might be led into thinking that it would offer something better than they now have.
(*Daily Telegraph, March 12, 1977*)

KARL POPPER
We must plan for freedom, and not only for security, if for no other reason than that only freedom can make security secure.
(*The Open Society and its Enemies*)

JOHN POULSON
Freedom I now realise is something to be treasured.
(*Evening Standard, May 13, 1977*)

PIERRE JOSEPH PROUDHON
Liberty — the mother not the daughter of order.

FRANKLIN D. ROOSEVELT
A world founded upon four essential freedoms. The first is freedom of speech and expression — everywhere in the world. The second is freedom of every person to worship God in his own way — everywhere in the world. The third is freedom from want . . . everywhere in the world. The fourth is freedom from fear . . . anywhere in the world.
(*Speech, January 6, 1941*)

ST JOHN
Everyone who acts sinfully is a slave of sin, and the slave cannot make his home in the house for ever . . . Why then, if it is the Son who makes you free men, you will have freedom in earnest.
(*The New Testament*)

If you continue faithful to my word, you are my disciples in earnest, so you will come to know the truth, and the truth will see you free.
(*The New Testament*)

(Jesus) . . . "and you will know the truth, and the truth will make you *free*." They answered him, "We are descendants of Abraham, and have never been in bondage to anyone. How is it that you say. 'you will be made free'?" Jesus answered them, "Truly, truly, I say to you everyone who commits sin is a *slave* to sin. The slave does not continue in the house for ever; the son continues for ever. So if the Son makes you free, you will be free indeed."
(*The New Testament*)

The truth shall make you free.
(*The New Testament*)

ST PAUL
Not that we have dominion over your faith, but are keepers of your joy.
(*Corinthians; The New Testament*)

SAYINGS OF THE FATHERS
Whom do men honour?
The man who honours his fellow men.

FRIEDRICH von SCHILLER

Man is created free and is free, even though born in chains.
(*Die Wörte des Glaubens*)

All the arts of pleasure grow when suckled by freedom.
(*Der Spazlergang*)

Free will I live, and as freely die.
(*Wallenstein's Lager*)

WILLIAM SHAKESPEARE

Brutus: Let's all cry, "Peace, freedom, and liberty!"
(*Julius Caesar*)

PERCY BYSSHE SHELLEY

The glorious joy of thy name — Liberty!
(*The Revolt of Islam*)

To suffer woes which hope thinks infinite;
To forgive wrongs darker than death or night;
To defy power, which seems omnipotent;
To love, and bear; to hope till hope creates
From its own wreck the thing it contemplates;
Neither to change, not falter, nor repent;
This, like thy glory, Titan, is to be
Good, great and joyous, beautiful and free;
This is alone life, joy, empire, and victory.
(*Prometheus Unbound*)

JAMES STEPHENS

. . . every thing must come from Liberty into the Bondage, that it may
return again to the Liberty.
(*The Crock of Gold*)

As hated husband and hateful wife,
Who must suffer till they see
Love is crowned by liberty.
(*Mount Derision from The Hill of Vision*)

FRANZ-JOSEF STRAUSS

It is not our task as politicians to make out prescriptions of other
people's happiness against their will. That would be the end of
freedom.
(*Speech in Augsburg, May 15, 1976*)

MICHAEL SWANN

Freedom of speech is not just freedom to express one's view in a newspaper or on the air; it is freedom also to speak one's mind to friends or neighbours, to write letters, and to circulate what one has written; all things that are dangerous, to say the least, in authoritarian countries.

(*Lecture, Are The Lamps Going Out?; BBC*)

TIBOR SZAMUELY

We have become accustomed to the idea that Britain no longer counts. This is untrue. From the point of view of freedom Britain matters a great deal — the very idea of freedom is, for anyone in any country of the world, inalienably tied to Britain.

(*Communism and Freedom*)

ALEXIS DE TOCQUEVILLE

I should have loved freedom, I believe, at all times, but in the time in which we live I am ready to worship it.

Nothing is more fertile in prodigies than the art of being free; but there is nothing more arduous than the apprenticeship of liberty . . . Liberty is generally established with difficulty in the midst of storms; it is perfected by civil discords; and its benefit cannot be appreciated until it is already old.

(*Democracy in America*)

UNIVERSAL DECLARATION OF HUMAN RIGHTS (1948)

Everyone has the right to freedom of peaceful assembly and association.

No one may be compelled to belong to an association.

All human beings are born free and equal in dignity and rights. They are endowed with reason and conscience and should act towards one another in a spirit of brotherhood.

Everyone has the right to own property alone as well as in association with others . . . No one shall be arbitrarily deprived of his property . . . Everyone has the right to freedom of thought, conscience and religion . . . Everyone has the right to freedom of opinion and expression; this right includes freedom to hold opinions without interference and to seek, receive and impart information and ideas through any media and regardless of frontiers . . . Everyone has the right to take part in the government of his country, directly or through freely chosen representatives . . . The will of the people shall be the basis of the authority of government; this will shall be expressed in periodic and genuine elections which shall be by universal and equal suffrage and shall be held by secret vote or by equivalent free voting procedures.

GUISEPPA VACCA
Our (Italian Communist Party) fundamental aim is the development of individual freedoms; the plurality of parties both in power and in opposition and parliament must have a full role in the democratic transformation of our society.
(*Morning Star, November 1, 1976*)

HANS VAIHINGER
On the threshold of the moral world we meet the idea of Freedom, "one of the weightiest conceptions man has ever formed," once a dogma, in the course of time a hypothesis, now in the eyes of many a fiction, yet we cannot do without it, even although we may be firmly convinced that our acts are determined by laws that cannot be broken.
(*The Philosophy of "As If"*)

HELEN WADDELL
Tradition is for ever in the making. We are the heirs of it: but the capital is not ours to squander. Or rather, it is ours to squander: that is the danger and the challenge. Justice, the freedom of the press, religious and political tolerance, humanity, charity, these things were not lightly won, nor are they lightly maintained.
(*More Latin Lyrics, from Virgil to Milton*)

GRAHAM WALLAS
Freedom is the opportunity for continuous initiative.

VERNON WATKINS
Verse tests the very marrow in the bone,
Yet man, being once engaged by song, is freed:
The act itself is prayer, deliberate in its speed.
(*The Interval; from Affinities*)

A. N. WHITEHEAD
When we think of freedom we are apt to confine ourselves to freedom of thought, freedom of the press, freedom of religious opinion . . . This is a thorough mistake . . . In fact freedom of action is the primary need.
(*Adventure of Ideas*)

WILLIAM WORDSWORTH
Two voices are there; one is of the sea,
One of the mountains; each a mighty voice;
In both from age to age thou didst rejoice,
They were thy chosen music, Liberty!
(*National Independence and Liberty*, *"On the Subjugation of Switzerland"*)

Betrayers

ALCUIN
Nor should we listen to those who say, "The voice of the people is the voice of God", for the turbulence of the mob is always close to insanity.
(*Epistolae, 166-9*)

COMMUNIST PARTY OF THE SOVIET UNION
Peaceful co-existence serves as the basis for peaceful competition between socialism and capitalism on an international scale, and constitutes a special form of class struggle between them.
(*Programme adopted at 22nd Congress, 1961*)

MALCOLM MUGGERIDGE
If there is one thing more unedifying than a ruling class in a position of dominance, it is a ruling class like ours on the run.
(*Jesus Rediscovered*)

GEORGE WILLIAM RUSSELL (A.E.)
In the lost boyhood of Judas
Christ was betrayed.
(*Germinal*)

WILLIAM SHAKESPEARE
Is it possible that he should know what he is, and be that he is?
(*All's Well That Ends Well*)

JAMES STEPHENS
"The idea of virtue," said the Philosopher, with some indignation, "has animated the noblest intellects of the world."

"It has not animated them," replied Pan; "it has hypnotised them so that they have conceived virtue as repression and self-sacrifice as an honourable thing instead of the suicide which it is."
(*The Crock of Gold*)

23

PERCY BYSSHE SHELLEY
To meet his pensioned Parliament.
(*The Mask of Anarchy*)

Flattering the thing they feared.
(*Prometheus Unbound*)

A Bundle of Contradictions

LORD ACTON
The finest opportunity ever given to the world was thrown away because the passion for equality made vain the hope for freedom.

H. AGAR
The truth that makes men free is for the most part the truth which men prefer not to hear.
(*A Time for Greatness*)

GEORGE BARKER
"Only the truly unhappy are at liberty," said Magog, "to step blindfold off the pavement harmlessly into the line of advancing hordes of statistics which prove this cannot be done with complete impunity by any save suicides."

J. M. BARRIE
His lordship may compel us to be equal upstairs, but there will never be equality in the servants' hall.
(*The Admirable Crichton*)

ERNEST BECKER
The critique of guru therapies also comes to rest here: you can't talk about an ideal of freedom in the same breath that you willingly give it up.
(*The Denial of Death*)

EDUARD BENES
It should be stressed that in their actions against democracies the totalitarian regimes were always offensive and were consistent in their mutual support; the democratic regimes were not consistent in this respect and at critical moments in their difficult fight they deserted and betrayed each other.

NICHOLAS BERDYAEV
Utopias now appear to be much more realisable than we had previously thought. We find ourselves nowadays confronted with a question agonising in quite a different way: How can we avoid their final realisation?

MARTIN BUBER
Spirit and life have fallen apart from one another more radically perhaps than in any earlier time.
(*A Believing Humanism*)

EDMUND BURKE
Liberty, too, must be limited in order to be possessed.
(*Letter to the Sheriffs of Bristol*)

G. K. CHESTERTON
"There again," said Syme irritably, "what is there poetical about being in revolt? You might as well say that it is poetical to be seasick. Being sick is a revolt. Both being sick and being rebellious may be the wholesome thing on certain desperate occasions; but I'm hanged if I can see why they are poetical. Revolt in the abstract is — revolting. It's mere vomiting."
(*The Man who was Thursday*)

A progressive is always a conservative; he conserves the direction of progress. A reactionary is always a rebel.
(*Introduction to Carlyle's Past and Present*)

BRIAN CROZIER
It is widely assumed that there is little to choose between authoritarian and totalist governments; yet in one important sense, they are mutually antithetical. Authoritarian governments seek to abolish politics; totalist governments seek to involve the whole population in politics.

A. V. DICEY
Where the right to individual freedom is a right deduced from the principles of the constitution, the idea readily occurs that the right is capable of being suspended or taken away.

FYODOR DOSTOYEVSKY
There is nothing more alluring to man than this freedom of conscience, but there is also nothing more tormenting, either.
(*Ivan Karamazov's Grand Inquisitor in The Brothers Karamazov*)

JOHN S. DUNNE
The sense of a complete relativity of standpoints, however, a relativity such that no standpoint, fixed or shifting, is the true standpoint, seems characteristic of the twentieth century.
(*A Search for God in Time and Memory*)

Doubt carried to the limit will end in the doubt of doubt, despair likewise will end in the despair of despair.
(*A Search for God in Time and Memory*)

WILSON van DUSEN
Because of the limitations of our existence we are partially bound and partially free.
(*The Presence of Other Worlds*)

MIRCEA ELIADE
Everything depends upon what is meant by freedom.
(*Yoga, Immortality and freedom*)

DANIEL GEORGE
O Freedom, what liberties are taken in thy name!
(*The Perpetual Pessimist*)

JOHANN WOLFGANG von GOETHE
Law givers or revolutionaries who promise equality and liberty at the same time are either utopian dreamers or charlatans.

YVAN GOLL
He crosses the bridges of all the ages
The bridges of all contradictions
From the left bank to the right bank
From yes to no from just to unjust.
(*Jean Sans Terre*)

LORD HALIFAX
In the contest between ease and liberty, the first hath generally prevailed.

ELIE HALEVY
The Socialists believe in two things which are absolutely different and perhaps even contradictory: freedom and organisation.
(*Quoted by W. R. Inge in The End of an Age*)

F. A. HAYEK
There is perhaps nothing more disheartening than the fact that there are still so many intelligent and informed people who in most other respects will defend freedom and yet are induced by the immediate benefits of an expansionist policy to support what, in the long run, must destroy the foundations of a free society.
(*The Constitution of Liberty*)

The intellectual leaders in the movement for liberty have all too often confined their attention to those uses of liberty closest to their hearts, and have made little effort to comprehend those restrictions of liberty which did not directly affect them.
(*The Constitution of Liberty — Introduction*)

To the Socialists of All Parties.
(*Dedication of The Road to Serfdom*)

HERMANN HESSE
As long as a man is well off, he can afford to do superfluous and foolish things. When well-being gives way to affliction, life begins to educate us.
(*The Path of Love, December, 1918; If the War Goes On*)

ZBIGNIEW HERBERT
The predictions of poetry are incorrect
Everything happened differently,
The fire in the poem was one thing
A town in flames was another.

W. E. INGE
Christianity promises to make men free; it never promises to make them independent.
(*The Philosophy of Plotinus*)

MICHAEL IVENS
... the businessman is not always a paragon of imaginative sympathy. He may be strong on freedom for activity; he may, in contrast, be illiberal on social and sexual innovation, on dress, on new political views.
(*Pressures for Conformity, article in Patterns of Prejudice, Jan/Feb 1977*)

PAUL JOHNSON
Liberty is when I am allowed to defy Mr Scanlon.
(*BBC Television, August 9, 1977*)

SAMUEL JOHNSON
Your levellers wish to level down as far as themselves, but they cannot bear levelling up to themselves.
(*Letter to Lord Chesterfield*)

It is better that some should be unhappy, than that none should be happy, which would be the case in a general state of equality.

BERTRAND DE JOUVENEL
One of the strangest intellectual illusions of the nineteenth century was the idea that toleration could be ensured by moral relativism.

ARTHUR KOESTLER
Every major principle in Gandhi's Back-to-Nature philosophy was self-defeating, stamped with tragic irony. (Even as President of Congress, he always insisted on travelling third-class; but he had a special coach to himself.)
(*The Heel of Achilles: Mahatma Gandhi — Yogi and Commissar, a Re-valuation*)

MACHIAVELLI
For the great majority of mankind are satisfied with appearances, as though they were realities, and are often more influenced by things that seem than by those that are.
(*quoted by Malcolm Muggeridge in Jesus Rediscovered*)

MORRISON OF LAMBETH
The profound dilemma of modern Russia is how to ensure that production goes up and yet not yield too far on what by its very outlook it must regard as dangerous liberty for the individual.
(*An Autobiography*)

MALCOLM MUGGERIDGE
How I envy the historian who, like Gibbon, will look back across the centuries at the hilarious spectacle of Marxist-Christian dialogues attempting to find common ground between the brutal atheism of the Communist Manifesto and the Sermon on the Mount.
(*Jesus Rediscovered*)

Turn your minds for a moment to the unhappy plight of those so-called
Christian Socialists who identified the rise of the Labour Party with the
coming of Christ's kingdom. What must be their feelings today? Or
those others who saw in Soviet Communism the fulfilment of Christian
hopes — what must they feel as the full villainy of Stalin's regime
becomes manifest?
(*Jesus Rediscovered*)

FRIEDRICH NIETZSCHE
What has become perfect, all that is ripe — wants to die.

GEORGE ORWELL
War is Peace
Freedom is Slavery
Ignorance is Strength.
(*1984*)

DAVID OWEN
The price of championing human rights is a little inconsistency from
time to time.
(*Sayings of the Week in The Observer, April 3, 1977*)

PLATO
Freedom creates rather more drones in the democratic than there were
in the oligarchical state.
(*The Republic*)

J. B. PRIESTLEY
A lot of the English . . . have left behind the challenging rocks of
discipline by circumstance, yet cannot reach the shining plateau of
self-discipline, and their freedom only entangles them with whims and
fancies, silliness and self-indulgence.
(*Prescription for Our Time*)

OTTO RANK
Thus the plight of modern man: a sinner with no word for it, or,
worse, who looks for the word for it in a dictionary of psychology and
thus only aggravates the problem of his separateness and hyper-
consciousness.

It seems to be difficult for the individual to realise that there exists a division between one's spiritual and purely human needs, and that the satisfaction or fulfilment for each has to be found in different spheres. As a rule, we find the two aspects hopelessly confused in modern relationships, where one person is made the god-like judge over good and bad in the other person.

HERBERT READ
It does not seem that the contradiction which exists between the aristocratic function of art and the democratic structure of modern society can ever be resolved. But both may wear the cloak of humanism, the one for shelter, the other for disguise. The sensitive artist knows that a bitter wind is blowing.

JEAN-FRANÇOIS REVEL
It seems to be indispensable to the peace of soul of most people to believe that the most powerful country in the world is also the most reactionary. We must believe that, if we are to believe that the reactionary trends in our own countries are an offshoot of American imperialism.
(*Without Marx or Jesus*)

RAINER MARIA RILKE
If my devils are to leave me, I am afraid my angels will take flight as well.
(*Letter 74, Briefe aus den Jahren 1907 bis 1914*)

MAXIMILIAN ROBESPIERRE
The government of the Revolution is the despotism of liberty against tyranny.
(*French National Convention, February 5, 1794*)

MME ROLAND
O liberty, O liberty, what crimes are commited in your name!
(*On passing the statue of Liberty, on her way to the scaffold*)

MURRAY N. ROTHBARD
Socialism is neither genuinely radical nor truly revolutionary. Socialism is a reactionary reversion.

BERTRAND RUSSELL
A fanatical belief in democracy makes democratic institutions impossible.

GEORGE SAVILE, MARQUESS OF HALIFAX (1633-95)

In a limited monarchy, Prerogative and liberty are as jealous of one another as any two neighbouring states can be of their respective encroachments. They ought not to part for small bickerings, and must bear little jealousies without breaking them.
(*The Political, Moral and Miscellaneous Reflections*)

Power is so apt to be insolent, and liberty to be saucy, that they are very seldom upon good terms. They are both so quarrelsome that they will not easily enter into a fair treaty. For indeed it is hard to bring them together; they ever quarrel at a distance.
(*The Political, Moral and Miscellaneous Reflections*)

HUGH SCANLON

Liberty is conforming to the majority.
(*BBC Television, August 9, 1977*)

GEORGE BERNARD SHAW

Freedom incurs responsibility; that is why so many men fear it.
(*Maxims for Revolutionists*)

THORNE SMITH

He was an institutional sort of animal, but not morbid. Not apparently. So completely and successfully had he inhibited himself that he veritably believed he was the freest person in the world.
(*The Jovial Ghosts*)

HERBERT SPENCER

The ultimate result of shielding men from the effects of folly is to fill the world with fools.

FRANZ-JOSEF STRAUSS

Freedom is the great aspiration and incentive but also one of the bogus slogans which have driven humanity from the very beginning.
(*Article in Bayernkurier, April 13, 1977*)

ALEXIS de TOCQUEVILLE

I think that democratic communities have a natural taste for freedom; left to themselves, they will seek it, cherish it, and view any privation of it with regret. But for equality, their passion is ardent, insatiable, incessant, invincible: they call for equality in freedom; and if they cannot obtain that, they still call for equality in slavery. They will endure poverty, servitude, barbarism; but they will not endure aristocracy.

MARK TWAIN
It is by the goodness of God that we have in our country three unspeakably precious things: freedom of speech, freedom of conscience, and the prudence never to practise either.

A. N. WHITEHEAD
It must be admitted that there is a degree of instability which is inconsistent with civilisation. But, on the whole, the great ages have been unstable ages.
(*Science and the Modern World*)

Unfortunately the notion of freedom has been eviscerated by the literary treatment devoted to it. Men of letters, artists in symphonies of pictorial imagination, have staged the shock of novel thought against tradition. The concept of freedom has been narrowed to the picture of contemplative people shocking their generation. When we think of freedom, we are apt to confine ourselves to freedom of thought, freedom of the press, freedom of religious opinions. Then the limitations to freedom are conceived as wholly arising from the antagonisms of our fellow men. This is a thorough mistake.
(*Science and the Modern World*)

In formal logic, a contradication is the signal of a defeat: but in the evolution of real knowledge it marks the first step in progress towards a victory. This is one great reason for the utmost toleration of variety of opinion.
(*Science and the Modern World*)

OSCAR WILDE
Democracy means simply the bludgeoning of the people by the people for the people.
(*Soul of Man under Socialism*)

CHARLES WILLIAMS
It is inhuman, and with the inhuman there can be no treaty. This is the difficulty of toleration; it is also the objection to toleration.
(*The Descent of the Dove*)

For generally those who have wanted liberty have not apprehended dogma, and those who have apprehended dogma have not wanted liberty. Liberalism in religion and liberalism in politics are not the same thing, however often they are confused, by the friends and the enemies of either.
(*The Descent of the Dove*)

. . . toleration had to be a necessity before it could be a virtue.
(*The Descent of the Dove*)

GERARD WINSTANLEY
There are few who act for freedom, and the actors for freedom are oppressed by the talkers and verbal professors of freedom.
(*Law of Freedom, 1652*)

Children's Freedom

MARIE BONAPARTE
The days of the child seem to unfold in some sense outside of our time.
These days of childhood — let us each recall them — seem to the child
as if they were eternal . . . Of course the important persons who bring
up the child strictly impose the scheme of their time on him . . . but he
feels the imposition of adult time by adults as an alien intrusion into
his own time, which is essentially in some sense infinite.
(*Chronos, Eros, Thanatos*)

ANGELA CARTER
And, like all grown ups, they were quite sure they always knew what
was best.
(*The Infernal Desire Machines of Doctor Hoffman*)

WILLIAM HENRY DAVIES
Girls scream,
Boys shout;
Dogs bark,
School's out.
(*School's out*)

GRAHAM HUTTON
There is not much "freedom from care" in darkest Africa, or in the
South Sea islands, or anywhere else on earth, where children can
suddenly die of preventible diseases.
(*All Capitalists Now*)

SAMUEL JOHNSON
That lad looks like the son of a schoolmaster, which is one of the very
worst conditions of childhood.
(*"Sir," said Dr Johnson; arranged by H. C. Biron*)

35

SOREN KIERKEGAARD
In an external respect it is easy to perceive when the moment has arrived that one ought to let the child walk alone; . . . the art is to be constantly present and yet not be present, to let the child be allowed to develop itself, while nevertheless one has constantly a survey clearly before one.
(*Dread*)

FATHER PETER LEVI
I say God's freedom is born in this child.
(*Christmas Sermon from Death is a Pulpit*)

FRIEDRICH NIETZSCHE
What child has not had reason to weep over its parents?
(*Thus Spake Zarathustra*)

HERBERT READ
Never yield to habit, especially to habits of thought which polish away the rough edges of truth; remain open, innocent, original. Put away childish things, but retain, all the same, a core of childhood, a slender vein of vital sap, which the rings of growth may hide, but never destroy.
(*Introduction to The Tenth Muse*)

PERCY BYSSHE SHELLEY
But children near their parents tremble now,
Because they must obey.
(*The Revolt of Islam*)

JAMES STEPHENS
Every child knows that every grown female person in the world has authority to wash children and to give them food; that is what grown people were made for.
(*The Crock of Gold*)

WILLIAM WORDSWORTH
O Heavens! how awful is the might of Souls,
And what they do within themselves, while yet
The yoke of earth is new to them, the world
Nothing but a wild field where they were sown.
(*The Prelude — Residence at Cambridge*)

Destroyers, Despots and Dangers

JOHN QUINCY ADAMS
Despotism or unlimited sovereignty is the same in a majority of a popular assembly, an aristocratical council, an oligarchical junta, and a single emperor.

RICHARD ALDINGTON
I disbelieve in bunk and despotism, even in dictatorship of the intelligentsia.
(*Introduction to Death of a Hero*)

ANDREI AMALRIK
Marxism has placed its stake on force, which Marx called the midwife of history. And even though the midwife perpetually delivers monsters . . . Marxists never tire of promising that the next child will be a splendid one.
(*Observer, February 13, 1977 — on receiving the 1976 Human Rights Award*)

Unless the Western States — and in the first instance the USA — can summon up enough political will to withstand the USSR in Europe and try to influence Soviet internal liberalisation . . . France and Britain may one fine day find themselves in the position of Hungary or Czechoslovakia.
(*Europe and the Soviet Union*)

CHARLES BAUDELAIRE
Certain patches of base flattery aimed at democracy.
(*Preface to The Flowers of Evil*)

ERNEST BECKER
Modern man is drinking and drugging himself out of awareness, or he spends his time shopping, which is the same thing.
(*The Denial of Death*)

Only scapegoats can relieve one of his own stark death fear: "*I am threatened with death* — let us kill plentifully."
(*The Denial of Death*)

If repression makes an untenable life liveable, self-knowledge can entirely destroy it for some people.
(*The Denial of Death*)

The problem with all the scientific manipulators is that somehow they don't take life seriously enough; in this sense, all science is "bourgeois", an affair of bureaucrats.
(*The Denial of Death*)

MAX BEERBOHM
Humilité, Servilité, Lavalité.
(*letter to Helen Waddell, 1940*)

ANEURIN BEVAN
The Communist Party is the sworn inveterate enemy of the Socialist and Democratic Parties. When it associates with them, it does so as a preliminary to destroying them.
(*Introduction to "Curtain Falls"*)

Its relationship to democratic institutions is that of the death watch beetle — it (the Communist Party) is not a Party, it is a conspiracy.
(*Vincent Brome, "Aneurin Bevan"*)

WILLY BRANDT
The Berlin Wall forces the Soviets to admit that an imported government by coercion provides no platform stable enough for carrying on true political competition and economic co-existence with the West.
(*The Ordeal of Co-existence*)

LEONID BREZHNEV
For it is clear as can be that detente and peaceful co-existence relate to inter-state relations. Detente in no way rescinds, or can rescind, the laws of the class struggle.
(*Congress of Communist Party of Soviet Union, February 24, 1976*)

SAMUEL BRITTAN
The danger signal for the unwarranted expansion of the political sphere is provided by the word "society" in conjunction with "modern society", "society will not tolerate", "social needs" and similar phrases and slogans.

A. MOELLER VAN DEN BRUCK
All anti-liberal forces are combining against everything that is liberal.

MARTIN BUBER

An effective stand may be taken in the form of non-violence against unfeeling human beings in the hope of gradually bringing them thereby to their senses; but a diabolical steamroller cannot thus be withstood.
(*letter to Gandhi*)

JAKOB BURCKHARDT

Terrorism is essentially the rage of literati in its last stage.

EDMUND BURKE

Among a people generally corrupt, liberty cannot long exist.
(*Letter to the Sheriffs of Bristol*)

The concessions of the weak are the concessions of fear.
(*Speech on Conciliation with America, 1775*)

Dangers by being despised grow great.
(*Speech on the Petition of the Unitarians, 1792*)

He that wrestles with us strengthens our nerves, and sharpens our skill. Our antagonist is our helper.
(*Reflections on the Revolution in France*)

To innovate is not to reform.
(*A Letter to a Noble Lord, 1796*)

ROBERT F. BYRNES

To present conflict between the states established on Lenin's ideas and those of Jefferson is also a struggle between power and freedom. The concentration camp and the Berlin Wall, the open library and the travelling scholar are its appropriate symbols.
(*Soviet-American Academic Exchange (Survey Magazine)*)

GUSTAV CASSEL

The arbitrariness, the mistakes and the inevitable contradictions of such policy (the Planned Economy) will, as daily experience shows, only strengthen the demand for a more rational co-ordination of the different measures and, therefore, for unified leadership. For this reason the Planned Economy will always tend to descend into Dictatorship.
(*From Protectionism Through Planned Economy to Dictatorship*)

CHRISTOPHER CAUDWELL
In a society which is based on co-operation, not on compulsion, and which is conscious, not ignorant, of necessity, desires as well as cognitions can be socially manipulated as part of the social process.
(*Concept of Freedom*)

WINSTON S. CHURCHILL
We do not wish the people of this ancient island reduced to a mass of State-directed proletariats, thrown hither and thither, housed here and there, by an aristocracy of privileged officials or privileged party, sectarian or trade union bosses.

ANTHONY CROSLAND
Marx has little or nothing to offer the contemporary socialist, either in respect of practical policy, or of the correct analysis of our society, or even of the right conceptual tools or framework. His prophecies have been almost without exception falsified, and his conceptual tools are now quite inappropriate.

MARQUIS DE CUSTINE
In Russia fear replaces, that is, paralyses thought.
(*The Empire of the Czar*)

DANIEL DEFOE
Nature has left this tincture in the blood,
That all men would be tyrants if they could.
(*The Kentish Petition*)

DEMOCRATS OF RUSSIA, THE UKRAINE AND THE BALTIC REGION
The Socialism established in Russia and her satellites has undermined the position of man in society by limiting or depriving him of property, of rights and of power — i.e. of all the blessings which alone enable man to maintain his being and uphold his position in the world. It has brought with it the denial of human liberties — at times reaching the stage of State slavery — and, even of a modest prosperity, lagging far behind most capitalist countries, despite the vast sacrifices and intensive effort of 200 million people in the richest country in the world.
(*Programme of the Democratic Movement of the Soviet Union, 1969*)

MILOVAN DJILAS

Throughout history there have been no ideal ends which were attained with non-ideal, inhumane means, just as there has been no free society built by slaves. Nothing so well reveals the reality and greatness of ends as the methods used to attain them.
(*The New Class*)

Tyranny over the mind is the most complete and most brutal type of tyranny: every other tyranny begins and ends with it.
(*The New Class*)

Despotisms, even when they are opposing ones, justify themselves in the same way: they cannot even avoid the same words in doing so.
(*The New Class*)

Persecutions, prohibitions, the imposition of forms and ideas, humiliations, and insults, the doctrinaire authority of semi-literate bureaucrats over geniuses; all this is done in the name of the people and for the people. Communist ''Socialist Realism'' is not different even in terminology from Hitler's National Socialism.
(*The New Class*)

History, especially of its own, the Communist period, does not exist. Imposition of silence and falsification are not only permitted but are general phenomena.
(*The New Class*)

Absolute despotism equates itself with the belief in absolute human happiness, though it is an all-inclusive and universal tyranny.
(*The New Class*)

The proposition that Marxism is a universal method, a proposition upon which Communists are obliged to stand, must in practice lead to tyranny in all areas of intellectual activity . . . What of the astronomers, if the cosmos is apathetic to Communist dialectics?
(*The New Class*)

They squander the nation's wealth as though it were someone else's, and dip into it as though it were their own.
(*The New Class*)

PETER DRUCKER
The complete collapse of the belief in the attainability of freedom and equality through Marxism has forced Russia to travel the same road towards a totalitarian, purely negative, non-economic society of unfreedom and inequality which Germany has been following.
(*The End of Economic Man, 1939*)

MAX EASTMAN
Instead of being better, Stalinism is worse than fascism, more ruthless, barbarous, unjust, immoral, anti-democratic, unredeemed by any hope or scruple.
(*Stalin's Russia and the Crisis of Socialism*)

LINCOLN EVANS
. . . the British people . . . are allergic to tyranny regardless of whether it wears a top hat or a cloth cap.
(*Journey to Coercion*)

GEORGE EVERY
Civilisation contracts, as when at evening men looked west from the Bosphorus and saw the smoke of Hun camps in Thrace.
(*Civilisation contracts*)

MILTON FRIEDMAN
Many countries are today experiencing socially destructive inflation, abnormally high unemployment, misuse of economic resources, and in some cases, the suppression of human freedom not because evil men deliberately sought to achieve these results, but because of erroneous judgements about the consequences of government measures.
(*Inflation and Unemployment, Alfred Nobel Memorial Lecture, 1976*)

The excuse for the destruction of liberty is always the plea of necessary — that there is no alternative.
(*Morality and Controls, New York Times, October 29, 1971*)

KARL J. FRIEDRICH and ZBIGNIEW K. BRZEZINSKI
Totalitarian dictatorship, in a sense, is the adaptation of autocracy to twentieth-century industrial society.
(*Totalitarian Dictatorship and Autocracy*)

The degree to which a totalitarian movement succeeds in politicising the army is indicative also of the extent to which the society itself has become totalitarian.
(*Totalitarian Dictatorship and Autocracy*)

Whether the battle cry is ''expropriation of the exploiters'' or ''the common good before selfishness,'' the totalitarian dictatorships develop a centrally-directed economy as the feature in their syndrome of traits.
(*Totalitarian Dictatorship and Autocracy*)

Confessions are the key to . . . psychic coercion. Nowhere else (than in China) has totalitarian terror so perfected this instrumentality. It is practised in two contexts: the prison and the revolutionary university.
(*Totalitarian Dictatorship and Autocracy*)

The psychic fluidum — that is, the peculiar atmosphere — of totalitarian dictatorship is created by two closely related phenomena, propaganda and the terror.
(*Totalitarian Dictatorship and Autocracy*)

KLEMENT GOTTWALD
You asked me why we Communist leaders travel so often to Moscow? I will tell you. We go there to learn how better to wring your capitalist necks.
(*In the Czechoslovak Parliament between two World Wars*)

JOHN KENNETH GALBRAITH
Long-run salvation by men of business has never been highly regarded if it means disturbance of orderly life and convenience in the present. So inaction will be advocated in the present even though it means deep trouble in the future. Here, at least equally with communism, lies the threat to capitalism. It is what causes men who know that things are going quite wrong to say that things are fundamentally sound.
(*The Great Crash 1929*)

DAVID GASCOYNE
Whereon He hangs and suffers still:
See, the centurions wear riding-boots,
Black shirts and badges and peaked caps.
(*Ecce Homo*)

PIETER GEYL
Exactly at which point co-operation became collaboration was a question that could not be answered offhand. It was apt to involve serious-minded and patriotic men in the most painful conflicts of conscience.
(*Encounters in History*)

ANDRÉ GIDE
As it always happens that we recognise the value of certain advantages after we have lost them, there is nothing like a stay in the USSR to help us appreciate the inappreciable liberty of thought we still enjoy in France.
(*Back from the USSR*)

JO GRIMOND
Bureaucracy is the antithesis of democracy.
(*The Bureaucratic Blight*)

DUSAN HAMSIK
Censorship is catastrophic for all concerned: for society, for the creative artist, and for the very political leaders who install it. The more they restrict intellectual expression, the more firmly do they condemn themselves to stagnation.
(*Index on Censorship, London; Vol. 5/No. 3*)

F. A. HAYEK
The future historian will probably say that the destruction of Britain's economic position is the result of an obsession of democratic government with the creation of jobs.
(*The Daily Telegraph, August 26, 1976*)

All the suspected defects of the economic establishment would be quickly eliminated if others were allowed to go ahead with more economical methods.
(*The Daily Telegraph, August 26, 1976*)

Though the concept of national freedom is analogous to that of individual freedom, it is not the same . . . it has often provided the pretext for ruthless restrictions of the individual liberty of the members of minorities.
(*The Constitution of Liberty*)

While to the Nazi the communist, and to the communist the Nazi, and to both the socialist, are potential recruits who are made of the right timber, although they have listened to false prophets, they both know that there can be no compromise between them and those who really believe in individual freedom.
(*The Road to Serfdom*)

The uncritical transfer to the problems of society of habits of thought engendered by the preoccupation with technological problems, the habits of thought of the natural scientist and the engineer.
(*The Road to Serfdom*)

How many features of Hitler's system have not been recommended to us for imitation from the most unexpected quarters, unaware that they are an integral part of that system and incompatible with the free society we hope to preserve?
(*The Road to Serfdom*)

The rise of Fascism and Nazism was not a reaction against the socialist trends of the preceding period, but a necessary outcome of those tendencies.
(*The Road to Serfdom*)

In Germany it was largely people of goodwill, men who were admired and held up as models in this country, who prepared the way, if they did not actually create, the forces which now stand for everything they detest.
(*The Road to Serfdom*)

The promise of greater freedom has become one of the most effective weapons of socialist propaganda.
(*The Road to Serfdom*)

The positions in a totalitarian society in which it is necessary to practice cruelty and intimidation, deliberate deception and spying, are numerous.
(*The Road to Serfdom*)

It may indeed be said that it is the paradox of all collectivist doctrine and its demand for the ''conscious'' control or ''conscious'' planning that they necessarily lead to the demand that the mind of some individual should rule supreme.
(*The Road to Serfdom*)

The moral consequences of totalitarian propaganda . . . are destructive of all morals because they undermine one of the foundations of all morals, the sense of and the respect for truth.
(*The Road to Serfdom*)

ADOLF HITLER
When we possess all constitutional rights we shall then mould the state into that form which we consider to be the right one.

SIDNEY HOOK
Polycentric communism means not the demise of Communist ideology but rather a polycentric ideology more complicated than the monolithic ideology of the past but not less effective.
(*Introduction to Revolution, Reform, and Social Justice*)

GRAHAM HUTTON
If the entire economic and political system depends on regularly taking away the fruits of people's labour, the Government and its leaders soon come under suspicion, disbelief and non-co-operation. That was happening at the end of Stalin's own iron rule over the Russians. And his system had to be abruptly changed, in the face of the whole world as well as of the Russian people.
(*All Capitalists Now*)

State control of everyone and everthing denies basic human freedoms: not only the four great freedoms, but also freedom to choose jobs, to move about, save, to engage in any business, to invest in this or that, to make a profit or a loss.
(*All Capitalists Now*)

Communist managers have been the most ruthless this century — with their work people as well as with their local managers — if an industry or firm fell down on its scheduled performance.
(*All Capitalists Now*)

ALDOUS HUXLEY
People are happy . . . they get what they want, and they never want what they can't get. They're well off; they're safe; they're never ill: . . . they're plagued with no mothers or fathers; they've got no wives, or children, or loves to feel strongly about; they're so conditioned that they practically can't help behaving as they ought to behave.

THOMAS HENRY HUXLEY
The despotism of a majority is as little justifiable and as dangerous as that of one man.
(*On the National inequality of Men, The Nineteenth Century, January, 1890*)

HENRIK IBSEN
The most dangerous foe to truth and freedom in our midst is the compact majority. Yes, the damned, compact, liberal majority.

W. R. INGE
The enemies of Freedom do not argue; they shout and they shoot.
(*The End of an Age*)

MICHAEL IVENS
In an Eastern European country for example, there are more cogent arguments for the relationship between economic and cultural freedoms — when the police were not around — than in Britain. The reasons are obvious. If you wanted to publish a book or a film, make a record, or create and sell a dress, and the State does not approve — then you don't do it.
(*Pressures for Conformity, article in Patterns of Prejudiced, Jan/Fev, 1977*)

PAUL JOHNSON
The tramp, tramp of totalitarian feet marching into the constituency parties has been accompanied by the pitter-patter of middle-class liberals scuttling out.
(*New Statesman, February 11, 1977*)

SAMUEL JOHNSON
Let the authority of the English government perish rather than be maintained in iniquity.
(*"Sir," said Dr Johnson; arranged by H. C. Biron*)

SIR KEITH JOSEPH
What . . . do regimes founded and ruled by socialists in the name of socialism since the First World War have to offer? They have produced no new amenities, rights, facilities, improvements in the human condition. On the contrary, their trade mark so far has been trumped-up show trials, Gulag, mass murder, the use of mental asylums to punish dissidents, cultural revolution, enforced assent far worse than the old forms of dictatorial suppression, conscription of labour, brainwashing, intensified xenophobia and power struggles reminiscent of the middle ages.
(*The Times, November 3, 1976*)

BERTRAND de JOUVENEL

The small society, as the milieu in which man is first found, retains for him an infinite attraction; but . . . any attempt to graft the same features on large society is utopian and leads to tyranny.
(*Sovereignty*)

C. G. JUNG

Nothing has a more divisive and alienating effect upon society than . . . moral complacency and lack of responsibility.
(*The Undiscovered Self*)

The leaders of the mass State cannot avoid being deified, and wherever crudities of this kind have not yet been put over by force, obsessive factors arise in their stead, charged with demonic energy — for instance, money, work, political influence, and so forth.
(*The Undiscovered Self*)

Since every tyranny is *ipso facto* immoral and ruthless, it has much more freedom in the choice of its methods than an institution which still takes account of the individual.
(*The Undiscovered Self*)

JOHN MAYNARD KEYNES

When the accumulation of wealth is no longer of high social importance, there will be great changes in the code of morals . . . The love of money as a possession — as distinguished from the love of money as a means to the enjoyments and realities of life — will be recognised for what it is, a somewhat disgusting morbidity, one of those semi-criminal, semi-pathological propensities which one hands over with a shudder to the specialists in mental disease.
(*Essays in Persuasion*)

There is no subtler, no surer means of overturning the existing basis of society than to debauch the currency.
(*The Economic Consequences of the Peace*)

ARTHUR KOESTLER

The 1980s may easily turn into the Decade of the Demagogues. But not here. We shall more likely have a Decade of the Dentists, so called to commemorate the first member of that profession to become Prime Minister — a profession notoriously expert in depriving people of their bite.
(*Life in 1980 — The Rule of the Mediocracy; The Times*, October 2, 1969. *Repeated in The Heel of Achilles*)

Anthony Grey: What about when one arrives back on the trivial plane? What do you think are the most threatening things to individual freedom in normal society?

Arthur Koestler: To go to the other extremes, suddenly, and to throw away everything and say, oh, these were just overwrought nerves and silly thoughts. To diminish and thereby to destroy the genuineness of the experience.
(Discussion on solitary confinement — from One Pair of Eyes television programme reported by Arthur Koestler in The Heel of Achilles)

NIKITA S. KRUSHCHEV

It does not follow at all from the fact that we stand for peaceful coexistence and economic competition with capitalism that the struggle against bourgeois ideology, against bourgeois survivals, can be relaxed. Our task is tirelessly to expose bourgeois ideology, reveal how inimical it is to the people, and show up its reactionary nature.
(Twentieth Congress of the Communist Party of the Soviet Union)

We will bury you.

D. H. LAWRENCE

Every race that has become self-conscious and idea-bound in the past has perished.
(Fantasia of the Unconscious)

ANTHONY LEJEUNE

Every limitation in freedom makes the next limitation seem less shocking and more acceptable.
(Freedom and the Politicians)

VLADIMIR ILYITCH LENIN

The scientific concept of dictatorship means nothing else but power based directly on violence, unrestrained by any laws, absolutely unrestricted by any rules.

It is true that liberty is precious — so precious that it must be rationed.
(attributed)

Thousands of practical forms and methods of accounting and controlling the rich, the rogues, and the idlers should be devised and put to a practical test by the communes themselves, by small units in town and country . . . In one place half a score of rich, a dozen rogues, half a dozen workers who shirk their work (in the hooligan manner in which many compositors in Petrograd, particularly in the Party printing shops, shirk their work) will be put in prison. In another place they will be put to cleaning latrines. In a third place they will be provided with ''yellow tickets'' after they have served their time, so that all the people shall have them under surveillance, as *harmful* persons, until they reform. In a fourth place, one out of every ten idlers will be shot on the spot.
(*Selected Works, quoted by Sidney Hook in Revolution, Reform and Social Justice*)

BERNARD LEVIN
Let us never allow ourselves to think that poverty is an excuse for an invitation to totalitarianism, and if we should be tempted to think as much, let us remind ourselves that totalitarianism not only extinguishes liberty but institutionalises poverty as well.
(*The Times, July 28, 1976*)

FREDERICO GARCIA LORCA
With their souls of patent leather
they come down the road . . .
Where they breathe they impose
silence of dark rubber
and fear of fine sand.

MRS E. LYNN LINTON
Their idea of freedom is their own preponderance so that they shall do all they wish to do without let or hindrance from outside regulation or the restraints of self-discipline; their idea of morality, that men shall do nothing they choose to disallow.
(*The Wild Women as Politicians, The Nineteenth Century, July, 1891*)

THOMAS MACAULAY
The Puritan hated bear-baiting, not because it gave pain to the bear, but because it gave pleasure to the spectators.
(*History of England*)

FRANK McFADZEAN

The preservation of democracy and even elementary efficiency requires that the horizons of politicians and civil servants should be contained and then pushed back. They have been playing God in the market place for too long with the disastrous consequences which are all around for us to see.

(*Saying of the Week, Observer, November 21, 1976*)

LOUIS MACNEICE

The little sardine men crammed in a monster toy
Who tilt their aggregate beast against our crumbling Troy.

(*Turf-stacks*)

MAO TSE-TUNG

Both in the army and in the local organisations, inner-party democracy is meant to strengthen discipline and increase combat effectiveness, not to weaken them.

(*Selected Works Vol. II*)

In the sphere of theory, destroy the roots of ultra-democracy. First it should be pointed out that the danger of ultra-democracy lies in the fact that it damages or even completely wrecks the party or organisation and weakens or even completely undermines the party's fighting capacity, rendering the party incapable of fulfilling its fighting tasks and thereby causing the defeat of the revolution.

(*Selected Works Vol. II*)

Liberalism is extremely harmful in a revolutionary collective. It is a corrosive which eats away unity, undermines cohesion, causes apathy and creates dissension.

(*Selected Works, Vol. II*)

WALTER DE LA MARE

O yes, thou most blessed, from Monday to Sunday
Has lived on me, preyed on me, Mrs Grundy.

(*Mrs Grundy*)

KARL MARX

It is secrecy, mystery, that is everywhere the soul of bureaucracy.

ROLLO MAY

If our freedom is left over, what the machine *can't* do, the whole issue is lost to start with: we are doomed when, in some future day, a machine can be invented to do it.
(*Love and Will*)

H. L. MENCKEN

Puritanism: the haunting fear that someone, somewhere, may be happy.

HENRY MEULEN

Socialists face the knotty problem that they must strive by every means to stimulate people to criticise the government in order to get control; but once that control is secured, criticism must be stifled.
(*The Individualist, October 1976*)

JOHN STUART MILL

A fixed rule, like that of equality, might be acquiesced in, and so might chance, or an external necessity; but that a handful of human beings should weigh everybody in the balance, and give more to one and less to another at their sole pleasure and judgment, would not be borne unless from persons believed to be more than men, and backed by supernatural terrors.
(*Principles of Political Economy*)

Under this (a bureaucratic) machine, not only is the outside public ill qualified to criticise or check the mode of operation of the bureaucracy but even if . . . popular institutions raise a ruler or ruler of reforming inclinations, no reform can be effected which is contrary to the bureaucracy.
(*On Liberty*)

Evil for evil, a good despotism, in a country at all advanced in civilisation, is more noxious than a bad one; for it is far more relaxing and enervating to the thoughts, feelings and energies of the people.
(*Representative Government*)

LUDWIG von MISES

"Planning for Freedom," has lately become the most popular slogan of the champions of totalitarian government and the Russification of all nations.
(*Human Action*)

Habeas corpus and trial by jury are a sham if, under the pretext of economic expediency, the authority has full power to relegate every citizen it dislikes to the arctic or to a desert and to assign him "hard labour" for life.
(*Human Action*)

The naive advocates of government interference with consumption delude themselves when they neglect what they disdainfully call the philosophical aspect of the problem. They unwittingly support the case of censorship, inquisition, religious intolerance and the persecution of dissenters.
(*Human Action*)

Governments which are eager to keep up the outward appearance of freedom even when curtailing freedom disguise their direct interference with consumption under the cloak of interference with business.
(*Human Action*)

The Reich of the Nazis and the commonwealth of the Marxians are planned as societies of undisturbed peace. They are to be created by pacification, i.e. the violent subjugation of all those not ready to yield without resistance.
(*Human Action*)

When the monopolist controls one of the vital conditions of human survival, he has the power to starve to death all those who do not obey his orders.
(*Human Action*)

In a totalitarian system there is nothing to which the attribute "free" could be attached but the unlimited arbitrariness of the dictator.
(*Human Action*)

MALCOLM MUGGERIDGE

It's silly to say the Brown Terror is worse than the Red Terror. They're both horrible. They're both Terrors. I watched the Nazis march along Unter Den Linden and realised — of course, they're Komsomols, the same people, the same faces. It's the same show.
(*Chronicles of Wasted Time: The Green Stick*)

There were plenty of enlightened people then to contend that Alaric was a fine fellow, and that hope lay in a dialogue with him.
(*Jesus Rediscovered*)

When the lawlessness and destruction have been achieved, the choice is between chaos and tyranny, and, faced with such a choice, the great majority of human beings will always choose tyranny, or have it imposed upon them.
(*Jesus Rediscovered*)

BENITO MUSSOLINI
Un apostolo di violenzo.

GEORGE ORWELL
The first and simplest stage in the discipline, which can be taught even to young children, is called, in Newspeak, crimestop. Crimestop means the faculty of stopping short, as though by instinct, at the threshold of any dangerous thought . . . Crimestop . . . means protective stupidity.
(*1984*)

CHARLES PEGUY
Tyranny is always better organised than freedom.

The triumph of demagogues is short-lived. But the ruins are eternal.

JOHN PEYTON
Freedom is perhaps threatened above all, by the fact that a small minority has realised that its own resolve enables it to cut like a hot knife through the butter of the great uncertain and irresolute majority.
(*The Daily Telegraph, March 12, 1977*)

WILLIAM PITT the Younger
Necessity is the plea for every infringement of human freedom. It is the argument of tyrants, it is the creed of slaves.
(*Speech, House of Commons*)

ENOCH POWELL
It is through false security that men lose their property and nations lose their liberty.
(*Freedom and Reality*)

J. B. PRIESTLEY
Unless a fairly large section makes some attempt to arrive at self-discipline and a sense of responsibility towards the community, our country can stagger into bankruptcy and lose the very liberty it has guarded for centuries.
(*Prescription for Our Time*)

G. D. PROSSER
When did appeasement work? Who of the many tyrants who built on force were defeated except by force? Napoleon? Hitler? And so on in history.
(*Letter, Daily Mail, January 17, 1977*)

KATHLEEN RAINE
But to deny the reality of evil may be to give power to principalities and powers of the collective mind.

AYN RAND
In 1917, the Russian peasants were demanding: "Land and Freedom!" But Lenin and Stalin is what they got.
(*Capitalism, the Unknown Ideal*)

WILHELM REICH
The received masses run away from you, and you run after them, yelling: "Stop, stop, your proletarian masses! You just can't see yet that I am your liberator!
(*Listen, Little Man!*)

LORD ROBBINS
I confess to considerable doubts about the eventual stability of democracy, unless buttressed by constitutional safeguards and a general climate of opinion which thoroughly understands the case for liberty in general — which is certainly not present in very many contemporary societies including our own.
(*Liberty and Equality, Institute of Economic Affairs, 1977*)

JEAN-JACQUES ROUSSEAU
The most absolute authority is that which penetrates into a man's innermost being and concerns itself no less with his will than with his actions.

BERTRAND RUSSELL
Most human beings, though in varying degrees, desire to control, not only their own lives but also the lives of others.
(*Freedom and Government*)

ST. JEROME
Our sins are what makes the barbarians strong . . . Our vices are what bring about the defeat of Roman armies . . .

MASSIMO SALVADORI

The errors and horrors of Sulla's patricians, Isabella of Spain's clergy and Lenin's vanguard of the proletariat should be enough to dispel what confidence people may have in the wisdom and restraint of elites.
(*Liberal Democracy*)

SAMUEL

And he will take your fields and your vineyards and give them to his supporters. He will take a tenth of your produce and give it to his staff. He will take the tenth of your sheep: and you shall be his servants. And you shall cry out in that day because of your king which you shall have chosen.
(*The Bible*)

GEORGE SANTAYANA

The blind extirpating the mad may plant a new madness.
(*My Host the World*)

Merciless irrational ambition has borrowed the language of brotherly love.
(*My Host the World*)

JEAN-PAUL SARTRE

I hate victims who respect their executioners.

The most serious error has doubtless been Khrushchev's report, his solemn and public denunciation (of Stalin), the detailed exposure of all the crimes of a sacred person who has long been the symbol of the regime; this is madness when such frankness has not been preceded by any appreciable rise in the standard of living of the population . . . The masses were not prepared for this sort of revelation of the truth.

Evil is the systematic substitution of the abstract for the concrete.

Historic experience of the countries in which Communists took power has revealed undeniably that the first stage of socialist society in construction — to consider it from the still abstract view of power — cannot be anything else than the indissoluble aggregation of bureaucracy, the Terror, and the cult of personality.
(*Critique de la raison dialectique*)

JOHN SELDEN
At this little gap every man's liberty may in time go out.
(*Proceedings in Parliament Relating to the Liberty of the Subject*)

WILLIAM SHAKESPEARE
You speak o' the people,
As if you were a god to punish, not
A man of their infirmity.
(*Coriolanus*)

BERNARD SHAW
The world is to the big and powerful states by necessity; and the little
ones must come within their border or be crushed out of existence.

PERCY BYSSHE SHELLEY
... The Tyrant's gem-wrought chariot ...
(*The Revolt of Islam*)

For traitorously did that foul Tyrant robe
His countenance in lies.
(*The Revolt of Islam*)

The Tyrant is amongst us.
(*The Revolt of Islam*)

No — in countries that are free
Such starvation cannot be
As in England now we see.
(*The Mask of Anarchy*)

Alas! for Liberty!
If numbers, wealth, or unfulfilling years,
Or fate, can quell the free!
(*Hellas*)

... the despot's bloodhounds with their prey
Unarmed and unaware, were gorging deep
Their gluttony of death.
(*The Revolt of Islam*)

SOCIALIST WORKER
There is no parliamentary road.

ALEXANDER SOLZENITSYN

Westerners will need a great deal of strength, of resolution, to see and accept the evidence of the implacable tide of violence and bloodshed that has methodically, steadily, triumphantly radiated out from a single centre for nearly 60 years, and to locate the countries already lined up for the next holocaust.

Socialism has created the illusion of quenching people's thirst for justice; socialism has lulled their conscience into thinking that the steamroller which is about to flatten them is a blessing in disguise, a salvation. And socialism, more than anything else, has caused public hypocrisy to thrive; it has enabled Europe to ignore the annihilation of 66 million people on its very borders.

It's an astonishing phenomenon that communism has been writing about itself in the most open way — in black and white — for 125 years. And even more openly, more candidly in the beginning . . . It's perfectly amazing. The whole world can read, everyone is literate, but somehow no one wants to understand. Humanity acts in such a way as if it didn't understand what communism is, and doesn't want to understand, is not capable of understanding.

JAMES STEPHENS

Every extreme is bad, in order that it may swing to and fertilize its equally horrible opposite.
(*The Crock of Gold*)

PAUL M. SWEENY

Intellectual freedom and personal security guaranteed by law have been virtually unknown to the peoples who are now blazing the trail to socialism; in the advanced countries, they are seriously jeopardized by the fierce onslaughts of reaction and counter-revolution. No one can say whether they will survive the period of tension and strife through which we are now passing, or whether they will have to be rediscovered and recaptured in a more rational world of the future.

The passage is dangerous and difficult, the worst may be yet to come.
(*The Communist Manifesto after 100 years; from Monthly Review, August 1949*)

MARGARET THATCHER

I reject Marxism because its doctrines seem to me false. It is the negation of human dignity. Wherever you have Marxist Government you have tyranny, oppression and drabness.
(*National Press Club, Washington, 1975*)

We did not lose the Cold War. But we are losing the Thaw in a subtle and disturbing way. We are losing the Thaw politically.
(*National Press Club, Washington, 1975*)

ALEXIS de TOCQUEVILLE
How can a populace, unaccustomed to freedom in small concerns, learn to use it temperately in great affairs? What resistance can be offered to tyranny in a country where each individual is weak, and where the citizens are not united by a common interest?
(*Democracy in America*)

Despots themselves do not deny the excellence of freedom, but they wish to keep it all to themselves.
(*France Before the Revolution of 1789*)

It may be said with strict accuracy, that the taste a man may share for absolute government bears an exact ratio to the contempt he may profess for his countrymen.
(*France Before the Revolution of 1789*)

EMMANUEL TODD
The Soviet system . . . fascism speaking a neo-Marxist language that none of its leaders really believe in.
(*La Chute Finale*)

LEON TROTSKY
Armed insurrection stands in the same relation to revolution that revolution as a whole does to evolution. It is the critical point when accumulating quantity turns with an explosion into quality.

It was the supreme expression of the mediocrity of the apparatus that Stalin himself rose to his position.

MARINA TSVETAYEVA
Thinking him human they
decided to kill him, and
now he's dead. For ever.
— Weep. For the dead angel.
(*Poems for Blok*)

KORNEL UJEJSKI
Great tyrants fall, and meaner ones remain,
As godless and more arrogant than they.
(*The Polish Eagle; version by Helen Waddell of prose translated by Xavier Zaleski*)

JOHN VAIZEY
Fascism, in any of its forms, was a cult of violence and irrationality that was alien to the forms of government and independence of thought which had characterised capitalist regimes.
(*Revolutions of our Time: Capitalism*)

VOLTAIRE
To succeed in chaining the crowd you just seem to wear the same fetters.

KURT VONNEGUT Jr.
I have never seen a more sublime demonstration of the totalitarian mind, a mind which might be likened unto a system of gears where teeth have been filed off at random. Such snaggle-toothed thought machine, driven by a standard or even a substandard libido, whirls with the jerky, noisy, gaudy pointlessness of a cuckoo clock in Hell.
(*Mother Night*)

HELEN WADDELL
The power of physical violence to cripple men's minds.
(*More Latin Lyrics, from Virgil to Milton*)

HENRY C. WALLICH
Where tyrants rule, liberty is high drama. Where the drama has reached its happy end, liberty become habitual and a little dull it nonetheless remains liberty.
(*The Cost of Freedom*)

H. G. WELLS
The coming of the aristocrat is fatal and assured. The end will be the Over-man — for all the mad protests of humanity.

E. G. WEST
At what point does the purpose of "social solidarity" lead us to the slippery slope towards the kind of uniform and homogenised society beloved by totalitarian regimes?
(*Education: A Framework for Choice*)

PEREGRINE WORSTHORNE
A powerful group whose strength depends on its members acting uniformly is scarcely likely to be very interested in the principles of individual freedom.

Individual freedom, let it be bluntly said, is too important a matter to be left to the tender mercies of those who make use of only one aspect of it.

WILLIAM WORDSWORTH
The insinuated scoff of coward tongues.
(*The Prelude — School-time*)

LUBOR J. ZINK
Now, as then, the decline — including economic disarray — and retreat of the democracies has been whetting the appetite of the advancing totalitarianism. This, of course, raises the risk of a general explosion the policy of appeasement, or detente as it is now called, is supposed to remove.
(*Freedom Down the Drain, Toronto Sun, October, 1975*)

V. ZAGLADIN
It is because of detente that the workers' movement in the Western world acquired an unprecedented swing, that the Communist parties of various countries have achieved a spectacular progress.
(*Novoie Vremya, May, 1976*)

Exiles

PETRONIUS ARBITER
When they beat the old man up, sent him to exile,
It was no man they banished,
It was the honour and the power of Rome.
(*Satyricon, trans. Helen Waddell*)
(*More Latin Lyrics from Virgil to Milton*)

DALAI LAMA
The hope of all men in the last analysis, is simply for peace of mind.
My hope rests in the courage of Tibetans, and the love of truth and
justice which is still in the heart of the human race; and my faith is in
the compassion of my Master.
(*My Land and My People*)

HILDEBERT
Thou art the chant of exiles in their sorrow.
(*In honour of the Holy Spirit; trans. Helen Waddell*)
(*More Latin Lyrics, from Virgil to Milton*)

The songs you sent me I have read
And read again . . .
And such divinity encompassed them,
I for a while forgot an exile's pain.
(*To Peter, Bishop of Poitiers; trans. Helen Waddell*)
(*More Latin Lyrics, from Virgil to Milton*)

JOCELIN
He walked an exile in an alien land
As on the hills of home.
(*Vita Kentigern; trans. Helen Waddell*)
(*More Latin Lyrics, from Virgil to Milton*)

RUDYARD KIPLING
"How far is St. Helena from the field of Waterloo?"
A near way — a clear way — the ship will take you soon.
A pleasant place for gentlemen with little left to do.
(*Morning never tries you till the afternoon!*)
(*A St. Helena Lullaby*)

CARMINA BURANA
Exile is sweet to me
With a girl's memory.
(*trans. Helen Waddell: More Latin Lyrics, from Virgil to Milton*)

RABBI NACHMAN
Through joy the spirit becomes settled, but through sadness it goes
into exile.
(*Sayings of Rabbi Nachman, from The Tales of Rabbi Nachman, by
Martin Buber*)

NORMAN NICHOLSON
Herod's men were searching the back alleys,
They did not see the refugees go,
Nor how when the child's hands fluttered like sparrows
His fingers blessed the casual snow.
(*Carol for Holy Innocents' Day*)

PAUL THE DEACON
Give back the captive to his fatherland,
To his own familiar fields.
(*trans. Helen Waddell; More Latin Lyrics, from Virgil to Milton*)

Fear of Freedom

MÉDARD BOSS
. . . the essential basic arch-anxiety (is) innate to all isolated, individual forms of human existence. In the basic anxiety human existence is afraid of as well as anxious about its "being-in-the-world" . . . Only if we understand . . . (this can we) conceive of the seeing paradoxic phenomenon that people who are afraid of living are also especially frightened of death.
(*Meaning and Content of Sexual Perversions*)

NORMAN O. BROWN
The essential point in the Freudian diagnosis of human sociability was seen by Róheim: men huddle into hordes as a substitute for parents, to save themselves from independence, from "being left alone in the dark".
(*Life Against Death, quoting Róheim: The Origin and Function of Culture*)

RICHARD BRATHWAITE
To Banbery came I, O profane one!
Where I saw a Puritane-one
Hanging of his cat on Monday,
For killing of a mouse on Sunday.
(*Barnabee's Journal*)

ELIAS CANETTI
For, since he fears power in any form, since the real aim of his life is to withdraw from it, in whatever form it may appear, he detects it, identifies it, names it, and creates figures of it in every instance where others would accept it as being nothing our of the ordinary.
(*Kafka's Other Trial — the Letters to Felice*)

WILSON van DUSEN
In a sense our freedom is dreadful. Though we have sufficient road signs or guides . . . it is easy enough to doubt them and get lost with or without them. This freedom implies that it was meant that we should struggle, and each find his way on his own.
(*The Presence of Other Worlds*)

64

FRANZ KAFKA

Had you not been lying on the ground among the animals, you would have been unable to see the sky and the stars and wouldn't have been set free. Perhaps you wouldn't have survived the terror of standing upright.
(*Letter to Felice Bauer, quoted by Elias Canetti in Kafka's Other Trial — the Letters to Felice*)

SÖREN KIERKEGAARD

I say it is especially the daily newspaper which labours at degrading men to be mere copies. As in a paper factory the rags are worked together into a mass, so the newspapers tend to smooth out every individual difference in men, all spirit (for spirit is differentiation in itself, and consequently also from others), in order to make them happy *qua numerus*, by means of the life which is peculiar to the number — in everything, like the rest. Here the animal creature finds peace and rest, in the herd.
(*Journals*)

CARLO LEVI

. . . men, capable of liberty — who cannot stand the terror of the sacred that manifests itself before their open eyes — must turn to mystery, must hide . . . the . . . truth.
(*Of Fear and Freedom*)

NORMAN MAILER

Willy-nilly I had had existentialism forced upon me. I was free, or at least whatever was still ready to change in my character had escaped from the social obligations which suffocate others. I could seek to become what I chose to be, and if I failed — there was the ice pick of fear! I would have nothing to excuse failure. I would fail because I had not been brave enough to succeed. So I was much too free.
(*Introduction to Barbary Shore*)

YEHUDI MENUHIN

If we all fear a common enemy, or suspect a common evil, we share something, however negative. But if we fear and suspect eath other, what hope is there then?
(*Theme and Variations*)

PERCY BYSSHE SHELLEY

But more he loathed and hated the clear light
Of Wisdom and free thought.
(*The Revolt of Islam*)

BENEDICT SPINOZA

Harmony is often the result of fear; but such harmony is insecure.
(*Ethics*)

WILLIAM WORDSWORTH

Me this unchartered freedom tires;
I feel the weight of chance-desires;
My hopes no more much change their name,
I long for a repose that ever is the same.
(*Ode to Duty*)

Fighting for Freedom

THOMAS AQUINAS
Give us the strength to fight.
(*trans. Helen Waddell; More Latin Lyrics, from Virgil to Milton*)

AUGUSTINE
A liberty . . . protected and made firm by the gift of perseverance, that this world should be overcome, the world, that is, in all its deep loves, in all its terrors, in all its countless ways of going wrong.

GEORGE BARKER
When will men again
Lift irresistible fists
Not bend from ends
But each man lift men
Nearer again.
(*The leaping Laughers; Collected Poems*)

JACQUES BARZUN
Intellect deteriorates after every surrender as folly, unless we consciously resist, the nonsense does not pass by but into us.
(*The House of Intellect*)

R. BERGER-PERRIN
Liberals today have solid reasons for thinking that a future — perhaps not far away — will offer them this big chance to build a free world, which Europe has allowed to escape after having half succeeded between 1815 and 1914.
(*Vitalité Libérale*)

WILLIAM BLAKE
No, no, let us play.
(*Songs of Innocence: Nurse's Song*)

Struggling in my father's hands,
Striving against my swaddling bands.
(*Songs of Experience: Infant Sorrow*)

BOETHIUS

Give the spirit power to climb.
(*trans. Helen Waddell; More Latin Lyrics from Virgil to Milton*)

HENRY ST. JOHN, VISCOUNT BOLINGBROKE

Now, the greatest good of a people is their liberty . . . without liberty
no happiness can be enjoyed by society. The obligation, therefore, to
defend and maintain the freedom of such constitutions will appear most
sacred to a Patriot King.
(*The Idea of a Patriot King, 1742*)

WILLY BRANDT

I believe that it is desirable and necessary to free men and nations from
tutelage and dependence, and then to assist them. But I do not believe
that we have the right to coerce them into happiness as we conceive it.
(*The Ordeal of Co-existence*)

I do not want to force anyone to his knees. Nor will I let anyone force
me to kneel.
(*The Ordeal of Co-existence*)

ROBERT BROWNING

Yet we trusted thou shouldst speak
The message which our lips, too weak,
Refused to utter . . .
(*Songs from Paracelsus*)

But little do or can the best of us:
That little is achieved through Liberty.

WILLIAM JENNINGS BRYAN

The humblest citizen of all the land, when clad in the armour of a
righteous cause, is stronger than all the hosts of error.
(*Speech at the National Democratic Convention, Chicago, 1896*)

SIR ARTHUR BRYANT

Slavery — the opposite of freedom — is a thing absolute, definable and
degrading. It is that state in which man is left without any freedom of
choice. A poor man in this country, in a time of unemployment,
might think many times before leaving his job, but he could at least
leave it and continue to exist. He was free to express and organise his
opposition to government or to his economic lot, free to go where he

pleased, free to read whatever others chose to say against his rules or employers, free to strike against the terms of his employment, free to vote against the plans of his rulers, and, what is more, by his vote, to help dismiss them. These are no small liberties and have been won for free communities by centuries of struggle.
(*The Ultimate Evil; Illustrated London News, March 27, 1948*)

MARTIN BUBER
The real problem is how to humanise technology. This is a problem which the East will not be able to escape. And this is a difficult task: perhaps the gravest that has ever faced the human race.
(*Conversation with Rabindranath Tagore*)

For I cannot help withstanding evil when I see that it is about to destroy the good. I am forced to withstand the evil in the world just as the evil within myself. I can only strive not to do so by force. I do not want force. But if there is no other way of preventing the evil destroying the good, I trust I shall use force and give myself up into God's hands.
(*Two Letters to Gandhi*)

Every time one man helps another, the Hasidim say, an angel is born. I hope, my dear Albert Schweitzer, that fate will long allow you to hear the wings of many angels beating around you.
(*Letter to Albert Schweitzer, 1955*)

RUDOLF BULTMANN
There is only one possible way to become free from the past, free for a true hearing of the claim which comes to us in the present moment: that freedom is given to us through forgiveness.
(*Faith and Understanding*)

EDWARD GEORGE BULWER-LYTTON, BARON LYTTON
Take away the sword —
States can be saved without it!
(*Richelieu*)

EDMUND BURKE
Freedom and not servitude is the cure of anarchy; as religion, and not atheism, is the true remedy for superstition.
(*Speech on Conciliation with America, 1775*)

C. BURY
Among all the freedom goals, the goal of maximising everyone's freedom from coercion should take first priority.
(*The Structure of Freedom*)

LORD BYRON
Hereditary bondsmen! know ye not,
Who would be free, themselves must strike the blow!
(*Childe Harold*)

For Freedom's battle once begun,
Bequeathed by bleeding Sire to Son,
Though baffled oft is ever won.
(*The Giaour, 123*)

I dreamed that Greece might still be free
For, standing on the Persian's grave
I could not deem myself a slave.
(*Don Juan*)

ALBERT CAMUS
We all carry within us our places of exile, our crimes and our ravages. But our task is not to unleash them on the world; it is to fight them in ourselves and in others.
(*The Rebel; translated by Anthony Bower*)

JIMMY CARTER
The passion of freedom is on the rise. Tapping this new spirit, there can be no nobler nor more ambitious task for America to undertake on this day of a new beginning than to help shape a just and peaceful world that is truly humane.
(*Inaugural speech, January 20, 1977*)

PAUL CHAMBERS
. . . what economists should be doing is not fussing whether there should or should not be a merger here and there; what they should be fussing about is the absence of free trade throughout the world. There is a crying need for free trade.
(*Economics, Business and Government*)

WINSTON S. CHURCHILL
We must keep the flame of freedom burning strong and bright — as a beacon of hope to those struggling against the powers of totalitarian darkness. If we should falter, if we should succumb, all hope would be extinguished. Mankind as a whole would descend to the Gulag.
(*Speech to National Association for Freedom*)

SIR WINSTON CHURCHILL
What we have to consider today while time remains is the permanent prevention of war and the establishment of freedom and democracy as rapidly as possible in all countries. Our difficulties and dangers will not be removed by closing our eyes to them . . . They will not be removed by a policy of appeasement.
(*Sinews of Peace — Postwar Speeches*)

JOHN PHILPOT CURRAN
The condition upon which God hath given liberty to man is eternal vigilance; which condition if he break, servitude is at once the consequence of his crime, and the punishment of his guilt.
(*Speech on the Right of Election of Lord Mayor of Dublin, 1790*)

DANTE
The hottest places in hell are reserved for those who in a period of moral crisis maintain their neutrality.

DECLARATION OF ARBROATH
For it is not Glory; it is not Riches; neither is it Honour; but it is Liberty alone that we fight and contend for, which no honest man will lose but with his life.

MICHAEL DIXON
We need to be more aware than we are that freedom has no built-in preservatives of its own.

JOHN DONNE
And freely men confesse that this world's spent,
When in the Planets, and the Firmament
They seeke so many new.
(*The First Anniversay: An Anatomy of the World*)

FYEDOR DOSTOYEVSKY

I shall kill myself in order to assert my insubordination, my new and dreadful liberty.
(*Kivrilov in The Possessed*)

You want to go into the world and you are going empty handed, with some promise of freedom, which men in their innate simplicity and lawlessness cannot even comprehend, which they fear and dread — for nothing has even been more unendurable to man and human society than freedom!
(*Ivan Karamazov's Grand Inquisitor, to Christ, in The Brothers Karamazov*)

Everyone who desires supreme freedom must dare to kill himself . . . Beyond that there is no freedom; that's all, and beyond it there is nothing.
(*Kivrilov in The Possessed*)

RALPH WALDO EMERSON

'Tis man's perdition to be safe,
When for the truth he ought to die.
(*Sacrifice*)

WILLIAM NORMAN EWER

I gave my life for free — This I know;
For those who bade me fight had told me so.
(*Five Souls*)

BENJAMIN FRANKLIN

Those who would give essential liberty to purchase a little temporary safety deserve neither liberty nor safety.

KARL J. FRIEDRICH and ZBIGNIEW K. BRZEZINSKI

The Christian churches have shown themselves to be a real bulwark against the claim to total power of the totalitarian dictatorship, perhaps more real than any others. Whether Protestant or Catholic, the genuine Christian cannot accept totalitarianism.

PIETER GEYL

Liberty in the full sense of the word cannot, in the imperfect society in which we imperfect beings live, exist. All that we can do is to strive after conditions in which as much liberty as is practicable will be attained.
(*Encounters in History*)

Unless they had the courage to stand up for it, liberty has never remained the lot of men; and that to fight, or to be prepared to fight, may still prove to be the only way to retain it or as much as we have, the years in which we live have made abundantly plain.
(*Encounters in History*)

Resistance and nothing but resistance, resistance caring nought for all these nice distinctions and considerations, was a great moral asset. In France, too, it helped to save the soul of the nation. But it must always and everywhere be the affair of a minority.
(*Encounters in History*)

There were the working men of Amsterdam who in February, 1941, went on strike in protest against the anti-Jewish campaign then just opening. This, one should think, ought to have shaken Huizinga in his view as if the working men, "less civilised" or "less educated", were no more than a deadweight on civilisation, worse, a danger, now that they are trained by means of "organisation" (that modern pest) to "Soulless group egoism".
(*Encounters in History*)

JOHANN WOLFGANG von GOETHE
Freedom, to be real, must constantly be reconquered.

YVAN GOLL
O France you rhyme with sufferance
Your song will never come to silence.
(*Jean Sans Terre Sings an Ode to France in May, 1940; trans. Louise Bogan*)

I am the Man-of-Revolt
In my bagpipes I keep the cries of all the people
My heart in mourning beats the drum
Of the march to liberty.
(*Jean Sans Terre One-Man Band; trans. Babette Deitsch*)

JOHN GRIGG
The urgent task will be to induce the great majority of social democrats in the trade unions and local Labour parties to attend their branch meetings and to stay to the end, whatever the personal inconvenience. The price of Liberty is, alas, eternal boredom.
(*The Spectator, February 12, 1977*)

JO GRIMOND
If you want to run a free system, the people must feel that it gives them self-respect.
(*The Bureaucratic Blight*)

JORGE GUILLÉN
. . . Am one with all others
Whose shoulders resist and sustain
While their eyeballs grow great in their heads
And their wonderment cries that the world
Opens afresh to the onlooking ones.
(*Face to Face*)

F. A. HAYEK
If we are to succeed in the war of ideologies . . . we must first of all regain the belief in the traditional values for which this country stood in the past, and must have the moral courage stoutly to defend the ideals which our enemies attack.
(*The Road to Serfdom*)

PATRICK HENRY
Is life so dear or peace so sweet as to be purchased at the price of chains and slavery? Forbid it, almighty God! I know not what course others may take, but as for me, give me liberty or give me death.
(*Speech in Virginia Convention, 1795*)

HERMANN HESSE
The truth must be repeated for ever and ever in a thousand forms.
(*War and Peace, Spring, 1918; If the War Goes On*)

JOHN HICK
When something is "soul-destroying" it is values that are in danger of destruction. "Soul food" and "soul music" are symbols of the values of the black community in its search for justice and civil rights.
(*Death and Eternal Life*)

SIDNEY HOOK
It is when the cement of loyalty to a free society is dissolved that the greatest danger to its survival manifests itself. This loyalty need not be blind. Although its agglutinative character rests on habit, it also depends on awareness of historical achievement in the slow long march from the unfreedoms and evils of the past, and especially upon the insight into the social and political alternatives to existing society.
(*introduction to Revolution, Reform, and Social Justice*)

THOMAS HENRY HUXLEY
There are men . . . to whom the satisfaction of throwing down a triumphant fallacy is at least as great as that which attends the discovery of a new truth, who feel better satisfied with the government of the world when they have been helping Providence by knocking an imposture on the head, and who care even more for freedom of thought than for mere advancement of knowledge. These men are the Carnots who organise victory for truth.

HENRIK IBSEN
One should never put on one's best trousers to go out to battle for freedom and truth.
(*An Enemy of the People*)

ISAIAH
Arise, shine, for thy light is come.
(*The Bible*)

WILLIAM JAMES
Son of man, stand upon your own feet so that I may speak with you.

JOHN OF SALISBURY
For we also wrestle with the Angel, and the man in whom the love of eternity hath kindled, will go lame in the things of time. For not without the anguish of the struggle shall the facet of truth be seen, nor shall the day break without a benediction.
(*Policraticus*)

SAMUEL JOHNSON
In short, Sir, I have got no farther than this: every man has a right to utter what he thinks truth, and every other man has a right to knock him down for it. Martyrdom is the test.
(*"Sir,"* said Dr Johnson; arranged by H. C. Biron)

IMMANUEL KANT
Do what will make you worthy of happiness.
(*Critique of Pure Reason*)

JOHN F. KENNEDY
The war against hunger is truly mankind's war of liberation.
(*Speech at opening of World Food Congress, June 4, 1963*)

Pay any price, bear any burden, meet any hardship, support any friend or oppose any foe, to assure the survival and success of liberty.
(*The Sunday Times, (Kennedy Credo), September 3, 1967*)

To those people in the huts and villages of half the globe struggling to break the bonds of mass misery, we pledge our best efforts to help them help themselves, for whatever period is required — not because the communists may be doing it, not because we seek their votes, but because it is right.
(*Inaugural Presidential Address*)

JOHN MAYNARD KEYNES
The authoritarian state systems of today seem to solve the problem of unemployment at the expense of efficiency and of freedom . . . It may be possible by a right analysis of the problem to cure the disease whilst preserving efficiency and freedom.
(*The General Theory of Employment, Interest and Money, 1936-1947 edition*)

SÖREN KIERKEGAARD
A passionate, tumultuous age will overthrow everything, pull everything down; but a revolutionary age that is at the same time reflective and passionless leaves everything standing but cunningly empties it of significance.
(*Journals*)

MORRIS KLINE
By far the greatest value of the peliocentric theory to modern times is the contribution it made to the battle for freedom of thought and of expression.
(*Mathematics in Western Culture*)

HAROLD J. LASKI
Liberty is nothing if it is not the organised and conscious power to resist in the last resort
(*A Grammar of Politics*)

FATHER PETER LEVI
And words for happiness and freedom make my skull ring like a bell and my ribs shake.
(*Letter on the Art of Satire from Death is a Pulpit*)

ABRAHAM LINCOLN
The ballot is stronger than the bullet.
(*Speech 1856*)

LIN YUTANG

What threatens civilization today is not war, but the changing conception of life values entailed by certain political doctrines. Only by recapturing the dream of human freedom and restoring the importance of the common man's liberties can that undermining threat to modern civilization be averted.

(*Lin Yutang Memorial, Reader's Digest, 1976*)

The core of the cold war is not capitalist versus socialist, but the question, who is the oppressor of the masses? Whoever believes that the common people have as much right as the elite, and is willing to fight against injustices and indignities to them, will win in the end.

(*Lin Yutang Memorial, Reader's Digest, 1976*)

ROBERT H. BRUCE LOCKHART

In the democratic fortress of collective security the forward bastions are as important as the citadel. To let one fall without protest is to weaken the whole moral and physical structure of defence.

(*introduction to Czechoslovakia Accuses, by J. Josten*)

JAMES RUSSELL LOWELL

The only argument available with an east wind is to put on your overcoat.

(*Democracy and Addresses*)

ANTONIO MACHADO

It is more difficult to rise to the occasion than to stand above the conflict.

NORRIS McWHIRTER

If only people would realise that if a sizeable amount of people did a little, a few wouldn't have to bear the brunt of the battle for freedom.

(*Daily Mail interview, July 12, 1976*)

JAN MASARYK

A collective unit of free and contented people working for the welfare of all and thus for their own welfare — free, fully conscious manual and brain workers — that is our pledge, that is our duty.

(*Speaking to My Country — wartime BBC broadcasts*)

ROLLO MAY

We are the independent men who, often taking our powers too seriously, continuously act and react, unaware that much of value in life comes only if we don't press, comes in quietly when it is not pushed or required, comes not from a drive from behind or an attraction from in front, but emerges silently from simply being together.
(*Love and Will*)

JOHN STUART MILL

As practical beings it is our business to free human life from as many as possible of its difficulties, and not to keep up a stock of them as hunters preserve game, for the exercise of pursuing it.
(*Principles of Political Economy*)

Representative institutions necessarily depend for permanence on the readiness of the people to fight for them in case of their being endangered.
(*Representative Government*)

JOHN MILTON

Well hast thou fought
The better fight, who single has maintained
Against revolted multitudes the cause
Of truth.
(*Paradise Lost*)

It is the liberty, Lords and Commons, which your own valorous and happy counsels have purchased us, liberty which is the muse of all great wits . . . and cannot make us now less capable, less knowing, less lawfully pursuing of the truth, unless ye first make yourselves less the losers, less the founders of our true liberty.
(*Areopagitica*)

Is it just or reasonable, that most voices against the main end of government should enslave the less number that would be free? More just it is, doubtless, if it comes to force, that a less number compel a greater number to retain, which can be no wrong to them, their liberty, than that a greater number, for the pleasure of their baseness, compel a less most injuriously to be their fellow slaves. They who seek nothing but their own just liberty, have always the right to win it, whenever they have the power, be the voices never so numerous that oppose it.

LUDWIG von MISES
What alone can prevent the civilised nations of Western Europe, America and Australia from being enslaved by the barbarism of Moscow is open and unrestricted support of laissez-faire capitalism.
(*Anti-Capitalist Mentality*)

FRIEDRICH NIETZSCHE
To create freedom and a reverent ''No'' even in the face of duty: for this, my brothers, the lion is necessary.
(*Thus Spake Zarathustra*)

JOSÉ ORTEGA Y GASSET
We belong to an age in the proportion in which we feel capable of accepting its dilemma and arraying ourselves for battle on one side or the other of the trench it has dug. For the process of living is, in a very real sense, an enlistment under certain standards and a preparation for battle.

BORIS PASTERNAK
And never for a single moment
Betray your credo or pretend,
But be alive — this only matters —
Alive and burning to the end.
(*It Is Not Seemly; trans. Lydia Pasternak Slater, from Fifty Poems*)

PRINCE PHILIP
If you install a burglar alarm in your household, it is only the burglar who can get annoyed.
(*Atlantic Congress, 1959. Guildhall dinner*)

WILLIAM PITT (The Elder)
The poorest man may in his cottage bid defiance to all the forces of the Crown. It may be frail — its roof may shake — the wind may blow through it — the storm may enter — the rain may enter — but the King of England cannot enter — all his force dares not cross the threshold of the ruined tenement!
(*Speech*)

I rejoice that America has resisted. Three millions of people, so dead to all the feelings of liberty, as voluntarily to submit to be slaves, would have been fit instruments to make slaves of the rest.
(*Speech, House of Commons, January 14, 1766*)

PLATO
God alone is worthy of supreme seriousness, but man is made God's plaything, and that is the best part of him. Therefore every man and woman should live life accordingly, and play the noblest games . . . Life must be lived as a play, playing certain games, making sacrifices, singing and dancing, and then a man will be able to propitiate the gods, and defend himself against his enemies, and win in the contest.
(*Laws*)

KARL POPPER
To progress is to move towards some kind of end, towards an end which exists for us as human beings . . . only we, the human individuals, can do it; we can do it by defending and strengthening those democratic institutions upon which freedom, and with it progress, depends.

Only by planning, step by step, for institutions to safeguard freedom, especially freedom from exploitation, can we hope to achieve a better world.

Reason, like science, grows by way of mutual criticism; the only possible way of planning its growth is to develop those institutions that safeguard . . . the freedom of thought.
(*The Open Society and its Enemies*)

G. D. PROSSER
No civilisation can survive unless it is prepared to defend the laws on which it is built.
(*Letter, Daily Mail, January 17, 1977*)

HERBERT READ
To fight without hope is to fight with grace.
(*To a Conscript of 1940, from Collected Poems*)

RAINER MARIA RILKE
. . . only by suffering the rat-race in the arena can the heart learn to beat.
(*"Imitations" by Robert Lowell*)

ST. JOHN
If, my kingdom was of this world then would my servants fight that I should not be delivered to the Jews.
(*The Bible*)

ST. PAUL
A great price was paid to ransom you.
(*Corinthians; The Bible*)

For freedom Christ has set us free; stand fast therefore, and do not submit again to a yoke of slavery.
(*Galatians; The Bible*)

"SAKI" (HECTOR HUGH MUNRO)
It is one of the consolations of middle-age reformers that the good they inculcate must live after them if it is to live at all.
(*Beasts and Super-Beasts. The Byzantine Omelette*)

JEAN-PAUL SARTRE
We were never more free than under the German occupation . . . at each moment we were living to the full the meaning of that banal little phrase: "All men are mortal". The choice that each of us made of himself was authentic, because it was made in the presence of death, since it could always be expressed in the form, "Rather death than —."
(*Situations*)

DENIS SAURAT
The imperious need of their pride was liberty. And both extended to the whole of mankind in all its activities the benefit of that privilege.
(*on William Blake and John Milton*)

L. C. B. SEAMAN
They (the Allied princes), and not Bonaparte, were the Liberators, and to prove it they came armed not only with swords but with constitutions, much as the Allies of 1945 offered Four Freedoms and schemes of Social Insurance.
(*"From Vienna to Versailles"*)

WILLIAM SHAKESPEARE
Cinna: Liberty! Freedom! Tyranny is dead!
      Run hence, proclaim, cry it about the streets.
(*Julius Caesar*)

Jack Cade: Now show yourselves men, 'tis for liberty.
(*Henry VI*)

PERCY BYSSHE SHELLEY
I will arise and waken the multitude.
(*The Revolt of Islam*)

Shake your chains to earth like dew
Which in sleep had fallen on you —
Ye are many — they are few.
(*The Mask of Anarchy*)

Let a great Assembly be
Of the fearless and the free . . .
(*The Mask of Anarchy*)

ADAM SMITH
The natural effort of every individual to better his own condition,
when suffered to exert itself with freedom and security, is so powerful a
principle, that it is alone, and without any assistance, not only capable
of carrying the society on to wealth and prosperity, but of surmounting
a hundred impertinent obstructers . . . of human laws.
(*The Wealth of Nations*)

ALEXANDER SOLZHENITSYN
I am confident, of course, knowing that I shall fulfil my tasks as a
writer in any circumstances, and from my grave even more successfully
and incontestably than while I live. No one can bar truth's course, and
for its progress I am prepared to accept even death. But perhaps
repeated lessons will teach us, at least, not to arrest a writer's pen
during his lifetime.

JAMES STEPHENS
Curiosity will conquer fear even more than bravery will.
(*The Crock of Gold*)

A. J. P. TAYLOR
In a crisis good will and efficiency are not enough.

THE TALMUD
Condemn no man and consider nothing impossible, for there is no man
who does not have a future and there is nothing that does not have its
hour.

ABRAM TERTZ
Man is engaged in a constant process of dying, yet does nothing but dream of reaching a point where he will really begin to live.
(*Andrey Sinyavsky, A Voice from the Chorus*)

MARGARET THATCHER
I am for detente. Who is not! I am also for attente. For wanting to see results; for not letting down our guard: for keeping our powder dry.
(*Pilgrims' Dinner, New York, 1975*)

ALEXIS de TOCQUEVILLE
The nations of our time cannot prevent the conditions of men from becoming equal; but it depends upon themselves whether the principle of equality is to lead them to servitude or freedom, to knowledge or to barbarism, to prosperity or wretchedness.

ANTHONY TUKE
We cannot submit to pressure and must work to support tolerance against intolerance.
(*Annual Statement by Chairman of Barclays Bank, 1976*)

MARK TWAIN
Courage is resistance to fear, mastery of fear — not absence of fear.
(*Pudd'nhead Wilson's Calendar*)

KORNEL UJEJSKI
Man's will is broken only from within.
(*The Polish Eagle; version by Helen Waddell of prose trans. by Xavier Zaleski*)

Today we are in bondage, but our will
Unbroken is, and free.
(*The Polish Eagle; version by Helen Waddell of prose trans. by Xavier Zaleski*)

VOLTAIRE
I disapprove of what you say, but I will defend to the death your right to say it.
(*Attr. to Voltaire in S. G. Tallentyre: The Friends of Voltaire*)

I will not laugh while such things are done.

HENRY C. WALLICH

If laissez faire is no good, laissez George le faire is no good either. What we do not decide for ourself will be inevitably be decided for us by others. Freedom means not to have this happen.
(*Cost of Freedom*)

K. W. WATKINS

The challenge is to build a society which combines freedom, enterprise and incentive with social justice . . . If liberal democracy should fall, no return match would be permitted by the type of regime which would replace it. Thus its defence is the most important political and educational task for the last quarter of this century.

What is at stake is whether in Britain, the nineteenth century heir to the great heritage of Ancient Greece, democracy can be preserved.
(*The Practice of Politics*)

MAX WEBER

It is not for us to show our successors the way to peace and human contentment, but rather to show them the eternal struggle for the maintenance and cultivation of our national integrity.
(*Antrittsrede*)

WENDELL WILKIE

Freedom is an indivisible word. If we want to enjoy it, and fight for it, we must be prepared to extend it to everyone, whether they are rich or poor, whether they agree with us or not, no matter what their race or the colour of their skin.

WILLIAM WORDSWORTH

We must be free or die, who speak the tongue
That Shakspeare spake; the faith and morals hold
Which Milton held.
(*National Independence and Liberty,* "*London, 1802*")

Yea, our blind Poet, who, in his later day,
Stood almost single, uttering odious truth.
(*The Prelude — Residence at Cambridge*)

Freedom and Education

WILLIAM BLAKE
The eagle never lost so much time as when he submitted to learn of the crow.

MARK BLAUG
It is contradictory to argue that parents are too negligent or ignorant to make educational choices, even when provided with adequate finance and ample information, and at the same time to concede that they can be trusted to elect the sort of officials who will make sound educational choices.
(*Education: A Framework for Choice*)

RHODES BOYSON
It is time that the parent, who as the tax and rate payer finances the schools, is given more choice in where his son and daughter are to be educated.
(*Education: A Framework for Choice*)

SAMUEL BRITTAN
One of the few cases of inferior bargaining positions is that of school-children. They are unable to escape harsh treatment, petty rules, or uncongenial conditions by shopping around between schools.
(*Capitalism and the Permissive Society*)

LORD BROUGHAM
Education makes a people easy to lead, but difficult to drive; easy to govern, but impossible to enslave.
(*Attr.*)

The schoolmaster is abroad, and I trust more to him, armed with his primer, than I do to the soldier in full military array, for upholdings and extending the liberties of his country.
(*Speech in House of Commons, January 29, 1828*)

MARTIN BUBER

As teachers, you must dare. Everything in life is based on daring. For a man to father children in these times is daring. For a man to believe in God today — that is daring. All the teacher must do is to point the direction. Then it is up to the pupil himself.
(*Encounter with Martin Buber, Aubrey Hodes*)

The real struggle is not between East and West, or capitalism and communism, but between education and propaganda. Education means teaching people to see the reality around them, to understand it for themselves. Propaganda is exactly the opposite. It tells the people "You will think like this, as we want you to think!
(*Encounter with Martin Buber, Aubrey Hodes*)

G. K. CHESTERTON

It is arguable that we ought to put the State in order before there can really be such a thing as a State School.
(*All I Survey: On Education*)

ELIZA COOK

Better build schoolrooms for "the boy",
Than cells and gibbets for "the man".
(*A Song for the Ragged Schools*)

BENJAMIN DISRAELI

A University should be a place of light, of liberty, and of learning.
(*House of Commons, March 11, 1873*)

JOHN DRYDEN

By education most have been misled;
So they believe, because they were so bred.
(*The Hind and the Panther*)

EDUCATION ACT (1944)

So far as is compatible with the provision of efficient instruction and training and the avoidance of unreasonable public expenditure, pupils are to be educated in accordance with the wishes of their parents.

JULIAN GREEN

But isn't it the role of very great men to reveal us to ourselves? I mean that they teach us what we knew without knowing that we knew it.
(*Diary 1928-1957*)

MICHAEL IVENS

One argument for independent schools can be seen when you consider the total impossibility of their existing in countries like the Soviet Union and China. They would be an affront to the State concept of culture and the individual.
(*Pressures for Conformity, article in Patterns of Prejudice, Jan/Feb. 1977*)

SAMUEL JOHNSON

I am always for getting a boy forward in his learning; for that is a sure good. I would let him at first read *any* English book which happens to engage his attention; because you have done a great deal, when you have brought him to have entertainment from a book. He'll get better books afterwards.
(*"Sir," said Dr Johnson; arranged by H. C. Biron*)

Boarding schools were established for the conjugal quiet of the parents.
(*"Sir," said Dr Johnson; arranged by H. C. Biron*)

BERTRAND DE JOUVENEL

No university faculty could permit anyone under pretext of liberty, to teach that the earth is flat. The obviously false is ruled out, and occasionally it happens that a mistake is made. The obviously wicked is ruled out, and here our only guide is the moral opinions we profess ourselves.

JOHN STUART MILL

All that has been said of the importance of individuality of character, involves, as of the same unspeakable importance, diversity of education.
(*On Liberty*)

An education established and controlled by the State should only exist as one of many competing experiments . . . to keep the others up to a certain standard of excellence.
(*On Liberty*)

A general State education is a mere contrivance for moulding people to be exactly like one another.
(*Speech, 1859*)

Even education works by conviction and persuasion as well as by compulsion.
(*On Liberty*)

Any education which aims at making human beings other than machines, in the long run makes them claim to have control over their own actions.
(*Representative Government*)

JOHN MILTON
When God did enlarge the universal diet of man's body, saving ever the rules of temperance, He then also, as before left arbitrary the dieting and repasting of our minds.
(*Arcopagitica*)

MICHEL de MONTAIGNE
There is an alphabetical ignorance, which precedes learning; but there is also another kind of ignorance, which we might call doctoral, that is created by learning and replaces the alphabetical ignorance which has been destroyed.
(*Essais*)

F. MUSGROVE
It is the business of education in our social democracy to eliminate the influence of parents on the life chances of the young.
(*The Family, Education and Society*)

ALAN T. PEACOCK & JACK WISEMAN
A democratic society in particular depends for its continued and satisfactory life upon the existence of a sufficiently literate and informed electorate, which demands some minimum level of education.
(*Education for Democrats*)

The public provision of education facilities provides no obvious guarantee against the imposition of values.
(*Education for Democrats*)

We regard education as a means of safeguarding the family from too great reliance upon the state rather than as a means for the state to take over the responsibilities of the family.
(*Education for Democrats*)

BERTRAND RUSSELL
A generation educated in fearless freedom will have wider and bolder hopes than are possible to us.
(*On Education*)

Knowledge is the liberator from the empire of natural forces and destructive passions.
(*On Education*)

WILLIAM SHAKESPEARE
Her education promises her dispositions she inherits — which makes fair gifts fairer.
(*All's Well That Ends Well*)

PERCY BYSSHE SHELLEY
And Anarchy, the Skeleton,
Bowed and grinned to everyone,
As well as if his education
Had cost ten millions to the nation.
(*The Mask of Anarchy*)

JAMES STEPHENS
He who learns and teaches free
In heaven spends eternity.
(*from The College of Science in The Adventures of Seumas Beg*)

MICHAEL SWANN
It would be wise for us educators and broadcasters to do what we can to preserve and fortify the concept of freedom. It is too easily lost and only recaptured with great difficulty.

ALEXIS DE TOCQUEVILLE
In a country in which a woman is always free to exercise her choice, and where education has prepared her to choose rightly, public opinion is inexorable to her faults.

DOUGLAS TOBLER
History may well have decreed the eventual supremacy of democracy in the modern age, but if this was to be realised an educated, responsible and politically active citizenry was required.
(*Historians in Politics*)

ARNOLD TOYNBEE
If the people's souls are to be saved, the only way is to raise the standard of mass-education to a degree at which its recipients will be rendered immune against at any rate the grosser forms of exploitation and propaganda.
(*Study of History*)

E. G. WEST
The growing trend towards comprehensives as "community schools" serving their immediate neighbourhood seems to be emphasising . . . social stratification.
(*Education: A Framework for Choice*)

A. N. WHITEHEAD
We are too exclusively bookish in our scholastic routine . . . In the Garden of Eden, Adam saw the animals before he named them: in the traditional system, children named the animals before they saw them.
(*Science and the Modern World*)

Freedom and the State

LORD ACTON
Of all checks on democracy, federation has been the most efficacious and the most congenial . . . The federal system limits and restrains the sovereign power by dividing it and by assigning to government only certain defined rights. It is the only method of curbing not only the majority but the power of the whole people.

G. C. ALLEN
. . . the chief effect of government intervention between the wars was to defend the failure rather than to encourage the enterprising.
(*The British Disease*)

Governments must abandon their predilection for supporting the *status quo* in economic life, for curbing the innovators because they disturb entrenched interests.
(*The British Disease*)

W. H. AUDEN
      The Unknown Citizen
      (to JS/07/M/378)
      This Marble Monument
      Is erected by the State . . .
Was he free? Was he happy? The question is absurd:
Had anything been wrong, we should certainly have heard.

SIR ERNEST BARKER
The humming automatism of the State is about us and all our doings, engaged in constant service and constantly intending our good. The varied field is untidy, irregular, unregulated: it has many gaps: it has even more redundancies. But may the time never come when all our life spins round on the revolving wheels of legal regulation.
(*Principles of Social & Political Theory*)

LORD BEVERIDGE
The State is or can be master of money, but in a free society it is master of very little else.
(*Voluntary Action, A Report on Methods of Social Advance*)

The state in organising security should not stifle incentive, opportunity, responsibility; in establishing a national minimum it should leave room and encouragement for voluntary action by each individual to provide more than that minimum for himself and his family.
(*Social Insurance and Allied Services*)

J. BRYCE

It is surely carried to excess when men think only of the power and glory of their State and forget what they are to mankind at large.
(*University and Historical Addresses*)

MARTIN BUBER

We cannot do without the police, in the same way that we cannot do without a state and so on. But we should try to do as much as we can without them.
(*Encounter with Martin Buber, Aubrey Hodes*)

EDMUND BURKE

If any ask me what a free government is, I answer, that for any practical purpose, it is what the people think so.
(*Letter to Sheriffs of Bristol*)

The use of force alone is but *temporary*. It may subdue for a moment; but is does not remove the necessity of subduing again: and a nation is not governed, which is perpetually to be conquered.
(*Speech of conciliation with America, March 22, 1775*)

JAMES CALLAGHAN

Local government exists to provide services for the people, not to create jobs that otherwise would not be necessary.
(*November, 1976*)

ALBERT CAMUS

All modern revolutions have ended in a reinforcement of the power of the State.
(*The Rebel*)

GUSTAV CASSEL
The representative system cannot possibly be preserved, if parliaments are constantly over worked by having to consider an infinite mass of the most intricate questions relating to private economy. The parliamentary system can only be saved by wise and deliberate restrictions of the functions of parliaments.
(*From Protectionism Through Planned Eonomy to Dictatorship*)

The instrument of restriction or of complete suppression of a whole number of civil rights is the system of an effective subordination of all institutions and organisations in the state to the political directives by the apparatuses of the ruling party and the decisions of highly influential individuals.

SIR WINSTON S. CHURCHILL
It is in the interest of the wage-earner to have many other alternatives open to him than service under one all-powerful employer called the State.
(*Party Conference Speech, 1946*)

RICHARD CROSSMAN
. . . the real threat to British representative institutions — the ever-increasing and increasingly centralised power of the Whitehall bureaucracy — remains as great as ever . . .
(*Inside View: Three Lectures on Prime Ministerial Government*)

BRIAN CROZIER
It cannot be said too often that optimum freedom is incompatible with excessive government. This is true of all governments whether their particular myth is ''equality'' or ''freedom'', but it is clearly truer of the first category than the second.
(*Power in a Free Society, in The Master of Power*)

LORD DENNING
When the State itself is in danger, our cherished freedom may have to take second place and even natural justice itself may have to suffer a setback.
(*Sayings of the Week — The Observer, April 3 1977*)

BENJAMIN DISRAELI
The formation of a free government on an extensive scale, while it is assuredly one of the most interesting problems of humanity, is certainly the greatest achievement of human wit . . .

FREDERICK ENGELS

During the period when the proletariat still needs the State, it does not require it in the interests of freedom, but in the interest of crushing its antagonists.
(*Letters*)

FARMER'S ALMANAC

It's getting harder and harder to support the government in the style to which it has become accustomed.

MILTON FRIEDMAN

A majority rules in a political democracy, but the majority that rules is typically a coalition of special interests — not a majority promoting the general interest.
(*The Public be Damned, Newsweek, August 5, 1968*)

PIETER GEYL

Rousseau's spirit, Rousseau's *trick*, this horrifying adulteration of the word "liberty", this argument leading to the conclusion that the citizen must find his liberty in the submission of his will to the State — to the democratic State, it is true, the State founded by the surrender of each to all — this Rousseauan doctrine has become the property of quite a school of thought, and it has come to the Russians via intermediaries.
(*Encounters in History*)

EDWARD GIBBON

The principles of a free constitution are irrevocably lost, when the legislative power is nominated by the executive.
(*Decline and Fall of the Roman Empire*)

JOHAN WOLFGANG von GOETHE

What government is best? That which teaches us to govern ourselves.

BARRY GOLDWATER

A government that is big enough to give you all you want is big enough to take it all away.

JO GRIMOND

The natural bureaucrat is grieved if he has to spend his own money.
(*The Bureaucratic Blight*)

LORD HAILSHAM
I have never suggested that freedom is dead in this country, but only that it is diminishing, and that a principal cause of its impairment is, in truth, the unlimited legislative power confided to Parliament, now largely limited to a single chamber elected on a first past the post system.
(*Letter in The Times, April 14, 1977*)

F. A. HAYEK
National socialism is a common form, where the state becomes the dispenser of loot collected by force. The recipients lose their self reliance in the process and come to feel indebted forever to the collective for their very lives. They have by then become enslaved.
(*Of Freedom and Free Enterprise*)

The present tendency of governments to bring all common interests in large groups under their control tends to destroy real public spirit.
(*Law, Legislation and Liberty*)

The mischievous idea that all public needs should be satisfied by compulsory organization and that all the means that individuals are willing to devote to public purposes should be under the control of government, is wholly alien to the basic principles of a free society.
(*Law, Legislation and Liberty*)

F. HÖLDERLIN
What has always made the state a hell on earth has been precisely that man has tried to make it his heaven.

JOHAN HUIZINGA
A State is never a utilitarian institution pure and simple. It congeals on the surface of time like frost-flowers on a windowpane, and is as unpredictable, as ephemeral, and, in its pattern, as rigidly casual to all appearances as they.
(*Homo Ludens*)

It is, as we know from history, a sign of revolutionary enthusiasm when governments play at ninepins with names, the venerable names of cities, persons, institutions, the calendar, etc. *Pravda* reported that as a result of their arrears in grain deliveries three *kolkhozy* in the district of Kurks, already christened Budenny, Krupskaya, and the equivalent of Red Cornfield, have been rechristened Sluggard, Saboteur,

and Do-Nothing by the local soviet. Though this *trop de zèle* received an official rebuff from the Central Committee and the offensive soubriquets were withdrawn, the puerilistic attitude could not have been more clearly expressed.
(*Homo Ludens*)

DAVID HUME

In all cases, it must be advantageous to know what is the most perfect in the kind, that we may be able to bring any real constitution or form of government as near it as possible, by such gentle attentions and innovations as may not give too great a disturbance to society.
(*The Idea of a Perfect Commonwealth*)

GRAHAM HUTTON

Political leaders in a free or "open" society must be conservative about the basic principles of individual and corporate freedom but they must also be progressive by reducing obstacles to the advance of material welfare.
(*All Capitalists Now*)

There is no reason, there is only a lazy nonchalance, which makes the state so all-powerful in the citizens' private affairs today.
(*Agenda for a Free Society — The Individual and Society*)

THOMAS JEFFERSON

Governments are instituted among Men, deriving their just powers from the consent of the governed.
(*Declaration of Independence 1776*)

C. G. JUNG

The dictator State, besides robbing the individual of his rights, has also cut the ground from under his feet psychically by robbing him of the metaphysical foundations of his existence.
(*The Undiscovered Self*)

HOWARD E. KERSHNER

The totalitarian state demands the full allegiance of man. God is no longer the keeper of his conscience; but the state assumes that prerogative.
(*God, Gold and Government*)

LAURENCE KRODER
The state is merely a political institution. People invented it. There is nothing sacred or inevitable about its existence.
(*Formation of the State*)

ANTHONY LEJEUNE
The doctrine of minimum government is not an overreaching principle, but it is a sound principle.
(*Freedom and the Politicians*)

BERNARD LEVIN
There is no such thing, in the long run, as a state which is both collectivist and democratic.
(*The Times, March 23, 1977*)

ABRAHAM LINCOLN
That this nation, under God, shall have a new birth of freedom; and that government of the people, by the people and for the people, shall not perish from the earth.
(*Gettysburg Address*)

The State should do for the people what needs to be done, but which they cannot, by individual effort, do at all or do as well for themselves.

WALTER LIPPMAN
In a free society the state does not administer the affairs of men. It administers justice among men who conduct their own affairs.
(*An Enquiry into the Principles of a Good Society*)

ROGER L. MACBRIDE
It isn't accurate to say government "is composed of" good people; government *is* simply people. They may be good people, but they are very bad wizards. Mortals have no magic.
(*A New Dawn for America*)

JOSEPH de MAISTRE
Every country has the government it deserves.
(*Lettres et Opuscules Inédits*)

JOHN STUART MILL
The worth of a State, in the long run, is the worth of the individuals composing it.
(*On Liberty*)

A state which dwarfs its men, in order that they may be more docile instruments in its hands even for beneficial purposes — will find that with small men nothing great can be accomplished.
(*On Liberty*)

The government of a country is what the social forces in existence compel it to be, is true only in the sense in which it favours, instead of discouraging, the attempt to exercise among all forms of government practicable in the existing conditions of society, a national choice.
(*On Representative Government*)

LUDWIG von MISES
Government is the only agency that can take a useful commodity like paper, slap some ink on it, and make it totally worthless.

Modern civilization is a product of the philosophy of laissez-faire. It cannot be preserved under the ideology of government omnipotence.
(*Human Action*)

BENITO MUSSOLINI
Everything for the state, nothing outside the state, nothing against the state.

NEW YORK STATE SURROGATE COURT JUDGE
No man's life, liberty or property are safe while the legislature is in session.
(*1866*)

WILLIAM A. NISKANEN
A bureaucrat's life is not a happy one (tra la!), unless he can provide increasing budgets for his subordinate bureaucrats to disburse in salaries and contracts.
(*Bureaucracy: Servant of Master?*)

THOMAS PAINE
Government, even in its best state, is but a necessary evil; in its worst state, an intolerable one.
(*Common Sense*)

The more perfect civilisation is, the less occasion it has for Government.
(*The Rights of Man*)

JOHN PASSMORE
From Plato on, the setting up of a technically perfected State entails . . . that artistic innovation is simply not to be permitted.

JOHN PEYTON
Unless people wake up freedom will be on the retreat before the remorseless advance of the corporate state and the sprawl of bureaucracy.
(*The Daily Telegraph, March 12, 1977*)

KARL POPPER
Unlimited freedom means that a strong man is free to bully one who is weak and to rob him of his freedom . . . the state should limit freedom to a certain extent, so that everyone's freedom is protected by law.
(*The Open Society and its Enemies*)

Measures should be planned to fight concrete evils rather than to establish some ideal good. State intervention should be limited to what is really necessary for the protection of freedom.
(*The Open Society and its Enemies*)

ENOCH POWELL
The creative forces in a nation lie in the people themselves — in their determination, their effort, their hopefulness, their thrift, their readiness to venture and to change.

Lift the curtain and 'the State' reveals itself as a little group of fallible men in Whitehall, making guesses about the future, influenced by political prejudices and partisan prejudices, and working on projections drawn from the past by a staff of economists.

P. J. PROUDHON
To be governed is to be watched, inspected, spied upon, directed, law-ridden, regulated, penned up, indoctrinated, preached at, checked, appraised, seized, censured, commanded, by beings who have neither title, not knowledge, not virtue.

AYN RAND
Freedom, in a political context, means freedom from government, coercion. It does *not* mean freedom from the landlord, from the employer, or freedom from the laws of nature which do not provide men with automatic prosperity. It means freedom from the coercive power of the State — and nothing else.

MURRAY N. ROTHBARD
Private enterprise makes it its business to court the consumer and to satisfy his most urgent demands; government agencies denounce the consumer as a troublesome user of their resources. Only a government, for example, would look fondly upon the prohibition of private cars as a "solution" for the problem of congested streets.

LOUIS ROUGIER
When the individual is economically free, he is also politically free, for his life does not depend on the goodwill of a sole employer: the State.
(*Les Mystiques Economiques*)

BERTRAND RUSSELL
I am persuaded that there is absolutely no limit to the absurdities that can, by government action, come to be generally believed.
(*Unpopular Essays — An Outline of intellectual Rubbish*)

GEORGE SANTAYANA
He might have shown the world whether at least in England it were not possible for a modern civilisation to exist with a maximum of liberty and a minimum of government.
(*On Bertrand Russell; My Host the World*)

HELMUT SCHMIDT
The people are not only there on election day. Only if they devote themselves to the state, the champion and guardian of the rights and freedoms of all, will the state have the energy to assert the liberties and rights of the individual for the benefit of all against section interests.
(*Bundestag, May 17, 1974*)

ARTHUR A. SHENFIELD
It is very difficult to preserve liberty unless those who have power to legislate at any given moment are subject to general rules which express the most permanent purposes of the state.
(*Agenda for a Free Society — Law*)

ALFRED SHERMAN
The idea that public agencies themselves might need controlling was foreign to them. But it only takes a moment's reflection to realise that the worst vandalism — physical and social — has been perpetrated by public authorities.
(*Right Turn, the End of Local Government*)

ADAM SMITH
By a perpetual monopoly all the other subjects of the state are taxed absurdly . . . to enable the company to support the negligence and of their own servants.
(*The Wealth of Nations*)

The progressive state is in reality the cheerful and the hearty state to all different orders of society. The stationary is dull, the declining melancholy.
(*The Wealth of Nations*)

BENEDICT SPINOZA
The man who is guided by reason, is more free in a State, where he lives under a general system of law, than in solitude, where he is independent.
(*Ethics*)

JOSEPH STALIN
The state is an instrument in the hands of the ruling class for suppressing the resistance of its class enemies.

ALFRED, LORD TENNYSON
A land of settled government,
A land of just and old renown,
Where Freedom slowly broadens down
From precedent to precedent.
(*You ask me why*)

TIMES LITERARY SUPPLEMENT
A distaste for difference can drain life out of any society . . . it is a threat to freedom. The dislike of difference, of argument, of conflict, the wish for a quiet life at all costs with as little as possible to excite envy or ambition — almost a wish to get back to the peace of the womb — all this is an invitation to governments to extend their power.

ALEXIS de TOCQUEVILLE
I believe that provincial institutions are useful to all nations, but nowhere do they appear to me to be more necessary than amongst a democratic people.
(*Democracy in America*)

Everywhere the State acquires more and more direct control over the humblest members of the community, and a more exclusive power of governing each of them in his smallest concerns . . . Diversity, as well as freedom, is disappearing day by day.
(*Democracy in America*)

LEON TROTSKY
In a country where the sole employer is the State, opposition means death by slow starvation. The old principle: who does not work shall not eat, has been replaced by a new one: who does not obey shall not eat.

Freedom and the Law

FRANCIS BACON
One of the Seven was wont to say: "That laws were like cobwebs; where the small flies were caught, and the great break through."
(*Apothegms*)

JOHN BIGGS-DAVIDSON
Whether in Belfast or in London, there is no liberty without law, no freedom without order — only intimidation and oppression.
(*Address to Isle of Ely Conservatives, November 27, 1976*)

BILL OF RIGHTS (1791)
The right of the people to be secure in their persons, houses, papers, and effects, against unreasonable searches and seizures, shall not be violated.

SAMUEL BRITTAN
If some control is unavoidable, it is better that it should be through known laws rather than through exhortation or arm-twisting or through giving quasi-governmental powers to the CBI or TUC.
(*Government and the Market Economy*)

EDMUND BURKE
Bad laws are the worst sort of tyranny.
(*Speech at Bristol, 1780*)

People crushed by law have no hopes but from power. If laws are their enemies, they will be enemies to laws; and those, who have much to hope to nothing to lose, will always be dangerous, more or less.
(*Letter to the Hon. C. J. Fox, October 8, 1777*)

SAMUEL BUTLER
For Justice, though she's painted blind,
Is to the weaker side inclin'd.
(*Hudibras*)

G. K. CHESTERTON

When you break the big laws, you do not get liberty; you do not even get anarchy. You get the small laws.
(*Daily News, July 29, 1905*)

SIR EDWARD COKE

How long soever it hath continued, if it be against reason, it is of no force in law.
(*Institutes: Commentary upon Littleton. First Institute*)

LORD DENNING

The law (is) enacted by Parliament. It is, I take it, the will of Parliament that it shall be obeyed. Even by the most powerful. Even by the trade unions.
(*Appeal Court, January 27, 1977*)

We have but one prejudice. That is to uphold the law. And that we will do, whatever befall. Nothing shall deter us from doing our duty.
(*Appeal Court, January 27, 1977*)

THE ECONOMIST

The court must decide what the constitutional law of England is. But free people should have a debate on what it ought to be.
(*Editorial "Quis custodiet?", January 22, 1977*)

MILTON FRIEDMAN

The rule of law does not guarantee freedom, since general laws as well as personal edicts can be tyrannical. But increasing reliance on the rule of law clearly played a major role in transforming Western society from a world in which the ordinary citizen was literally subject to the arbitrary will of his master to a world in which the ordinary citizen could regard himself as his own master.
(*Morality and Controls, New York Times, October 28, 1971*)

C. G. HANSON

No changes in the law on their own can make people or organisations behave better. The traditions and attitudes developed over a century cannot be changed overnight.
(*Trade Unions: A Century of Privilege?*)

F. A. HAYEK
To say that in a planned society the Rule of Law cannot hold is, therefore, not to say that the actions of the government will not be legal or that such a society will necessarily be lawless.
(*The Road to Serfdom*)

The Rule of Law thus implies limits to the scope of legislation: it restricts it to the kind of general rules known as formal law, and excludes legislation either directly aimed at particular people, or at enabling anyone to use the coercive power of the state for the purpose of discrimination.
(*The Road to Serfdom*)

THOMAS HOBBES
As for other liberties, they depend on the silence of the law.

SAMUEL JOHNSON
The Law is the last result of human wisdom acting upon human experience for the benefit of the public.
(*"Sir," said Dr Johnson; arranged by H. C. Biron*)

IMMANUEL KANT
Man is free if he needs to obey no person but solely the laws.

JOHN LOCKE
Any man who seeks to overthrow a state based on law is guilty of the greatest crime of which a man is capable. He becomes the common enemy of all mankind and must be treated as such.

LORD JUSTICE MATHEWS
In England, justice is open to all, like the Ritz Hotel.

JOHN STUART MILL
Whenever there is definite risk of damage, either to the individual or the public, the case is taken out of the province of liberty, and placed in that of morality or law.
(*On Liberty*)

If a man through intemperance or extravagance, becomes unable to pay his debts, or, having undertaken the moral responsibility of a family, becomes from some cause incapable of educating or supporting them, he is deservedly reprobated, and might be justly punished. But it is for the breach of duty to his family or creditors, not for the extravagance.
(*On Liberty*)

BARON de MONTESQUIEU
Liberty is the right to do everything which the laws allow.
(*L'Esprit des Lois*)

SIR JOHN POWELL
Let us consider the reason of the case. For nothing is law that is not reason.
(*Coggs v. Bernard, 2 Lord Raymond, 911*)

THOMAS B. REED
One of the greatest delusions in the world is the hope that the evils of this world can be cured by legislation.

GEORGE SAVILE, MARQUIS OF HALIFAX
Men are not hanged for stealing horses, but that horses may not be stolen.
(*Political Thoughts and Reflections: Of Punishment*)

GEORGE BERNARD SHAW
Between life and death there are no degrees; between law and liberty there are many.
(*Everybody's Political What's What, 1944*)

PERCY BYSSHE SHELLEY
. . . where law is made the slave of wrong.
(*The Revolt of Islam*)

MARGARET THATCHER
Freedom under the law must never be taken for granted.
(*National Press Club, Washington, 1975*)

ALEXIS de TOCQUEVILLE

The legal profession is qualified by its attributes, and even by its faults, to neutralise the vices inherent in popular government.

UNIVERSAL DECLARATION OF HUMAN RIGHTS (1948)

All human beings are born free and equal in dignity and rights . . . Everyone has the right to life, liberty and security of person. All are equal before the law and are entitled without any discrimination to equal protection of the law . . . No one shall be subjected to arbitrary interference with his privacy, home or correspondence, nor to attacks upon his honour or reputation. Everyone has the right to the protection of the law against such interference or attacks.

Freedom and Property

I got a letter from my daddy; he bought
me a sweet piece of land;
I got a letter from my daddy, he bought
me a small piece of ground;
You can't blame me for leaving, Lawd,
I'm Florida bound.
(*Florida Bound Blues (Bessie, Empress of the Blues; Chris Albertson)*)

H. B. ACTON
The only sure way of being free is to have a private sphere into which
no-one can penetrate without permission. Private property is the chief
but not the sole means by which this independence is secured.
(*Agenda for a Free Society Objectives*)

LORD ACTON
A people averse to the institution of private property is without the
first elements of freedom.

ARISTOTLE
Great is the fortune of a state in which the citizens have a moderate
and sufficient property.

SIR ARTHUR BRYANT
To the medieval mind a liberty was a right to the enjoyment of a specific
property. It was a freedom to do something with one's own without
interference by the king or any other man.
(*The Makers of the Realm*)

G. K. CHESTERTON
It was my instinct to defend liberty in small nations and poor families;
that is, to defend the rights of man as including the rights of property;
especially the property of the poor.
(*Autobiography*)

THOMAS DRUMMOND
Property has its duties as well as its rights.
(*Letter to the Earl of Donoughmore, May 22, 1838*)

ROBERT FROST
Good fences make good neighbours.

MICHAEL IVENS
We talk of an Englishman's home being his castle. The freedom is, of course, relative. Bulldozers, Government orders and acts of God can demolish the largest pile. But his property rights do act as a bulwark — even his renting rights. It is hard to have the same feeling about a council flat.
(*Pressures for Conformity, article in Patterns of Prejudice, Jan/Feb 1977*)

THOMAS MACAULAY
An acre in Middlesex is better than a principality in Utopia.
(*Literary Essays Contributed to the Edinburgh Review, July 1837*)

LOUIS MACNEICE
What will happen to us when the State takes down the manor wall,
When there is no more private shooting or fishing, when the trees are all cut down.
(*An Eclogue for Christmas*)

MICAH
Woe to those who devise wickedness . . . they covet fields . . . and houses, and take them away; they *oppress* a man and his house . . . and his inheritance.
(*The Bible*)

MURRAY N. ROTHBARD
Pollution and overuse of resources stem directly from the failure of government to defend private property. If property rights were to be defended adequately, we would find that here, as in other areas of our economy and society, private enterprise and modern technology would come not as a curse to mankind but as its salvation.

JOHN RUSKIN
Whether we force the man's property from him by pinching his stomach or pinching his fingers, make some difference anatomically; morally, none whatsoever.

ARNOLD TOYNBEE
The institution of private property is so intimately bound up with all that is best in pre-industrial society that its sheer abolition could hardly fail to produce a disastrous break in the social tradition of our Western society.
(*Study of History*)

H. G. WELLS
It is paradoxical that different men seeking the same ends of liberty and happiness should propose on the one hand to make property as absolute as possible, and on the other to put an end to it altogether. But so it was. And the clue to this paradox is to be found in the fact that ownership is not one thing, but a multitude of different things.
(*A Short History of the World*)

Freedom and Enterprise
and Economics

H. B. ACTON
A centrally planned economy is bound to monopolise ideas and even to ration them, whereas in a society where competitive markets prevail it is not only trade, but also thoughts and men that are free.
(*The Morals of Markets*)

ANON
Bennery is penury.

ERNEST BARKER
An extension of the rights of political liberty must involve a similar extension to the rights of economic liberty.
(*Principles of Social and Political Theory*)

WALTER BAGEHOT
Capital must be propelled by self interest; it cannot be enticed by benevolence.
(*Economic Studies*)

FREDERIC BASTIAT
A protective duty is a tax directed against a foreign product; but we must never forget that it falls back on the home consumer. Then the State lays hold of one part of your income, we hand over another to the monopolists.
(*Economic Sophisms*)

HILAIRE BELLOC
Lord Finchley tried to mend the Electric Light
Himself. It struck him dead: And serve him right!
It is the business of the wealthy man
To give employment to the artisan.
(*Lord Finchley*)

The control of the production of wealth is the control of human life itself.

ERNEST BECKER
Commercial industrialism promised Western man a paradise on earth, described in great detail by the Hollywood Myth, that replaced the paradise in heaven of the Christian myth.
(*The Denial of Death*)

JEREMY BENTHAM
The desire of self preservation is called a natural propensity, that is to say regarded with approbation. The desire of gain is a propensity not less natural, but in this case although more useful, it is not regarded with the same approbation.
(*The Psychology of Economic Man*)

Free competition is equivalent to a reward granted to those who furnish the best goods at the lowest of prices. It offers an immediate and natural reward, which a crowd of rivals flatter themselves they shall obtain and cuts with greater efficiency than a distant punishment from which each may hope to escape.
(*Principles of Penal Law*)

MARK BLAUG
The fundamental link between economic and political freedom is rarely discussed, possibly because economists are embarrassed to admit that a definite piece of reasoning in political theory is what is really behind a widely shared preference for private over public ownership of industry
(*The Cambridge Revolution: Success or Failure?*)

SAMUEL BRITTAN
Political freedom depends on the existence of a large capitalist sector – a ''socialist market economy'' will not do.

NORMAN O. BROWN
Luther's identification of the spirit of capitalism with the Devil draws on this tradition of the Devil as Trickster.
(*Life Against Death*)

SIR ARTHUR BRYANT
The truth is that without the instrument of money-choice a free society cannot operate or a free man exist.
(*The Uses of Money, Illustrated London News, December 3, 1966*)

EDMUND BURKE

My opinion is against an overdoing of any sort of administration, and more especially against this most momentals of all meddling on the part of authority: the meddling with the subsistence of the people.
(*Thoughts and Details Upon Scarcity*)

The love of lucre, though sometimes carried to the ridiculous, sometimes to a vicious excess, is the grand cause of prosperity in all states.

If we command our wealth, we shall be rich and free;
if our wealth commands us, we are poor indeed.
(*Letters on a Regicide Peace, 1*)

LORD BYRON

Men are more easily made than machinery
Stockings fetch better prices than lives —
Gibbets on Sherwood will heighten the scenery,
Shewing how Commerce, how liberty thrives.
(*An Ode to the Framers of the Frame Bill*)

THOMAS CARLYLE

That brutish god-forgetting Profit-and-Loss Philosophy and Life-theory, which we hear jangled on all hands of us, in senate-houses, spouting-clubs, leading-articles, pulpits and platforms, everywhere as the Ultimate Gospel and candid Plain-English of man's Life, from the throats and pens and thoughts of all-but all men!
(*Past and Present*)

The progress of human society consists . . . in . . . the better and better apportioning of wages to work.
(*Past and Present*)

E. H. CARR

It is significant that the nationalisation of thought has proceeded everywhere *pari passu* with the nationalisation of industry.

SIR NORMAN CHESTER

The fact that the industries were publicly owned did not thereby ensure that they would not act like and be subject to the temptations of monopolies throughout the ages.
(*The Nationalisation of British Industry, 1945-51*)

A. J. CULYER

Economics . . . does not of itself show how to make a nation ''good'';
but whoever would be qualified to operate a social policy or to judge of
the means of creating social justice and of liberating the noble soul
from his base self, must first . . . be a political economist.
(*The Economics of Charity*)

SIR WINSTON CHURCHILL

Trade should be regulated mainly by laws of supply and demand and
. . . apart from basic necessaries in great emergencies, the price
mechanism should adjust and correct undue spending at home.
(*Speech, House of Commons, 1947*)

COLIN CLARK

Oft-repeated phrases about poverty in the midst of plenty, and the
problems of production having already been solved if only we understood the problem of distribution, turn out to be the most untruthful of
all modern cliches.
(*Conditions of Economic Progress*)

JOAN DICKINSON

Thus the universality of provision in the Welfare State, which is a
concept sacrosanct to Socialist philosophy is, in fact, a major if not the
prime cause of low wages and poverty.
(*The Daily Telegraph, April 4, 1977*)

Payment in kind, whether it is called the social wage or the ''truck''
system of the 19th century, is a form of slavery which prevents a
worker freely disposing of his earnings and ties him to one source for
his basic needs.
(*The Daily Telegraph, April 4, 1977*)

BENJAMIN DISRAELI

There can be no economy where there is no efficiency.
(*Letters, To Constituents, October 3, 1868*)

EDITH EFRON

The so-called American capitalist, today, usually does not know what
genuine free enterprise is.

PHILIP VANDER ELST
Individual liberty cannot in the long run survive unless the economic base of society is independent and separate from the State and buttresses the brittle self-restraint of men in power.
(*The Unsocial Socialist*)

DOULAS FAWCETT
It remains, however, for those who reject "unweeting Mind", who regard the much trumpeted evolution of the conscious from the subconscious as nonsense, to try to deal seriously with the colossal problem presented by the history of mankind. To what end is this long martyrdom, not only preponderantly painful but in large part offensive, squalid and foul? . . . Economic progress and a wealth of inventions will only free man for thinking, and bring him nearer to the fateful crisis.
(*Imaginism*)

RUDOLF FLESCH
Consider that good old expression free enterprise, used in hundreds of editorials every day. When the Gallup poll asked people what it meant, only 30 per cent had a clear idea. The others either could not define it or thought it meant freedom to put over a fast one in a business deal.
(*The Art of Readable Writing, Other People's Minds*)

BENJAMIN FRANKLIN
No nation was ever ruined by trade.
(*Essays: Thoughts on Commercial Subjects*)

MILTON FRIEDMAN
There is an invisible hand in politics that operates in the opposite direction to the invisible hand in the market. In politics, individuals who seek to promote only the public good are led by an invisible hand to promote special interests that it was no part of their intention to promote.
(*Government vs. The People from An Economist's Protest*)

The Pope clearly believes that central planning is the key to economic development; that free markets and private enterprise have at most a minor role to play . . . How can the Pope's views be so widely accepted? The intellectual subtlety of the argument for free markets is,

I believe, one part of the answer. The advantages of central planning
seem obvious . . . The advantages of the free market are more difficult
to grasp.
(*Papal Economics — on Pope Paul VI's Encyclical, On the Development of Peoples, Newsweek, April 24, 1967*)

Business can and does serve the consumer and serve him well — when
we force it to compete and when we deny it special government
favours.
(*A Silver lining? Newsweek, February 1, 1971*)

We have heard much these past few years of how the government
protects the consumer. A far more urgent problem is to protect the
consumer from the government.
(*An Economist's Protest (1972)*)

Many reformers have as their basic objection to a free market that it
frustrates them in achieving their reforms, because it enables people to
have what they want, not what the reformers want.
(*Talk: The Conventional Wisdom of J. K. Galbraith; 1976*)

I know of no example in time or place of a society that has been marked
by a large measure of political freedom, and that has not also used
something comparable to a free market to organise the bulk of economic
activity.
(*Capitalism and Freedom; the University of Chicago Press*)

HUGH GAITSKELL
It may be regrettable, but it seems to be a fact that people's enthusiasm
about almost any group to which they belong is enhanced by
competition.
(*Socialism and Nationalisation*)

JOHN KENNETH GALBRAITH
When people are least sure they are often most dogmatic . . . So it is in
economics.
(*The Great Crash 1929*)

JO GRIMOND
Inflation is the only possible result of a conspiracy among bureaucracies
to take more than they produce.
(*The Bureaucratic Blight*)

The market system must engage not only a handful of managers, nor a slightly larger handful of shareholders, but the majority of people. (*The Bureaucratic Blight*)

RALPH HARRIS

When governments set out to provide even the most essential social services on a universal basis, literally a free for all, their good intentions are frustrated by the accompanying ill effects on quality of service caused by monopoly on supply or chronic shortage caused by removal of price on incentives to work caused by the consequent burden on taxation and on consumer freedom caused by the suppression of choice.

RALPH HARRIS & ARTHUR SELDON

If the nation decides through the ballot box that it would like to maintain little shops . . . a special measure of retail derating could be justified. Such direct, discriminating methods are the proper way, rather than by artificial rigid structure of uniform pricing that . . . deprives the consumer of freedom of choice. (*Advertising in a Free Society*)

. . . competition prevents the abuse of powerful producer interests by giving the consumer the final say in determining their fortunes. (*Not From Benevolence . . .*)

SIR ROY HARROD

(Keynes believed that) the structure of the free economy with its scope for individual initiative must be preserved. Keynes remained essentially an individualist . . . His work may still prove to be the foundation of a new kind of free economy, if freedom is indeed preserved. (*The Life of John Maynard Keynes*)

F. A. HAYEK

A plant or industry cannot be conducted in the interest of some permanent distinct body of workers if it is at the same time to serve the interests of consumers. Moreover, effective participation in the direction of an enterprise is a full time job. It is not only from the point of view of the employers, therefore, that such a plan (industrial democracy) should be abandoned. (*The Constitution of Liberty — Labour Unions and Employment*)

"Full employment" has . . . become a fetish with the result that any addition to employment is regarded as a gain, however much harm it may do to the capacity of the country to earn its keep.
(*The Daily Telegraph, August 26, 1976*)

One cannot help a country to maintain its standard of life by assisting people to consume more than they produce.
(*The Daily Telegraph, August 26, 1976*)

I have indeed never felt so pessimistic about the chances of preserving a functioning market economy as I do at this moment — and this means also of the prospects of preserving a free political order.
(*Economic Freedom and Representative Government*)

Where effective competition can be created, it is a better way of guiding individual efforts than any other.
(*The Road to Serfdom*)

The Labour leaders who now proclaim so loudly that they have "done once and for all with the mad competitive system" are proclaiming the doom of the freedom of the individual.
(*The Road to Serfdom*)

Our freedom of choice in a competitive society rests on the fact that, if one person refuses to satisfy our wishes we can turn to another. But if we face a monopolist we are at his mercy. And an authority directing the whole economic system would be the most powerful monopolist conceivable.
(*Road to Serfdom*)

The recent growth of monopoly is largely the result of a deliberate collaboration of organised capital and organised labour when the privileged groups of labour share in the monopoly profits at the expense of the poorest, those employed in the less well organised industries and the unemployed.
(*The Road to Serfdom*)

The most important of the public good for which government is required is thus not the direct satisfaction of any particular needs but the securing of conditions in which the individuals and smaller groups will have favourable opportunities of mutually providing for their respective needs.
(*Law, Legislation and Liberty*)

The successful entrepreneur . . . is led by the invisible hand of the market to bring the succour of modern conveniences to the poorest homes he does not even know.
(*Law, Legislation and Liberty*)

HENRY HAZLITT
Capitalism, the system of private property and free markets, is not only a system of freedom and of natural justice — which tends in spite of exceptions to distribute rewards in accordance with production — but it is a great co-operative and creative system that has produced for our generation an affluence that our ancestors did not dare dream of.
(*The Future of Capitalism, in Towards Liberty*)

A. P. HERBERT
They do say capitalism is doomed: Karl Marx, I believe, made the same announcement 80 years ago. He might still be right: but the old clock ticks on; and it does not help very much to throw stones at it. It would be surprising if our system had survived quite unshaken the unprecedented upheaval of a world war. But it is infinitely adaptable and has not, I think, exhausted its resources.

JOHN HIBBS
Everything points to a competitive structure as the best means of securing the maximum choice for the consumer, combined with a real consumer's influence over the facilities with which he is provided.
(*Transport for Passengers*)

BRIAN HINDLEY
People engaged in business *are* likely to be the most competent to judge whether another business could be run more profitably.
(*Industrial Merger and Public Policy*)

When Britain erects high tariff barriers, or impedes the importation of foreign goods by any other artifice, she creates a situation in which monopoly is likely to become a much more important element in the economy than is inherently necessary.
(*Industrial Merger and Public Policy*)

SIDNEY HOOK
As a system Marxism is now invalid. Its theory of historical materialism was exploded by those most ''orthodox'' of Marxists, the Bolshevik-Leninists, who demonstrated that politics determines economics in our age, not vice versa.
(*Revolution, Reform, and Social Justice*)

The incontestable fact remains that the working masses of the Western democratic world have secured for themselves a greater freedom and a higher welfare at a far lesser cost than ''the blood, sweat, and tears'' paid by their Russian brothers for their present lot.
(*Revolution, Reform and Social Justice*)

. . . social justice without political democracy is impossible, since the greatest injustice of all is to impose rules upon adult human beings without their consent.
(*Revolution, Reform, and Social Justice*)

W. H. HUTT
The lesson of history, explained by classical economic analysis, is that disinterested market pressures, under the profit-seeking inducement, provide the only objective, systematic discipline that would dissolve traditional barriers and offer opportunities irrespective of race or colour.
(*The Economics of the Colour Bar*)

GRAHAM HUTTON
Economic progress towards meeting all the wants of all human beings everywhere can only come by cutting costs . . . That means we need more profits and other savings to be invested in research and new capital equipment.
(*All Capitalists Now*)

In Russia and other totalitarian countries, the scarce natural resources and capital are distributed to this, that, or other use by arbitrary decisions, which are then forced on all the human beings concerned, from workers to consumers. In Britain and other democratic, free countries, resources get used, and goods made and distributed by a more economical free and voluntary system of teamwork, competition and profitability.
(*All Capitalists Now*)

Big world-trading private concerns cannot expect to grow, develop and remain profitable unless they prove profitable to all concerned in all countries. The Communist ''international trade'' system . . . takes from Poland, Hungary, Czechoslovakia what ever is needed in Russia and returns to them only what is decreed by economic rulers in Moscow. Which looks more like exploitation?
(*All Capitalists Now*)

State monopolies usually run on taxes of one kind or another. Private enterprises pay taxes to the State or, it they fail to make profits, go out of business.
(*All Capitalists Now*)

Private enterprise = consumer freedom . . . If the State owns everywhere, it decides everything to be produced; so the people get what they are told to have, not necessarily what they would like. That is the true contrast between State monopolies and private enterprises.
(*All Capitalists Now*)

Bigness is free, competitive enterprise need not become the enemy of small business. On the contrary, it flourishes on competition, and it makes small businesses flourish, just as it helps to develop the underdeveloped resources of the less-developed countries abroad.
(*All Capitalists Now*)

The biggest savings, like the biggest outputs, are made by voluntary means: by individuals, by profits of firms re-invested to make more new equipment, by pension funds and insurance offices, by trade unions, and by savings banks, unit trusts and other institutions. All these savings have to be safeguarded for the future.
(*All Capitalists Now*)

Work, even forced labour, can always build up productive capital, in time. But like slavery, it does it very slowly and inefficiently. The most efficient way of building up capital quickly is by people freely working together.
(*All Capitalists Now*)

The basic difference between the Russian and the British or American economic system remains one of force rather than freedom for human beings.
(*All Capitalists Now*)

Prosperity comes quickest by freely pulling together. That remains as true for a family as it does for a nation, and for the whole family of nations in the world.
(*All Capitalists Now*)

MICHAEL IVENS

Mussolini's contribution to modern economic practice has, in fact, received a lack of acknowledgement. His creation of IRI in Italy as a means of buying into firms who were collapsing because of the demise of the banks who owned them, has spawned a number of children which are virtually identical to their elder brother.
(*Pressures for Conformity, article in Patterns of Prejudice, Jan/Feb 1977*)

. . . Just as Marx stood Hegel on his head, so it is necessary to stand Marx on his, and recognise that free enterprise and individual ownership are necessary to freedom.
(*Pressures for Conformity, article in Patterns of Prejudice, Jan/Feb 1977*)

THOMAS JEFFERSON

Were we directed from Washington when to sow and when to reap, we should soon want bread.

To take from one, because it is thought his own industry and that of his fathers has acquired too much, in order to spare to others who, or whose fathers, have not exercised equal industry and skill, is to violate arbitrarily the first principle of association, ''the guarantee to everyone a free exercise of his industry and the fruits acquired by it''.
(*Richard E. Ellis: Thomas Jefferson, The Man . . . His World . . . His Influence*)

JOHN JEWKES

The system of free markets . . . (is) one of the most brilliant institutional inventions of the Western World.
(*Growth through Industry*)

HARRY G. JOHNSON

By and large, the ever-rising standard of living generated for the majority by the modern industrial system implies not merely improvement in national standards of consumption, but greater personal freedom and broader opportunities for self-fulfilment.

SAMUEL JOHNSON

. . . the truth is that luxury produces much good.
(*''Sir,'' said Dr Johnson; arranged by H.C. Biron*)

A man cannot make a bad use of his money, so far as regards society, if he do not hoard it; for if he either spends it or lends it out, society has the benefit. It is in general better to spend money than to give it away; for industry was promoted by spending money than by giving it away.
(*"Sir,"* said *Dr Johnson;* arranged by *H.C. Biron*)

SIR KEITH JOSEPH

Laissez-faire was a phrase invented in France to mark the need to remove the controls and the taxes that were stifling the energies of the people. No one that I have ever met wants unrestrained laissez-faire. There must be a framework of laws and taxes and services within which the market system can do its work of raising the standard of living of the people.
(*The Enemies of Freedom*)

Monetary contraction in a mixed economy strangles the private sector unless the state sector contracts with it and reduces its take from the national income.
(*Monetarism is Not Enough, the 1976 Stockton Lecture*)

It seems to me that Keynes was certainly not a Keynesian, and that he was a monetarist by any reasonable definition of the term.
(*Monetarism is Not Enough, the 1976 Stockton Lecture*)

R. KELF-COHEN

Workers in nationalised industries have tended to regard consumers as persons who have no option but to take the product and must pay the price fixed by the producer . . .
(*20 Years of Nationalisation*)

The responsibility on the directors of a private enterprise is far more direct and harsh than it is on a board of nationalised industry.
(*20 Years of Nationalisation*)

TERENCE KELLY

. . . competition must be an essential ingredient of any remedy for the industry's troubles. It is not the role of the state to prop up private monopoly.
(*A Competitive Cinema*)

JOHN MAYNARD KEYNES

The ideas of economists and political philosophers, both when they are right and when they are wrong, are more powerful than is commonly understood. Indeed the world is ruled by little else. Practical men, who believe themselves to be quite exempt from any intellectual influences, are usually the slaves of some defunct economist. Madmen in authority, who heard voices in the air, are distilling their frenzy from some academic scribbler of a few years back. I am sure that the power of vested interests is vastly exaggerated compared with the gradual encroachment of ideas. Not, indeed, immediately, but after a certain interval; for in the field of economic and political philosophy there are not many who are influenced by new theories after they are twenty-five or thirty years of age, so that the ideas which civil servants and politicians and even agitators apply to current events are not likely to be the newest. But, soon or late, it is ideas, not vested interests, which are dangerous for good or evil.

(The General Theory of Employment, Interest and Money, 1936-1947 edition)

VLADIMIR ILYICH LENIN

The whole of society will have become a single office and a single factory with equality of work and equality of pay.

We recognise neither freedom, nor equality, nor labour democracy if they are opposed to the interests of the emancipation of labour from capital.

Politics cannot but have dominance over economics.

VERA LUTZ

France's rapid economic expansion since the war . . . has been associated with only mild interference by the authorities with the freedom or natural inducement to locate new businesses in the places which the entrepreneurs have thought best . . .

(Economic Miracles)

RICHARD LYNN

In Russia and Eastern Europe, although planning is an ideological commitment, they are now tumbling over one another to escape its meshes. The Communist experience is further evidence that psychological satisfaction and economic efficiency lie in the freedom of the market economy.

(National Planning and Industrial Frustration)

ROGER L. MACBRIDE
The United States has since the 1920s largely *built* the Soviet Union's technology with that developed in an enterprise society. If the Soviet Union stands on its own technical feet without our financial and technical subsidies, the inefficiencies of a socialist economy will effectively inhibit any overseas adventures it may contemplate.
(*A New Dawn for America*)

THOMAS MALTHUS
If a country can only be rich by running a successful race for low wages, I should be disposed to say at once, perish such wages.
(*Principles of Political Economy*)

KARL MANNHEIM
Recent studies in the sociology of law once more confirm that the fundamental principal of formal law by which every case must be judged according to general rational precepts, which have as few exceptions as possible and are based on logical subsumptions, obtains only for the liberal competitive phase of capitalism.

KARL MARX
Since the commencement of the 18th century there has been no serious revolution in Europe which had not been preceded by a commercial and financial crisis.
(*On Colonialism: Revolt in China and in Europe*)

The bourgeoisie has been the first to show what man's activity can bring about. It has accomplished wonders for surpassing Egyptian pyramids, Roman aqueducts and Gothic cathedrals . . . the bourgeoisie . . . draws all nations . . . into civilisation . . . it has created enormous cities and thus rescued a considerable part of the population from the idiocy of rural life . . . the bourgeoisie, during its rule of scarce one hundred years has created more massive and more colossal productive forces than have all the preceding generations together.

ANGUS MAUDE
Despite the pretentions of the planners, the fact is that it is only from the freedom of choice of the consumer, that real progress comes. This is not only true of industry and commerce. It is true of society as a whole.
(*Towards a Responsible Society*)

HENRY MEULEN
The reason for this disapproval of ''getting into debt'' springs from the fact that most people borrow only for consumption; it is a small minority that borrows for production.
(*The Individualist, October, 1976*)

JOHN STUART MILL
In the case of most men the only inducement which has been found sufficiently constant and unflagging to overcome the ever present influence of indolence and lose ease, and induce men to apply themselves unceasingly to work for the most part in itself dull and uninteresting, is the prospect of bettering their own economic condition and that of their family.
(*Chapters on Socialism*)

LUDWIG von MISES
When we call a capitalist society a consumers' democracy, we mean that the power to dispose of the means of production, which belongs to the capitalists and entrepreneurs, can only be acquired by means of the consumers' ballot, held daily in the market place.

In the market economy . . . the worker is free to find the employment that suits him best.
(*The Anti-Capitalist Mentality*)

The constitutions and bills of right do not create freedom. They merely protect the freedom that the competitive economic system grants to the individuals against encroachments on the part of the police forces.
(*The Anti-Capitalist Mentality*)

Where there is no market economy, the best intentioned provisions of constitutions and laws remain a dead letter.
(*Human Action*)

Capitalist society had no means of compelling a man to change his occupation or his place of work other than to reward those complying with the wants of consumers by higher pay.
(*Human Action*)

Even the crudest and dullest people achieve more when working of their own accord than under the fear of the whip.
(*Human Action*)

The history of capitalism in Great Britain as well as in all other capitalist countries is a record of unceasing tendency toward the improvement of the wage earner's standard of living.
(*Human Action*)

The outstanding fact about the Industrial Revolution is that it opened an age of mass production for the needs of the masses. The wage earners are no longer toiling merely for other people's well being . . . They themselves are the main consumers of the products the factories turn out.
(*Human Action*)

Servile labour disappeared because it could not stand the competition of free labour; its unprofitability sealed its doom in the market economy.
(*Human Action*)

It is not labour legislation and labour union pressure that have shortened hours of daily work and withdrawn married women and children from the factories; it is capitalism, which has made the wage earner so prosperous that he is able to buy more leisure time for himself and his dependents.
(*Human Action*)

In the political democracy only the votes cast for the majority candidate or the majority plan are effective in shaping the course of affairs. But on the market no vote is cast in vain. Every penny spent has the power to work upon the productive processes.
(*Human Action*)

ROBERT MOSS
Every Marxist knows (it is a pity that many non-Marxists appear to have forgotten) that economic pluralism is the essential precondition for political pluralism.
(*Freedom and Subversion*)

MALCOLM MUGGERIDGE
You clearly showed that You were against capitalism; if the money-changers had been nationalised like the Post Office, or state-registered like a betting shop, they would doubtless have been unobjectionable.
(*Jesus Rediscovered*)

D. R. MYDDLETON
There is no doubt that poorer citizens would gain far more by an increase in the national income than by trying to redistribute more of the "existing" national income.
(*IEA Readings*)

WILLIAM OF NASSAU (The Elder)
Though it is in the power of human institutions to make everybody poor, they cannot make everybody rich.
(*Journal*)

DUDLEY NORTH
No people ever yet grew rich by policies, but it is peace, industry and freedom that bring trade and wealth.
(*A Discourse Upon Trade*)

FRIEDRICH NIETZSCHE
When the State ceaseth, look, my brothers — do you not see the rainbow and the Bridge of the Beyond.
(*Thus Spake Zarathustra*)

THOMAS PAINE
When wages are fixed by what is called a law, the legal wages remain stationary while everything else is in progression; and as those who make that law still continue to lay on new taxes by other laws, they increase the expense of living and take away the means by another.
(*The Rights of Man*)

IVY PAPPS
There is no necessary conflict between freedom of choice and social concern . . . It is perfectly possible to argue for a free market and more individual choice whilst also demanding a redistribution of income.
(*Government and Enterprise*)

C. NORTHCOTE PARKINSON
We must never offer private monopoly as an alternative to public monopoly. We cannot defend the virtues of a competition which we have quietly abolished by trade agreements or merger.
(*Case for Capitalism — State Monopoly*)

OCTAVIO PAZ
I would gladly exchange all the speculations of modern Marxists with regard to dialectics, language, structure, or praxis among Lacedaemonians for a concrete analysis of the social relations of production in the Soviet Union or China.
(*Alternating Currents*)

PRINCE PHILIP
Innovation, risk and enterprise are incompatible with complete stability and security.
(*The Engineer, November 1976*)

GEORGE POLANYI
Man's economy, as a rule, is submerged in his social relationships. He does not act so as to safeguard his individual interest in the possession of material goods; he acts so as to safeguard his social standing, his social claims, his social assets. He values material goods, only in so far as they serve this end . . . The economic system will be run for non-economic motives.
(*The Greta Transformation*)

LOUIS POMMERY
It is false to say that the free economy leads to anarchy; there is no doubt that the regime by which people want to replace it would be the best harbinger of tyranny.
(*Aperçu d'Histoire Economique Contemporaine*)

KARL POPPER
We must construct social institutions, enforced by the power of the state, for the protection of the economically weak from the economically strong.
(*The Open Society and its Enemies: The Social System*)

KATHERINE ANNE PORTER
A man who has learnt to love the poor profitably.

ENOCH POWELL

The free enterprise economy is the true counterpart of democracy: it is the only system that gives everyone a say. Everyone who goes into a shop and chooses one article instead of another is casting a vote in the economic ballot box: with thousands of millions of others that choice is signalled through to production and investment and helps to mould the world just a tiny fraction nearer to people's desire. In the great and continuous general election of the free economy nobody, not even the poorest, is disfranchised.
(*Freedom and Reality*)

The collective wisdom and the collective will of the nation resides not in any little Whitehall clique but in the whole mass of the people — in the procedures, listening to the voice of the customer at home and abroad; in the savers and investors, using their eyes and their brains to lay out their resources to best advantage; in the consumers themselves, expressing through the complex nervous system of the market their wishes, their needs, their expectations.

When we look at the astonishing material achievements of the West . . . we see these things as the result, not of compulsion or government action or the superior wisdom of a few, but of that system of competition and free enterprise, rewarding success and penalising failure, which enables every individual to participate by his private decisions in shaping the future of his society.

It is no accident that wherever the State has taken economic decision away from the citizen, it has deprived him of his other liberties as well.

DAVID RICARDO

The friends of humanity cannot but wish that in all countries the labouring classes should have a taste for comforts and enjoyments and that they should be stimulated by all legal means to procure them. In those countries where the labouring classes . . . are contented with the cheapest food, the people are exposed to the greatest vicissitudes and miseries.
(*The Principles of Political Economy and Taxation*)

B. C. ROBERTS

If the unions are to make a constructive contribution to the future welfare of the nation they must come to terms with the market economy which is an essential feature of a free society, and not to seek to prevent it from working.
(*Trade Unions in a Free Society*)

B. A. ROGGE
The marketplace weeds out the dishonest.

HAROLD ROSE
. . . the pressure of open competition . . . provides the only workable and continuous solution to the conflict of economic interest and the accountability of managment to shareholders is an essential ingredient of a competitive economic system.
(*Disclosure in Company Accounts*)

MASSIMO SALVADORI
Monopoly capitalism is no more compatible with liberty than fascist corporatism or communist collectivism.
(*Liberal Democracy*)

J. A. SCHUMPETER
There exists no more democratic institution than the market.
(*Capitalism, Socialism and Democracy*)

WILFRID SENDALL
Political freedom only starts to appear with the separation of wealth and power, when sources of wealth arose which did not need physical power, in short with the development of commerce.
(*Prophets of Freedom and Enterprise*)

WILLIAM SHAKESPEARE
'Tis not so well that I am poor, though many of the rich are damned.
(*All's Well That Ends Well*)

BERNARD SHAW
Money . . . enables us to get what we want instead of what other people think we want.
(*The Intelligent Woman's Guide to Socialism*)

LORD SHAWCROSS
To enable personal freedom to survive private enterprise must continue to flourish. All experience so far has shown that individual freedom and complete socialisation cannot exist together.
(*Speech to Wider Share Ownership Council, May 18, 1977*)

ARTHUR A. SHENFIELD

If equity requires the redistribution of income and capital from the rich to the poor, our system does not achieve this result in any realistic sense . . . Above all it . . . undermines the rule of law because it stimulates tax avoidance out of all proportion to its capacity to produce revenue.
(*Right Turn — Trial by Taxation*)

ADAM SMITH

The statesman who should attempt to direct private people in what manner they ought to employ their capitals, would not only load himself with a most unnecessary attention, but assume an authority which could safely be entrusted to no council and senate whatever, and which would nowhere be so dangerous as in the hands of a man who had folly and presumption enough to fancy himself fit to exercise it.

By directing that industry in such a manner as its produce may be of the greatest value, and he is in this, as in many other cases, led by an invisible hand to promote an end there was no part of his intention . . . By pursuing his own interest he frequently promotes that of our society more effectually than when he really intends to promote it.
(*The Wealth of Nations*)

It is (ambition) which rouses and keeps in continual motion the industry of mankind. It is this which first prompted them to cultivate the ground, to build houses, to found cities and commonwealths, and to invent and improve all the sciences and arts which ennoble and embellish human life . . .
(*The Theory of Moral Sentiments*)

The great advantage of the market is that it is able to use the strength of self-interest to offset the weakness and partiality of benevolence, so that those who are unknown, unattractive or unimportant, will have their wants served.

The uniform, constant and uninterrupted effort of every man to better his condition, the principle from which public and national, as well as private opulence is originally derived, is frequently powerful enough to maintain the natural progress of things toward improvement, in spite of both the extravagance of government and of greater errors of administration.
(*The Wealth of Nations*)

Great nations are never impoverished by private though they sometimes are by public, prodigality and misconduct. The whole or almost the whole public revenue, is in most countries, employed in maintaining unproductive hands.
(*The Wealth of Nations*)

HENRY SMITH
If the communists will go back to what is fundamental in Marx, the insistence that economic freedom can only exist in conditions where capital is plentiful and productivity is high, they will be driven to see that the rising level of productivity in the West *lessens* tension in the world, and that the peaceful development of equipment and education in their own countries is the only permanent foundation on which socialism is possible.
(*Communist Economy under Change*)

JONATHAN SWIFT
He gave it for his opinion, that whoever could make two ears of corn or two blades of grass grow upon a spot of ground where only one grew before, would deserve better of mankind, and do more essential service to his country, than the whole race of politicians put together.
(*Gulliver's Travels*)

JEFFREY SWITZER
Public ownership does not necessarily provide a solution because it may substitute a bureaucracy that cannot be controlled for the private owner who can.

T. E. UTLEY
One argument of which the apologists of capitalism are inclined to make too little use is the unique value of an economy based on money and marketing as a means to personal freedom of all kinds. Nothing could be more equitable than a system which puts to the acid test of willingness to make sacrifices the desire to possess (scarce) commodities.
(*Capitalism and Morality: The Case for Capitalism*)

THORSTEIN VEBLEN
The time has come to ask liberal humanists — who, to their honour, entertain ''freedom from want'' as a goal — how they will deal with Plato's point that poverty consists not so much in small property as in large desires.
(*Theory of the Leisure Class*)

ANTHONY VICE

. . . take-over bids perform a useful function in a free economy where resources, human and other, are allocated by the price mechanism in accordance with underlying consumer preferences. Despite all the recent publicity and controversy, bids are essentially an old-fashioned method of industrial growth in a market economy.
(*Strategy for Take-overs*)

HENRY C. WALLICH

People accustomed to get what they want for their money are more likely to insist on the same for their vote.
(*Cost of Freedom*)

Consumer freedom is a rather prosaic version of our great ideal. The unobserving may be pardoned if he fails to recognise the housewife pushing her truck in the supermarket as a present-day incarnation of the goddess of liberty.
(*Cost of Freedom*)

The centralised economy puts a strain on democracy and freedom; the free economy does not.
(*Cost of Freedom*)

The consumer who can take his custom elsewhere, the worker who can check out and go, are symbols of freedom protected by the disposal of power.
(*Cost of Freedom*)

K. W. WATKINS

For those who, with justification, denounce the Watergate affair and other seamy aspects of American, British and other free enterprise economies there is a further point to be considered. In a free society such matters, however corrupt and revolting, can be exposed.
(*The Practice of Politics*)

Industry and private enterprise, by responsible social action and vastly improved communication with the man-in-the-street, can be its own best defender. But in conducting the defence it would err if it fought on a narrow business basis. What is at stake is freedom.
(*The Practice of Politics*)

H. G. WELLS
It is too hastily believed that the poor are poor because the rich have taken something away from them . . . It is not a process that can be remedied by selling up the rich man and giving up all that he has to the poor.
(*The Work, Wealth and Happiness of Mankind*)

PETER WILES
It appears that an effective desire for personal freedom really is generated by high income . . . Leninism is being recognised as a doctrine for backward peoples. For advanced ones Marxism suffices.
(*Leninism and Weltinnenpolitik; Survey Magazine*)

TOM WILSON
We may have, in some respects an increasingly permissive society; but we can scarcely claim to have an increasingly permissive economy.
(*The Contradiction in our Attitudes to Freedom, New Society, February 15, 1968*)

Individualism is a basic principle of those who wish to reform the criminal law. But those who want to secure attention for their views on economic policy had better avoid any reference to individual liberty lest they find their views dismissed out of hand as old-fashioned and even disreputable.
(*The Contradiction in our Attitudes to Freedom, New Society, February 15, 1968*)

The more he is a rebel, the more a man of letters can be assumed to be an opponent of private enterprise and an advocate of public ownership and state control. This is understandable in the light of history; but the lag in adjusting to changed circumstances seems a little excessive. Private enterprise, like the Conservative Party, has come to be identified with the establishment, and the establishment — though only vaguely defined — is assumed to be the natural enemy of the radical.
(*The Contradiction in our Attitudes to Freedom, New Society, February 15, 1968*)

VIRGINIA WOOLF
No force in the world can take from me my five hundred pounds . . . I need not hate any man; he cannot hurt me. I need not flatter any man; he has nothing to give me.
(*A Room of One's Own*)

B. S. YARNEY

It is not very likely that more than a small proportion of consumers might have to pay more for some of their purchases if retail price maintenance were abolished. It is certain, however, they would be able to buy things more cheaply.

(*Resale Price Maintenance and Shoppers' Choice*)

Freedom and Taxation

ALCUIN
Like a rascal tax collector than can never fill his name.
(*To Samuel, Bishop of Sens, in time of dearth; trans. Helen Waddell;
More Latin Lyrics, from Virgil to Milton*)

ANON
From a hundred thousand Pound Tax, to maintain knaves and whores.
(*A Free Parliament Litany*)

J. H. BREASTED
The financial burden of this vast organisation, begun under Diocletian
and completed under his successors, was enormous, for this multitude
of government officials and the clamorous army had all to be paid for
and supported.
The amount of a citizen's taxes continued to increase until finally
little that he possessed was free from taxation. The penalty of wealth
seemed to be ruin, and there was no motive for success in business
when such prosperity meant ruinous over-taxation.
The Emperor's unnumerable officials kept an eye upon even the
humblest citizen . . . staggering under his crushing burden of taxes, in
a state which was practically bankrupt, the citizen of every class had
now become a mere cog in the vast machinery of government. In so far
as the ancient world was one of progress in civilisation, its history
ended with the accession of Diocletian.''
(*Writing of the administrative organisation of the Roman Empire in
''Ancient Times''*)

COLIN CLARK
A large part of the effort of modern politicians is devoted to destroying
. . . the sense of responsibility among electors and to spreading the
futile and dishonest belief that somehow or other someone else will pay
for the good things for which electors are invited to vote.
(*Taxmanship*)

H. S. FERNS
The history of liberty and free enterprise in Britain begins with the refusal to pay taxes.

A. P. HERBERT
Well, fancy giving money to the Government!
Might as well have put it down the drain.
Fancy giving money to the Government!
Nobody will see the stuff again.
(*Too Much!*)

MICHAEL IVENS
Politicians have grasped that control of the currency gives unlimited powers. You can tax organisations and social classes out of existence.
(*Pressures for Conformity, article in Patterns of Prejudice, Jan/Feb 1977*)

W. E. H. LECKY
Highly graduated taxation realises most completely the supreme danger of democracy, creating a state of things in which one class imposes on another burdens which it is not asked to share.
(*Democracy and Liberty*)

LUDWIG von MISES
Many upholders of high taxation are sincere opponents of monopoly, but if taxation were lower and, especially if undistributed profits were exempt from taxation, many businesses would spring up which would compete actively with the established monopolies.
(*Human Action*)

J. PIERPOINT MORGAN
Income tax evasion is a legal, not a moral question. Anyone has a right to do anything the law does not say is wrong.

JAMES OTIS
Taxation without representation is tyranny.

CHARLES PRATT, EARL CAMDEN
Taxation and representation are inseparably united.
(*Speech, House of Lords, 1765*)

Freedom and Choice

WILFRED ALTMAN
. . . citizens who are expected to be capable of choosing their political governors should be capable of choosing their television programmes . . .
(*TV: from Monopoly to Competition*)

RHODES BOYSON
Poverty in this country progressively means not material shortages but the lack of choice. The good society must aim at widening choice for all, not least in education.
(*Education: A Framework for Choice*)

WILSON van DUSEN
One could really question the amount of freedom of choice involved if everyone ended up in heaven.
(*The Presence of Other Worlds*)

GEORGE ELIOT
The strongest principle of growth lies in human choice.

JOHAN HUIZINGA
History, and the advantages of diversity.
(*Letter to Julien Benda, 1933*)

RUDYARD KIPLING
Each to his choice, and I rejoice.
(*Sussex*)

JOHN MILTON
What wisdom can there be to choose, what continence to forbear without the knowledge of evil?
(*Areopagitica*)

God uses not to captivate under a perpetual childhood of prescription, but trusts him with the gift of reason to be his own chooser.
(*Areopagitica*)

When God gave (man) reason, he gave him freedom to choose, for reason is but choosing; he had been else a mere artificial Adam, such an Adam as he is in the nation.
(*Areopagitica*)

LUDWIG von MISES
The consumer is according to legend simply defenceless against high pressure advertising. If this were true, success or failure in business would depend upon the mode of advertising only. However nobody believes that any kind of advertising would have succeeded in making candle makers hold the field against the electric bulb.
(*Human Action*)

The owners of the material factors of production and the entrepreneurs are virtually mandatories or trustees of the consumers, revocably appointed by an election daily repeated.
(*Human Action*)

RABBI NACHMAN
The world was created only for the sake of the choice and choosing one.
(*Sayings or Rabbi Nachman, from The Tales of Rabbi Nachman, by Martin Buber*)

PRINCE PHILIP
Without diversity there would be no choice and without choice there is no freedom.
(*A Place for the Individual — Royal Society of Arts Lecture, 1976*)

SENECA, BISHOP OF PICENUM
. . . that man can achieve happiness by his free choice, supported by the goodness of human nature.

WILLIAM SHAKESPEARE
Thou hast power to choose.
(*All's Well That Ends Well*)

MARGARET THATCHER
My real reason for believing in the future of Britain and America is because freedom under the law, the essence of our constitutions — is something that both honours human dignity and at the same time provides the economic opportunity to bring greater prosperity to our people — a personal prosperity based on individual choice.
(*National Press Club, Washington, 1975*)

DENIS THOMAS

Freedom of the air means the right of people to listen to any broadcast of their choice, free from government dictation. To refuse people such freedom simply because unlicensed radio has knocked a hole in the fabric of state protectionism seems an abject denial of consumer wants — and voters' choice.

(*Competition in Radio*)

Freedom and the Unions

S. W. ALEXANDER

It is often argued that in the case of trade unions it is unfair that those who do not belong should have the advantages believed to be achieved by those in a majority. Those advantages are not, however, received at the expense of those who put on the pressure for higher wages but at the expense of the companies concerned, and they, too, are entitled to do what they wish. The right to individual freedom is paramount and the convenience of organisations is not.

(*Letter in Financial Times, December 15, 1976*)

MILTON FRIEDMAN

In general, I have little sympathy with trade unions. They have done immense harm by restricting the access to jobs, denying excluded workers the opportunity to make the most of their abilities, and forcing them to take less satisfactory jobs.

(*Morality and Controls, New York Times, October 29, 1971*)

GOTTFRIED HABERLER

The excessive power of labour unions should be curbed. There is simply no synthetic substitute for restoring a larger measure of competition in the labour market and elsewhere.

(*Inflation and the Unions*)

F. A. HAYEK

We have now reached a state where (the unions) have become uniquely privileged institutions to which general rules of law do not apply. They have become the only important instance in which governments signally fail in their prime function — the prevention of coercion and violence.

(*Constitution of Liberty*)

Whatever true coercive power unions may be able to wield over employers is a consequence of this primary power of coercing other workers; the coercion of employers would lose most of its objectionable character if unions were deprived of this power to exact unwilling support.

(*The Constitution of Liberty — Union Coercion and Wages*)

MICHAEL IVENS

If the businessman suffers from attacks on his freedom, his sufferings are nothing compared to those workers who fall out with the trade union system.
(*Pressures for Conformity, article in Patterns of Prejudice, Jan/Feb 1977*)

PAUL JOHNSON

The freedom of labour contracts is being removed by law . . . and the jaws of the corporate state once more close around us . . . The compulsory enforcement of the closed shop by parliamentary statute is the greatest disaster which has befallen liberty in my lifetime, a defeat of freedom comparable to those the Stuart kings attempted to inflict — and failed.
(*Towards the Parasite State, New Statesman, September 3, 1976*)

SIR KEITH JOSEPH

The socialist myth has served to rationalise and romanticise the most atavistic reactionary and anti-social currents among organised labour.
(*The Times, November 3, 1976*)

VLADIMIR ILYITCH LENIN

Pure and simple trade unionism means the ideological subordination of the workers to the bourgeoisie.
(*What is to be done?*)

JEAN-FRANÇOIS REVEL

. . . the oldest form of trade unionism is that of Britain. This means that the modern methods of acquiring and defending the rights of labour were first conceived and put into practice in the country where political liberalism had its start.
(*Without Marx or Jesus*)

B. C. ROBERTS

It is almost certain that a strike primarily directed against the government would be unlawful, and those taking part in it would be liable to legal action.
(*Trade Unions in a Free Society*)

It cannot be assured on the basis of mere existence of trade unions that a society is democratic, since the ruling oligarchies of both the right and left have made use of trade unions to suit their ends.
(*Trade Unions in a Free Society*)

Trade unions are vitally important institutions in a free society, since they serve as an instrument of democratic self-government. Their right to protect and promote the interest of their members should never be superseded by the state.
(*Trade Unions in a Free Society*)

H. C. SIMONS
Government, long hostile to other monopolies, suddenly sponsored and promoted widespread labour monopolies, which democracy cannot endure, cannot control without destroying, and perhaps cannot destroy without destroying itself.
(*Hanser on Fiscal Policy*)

HENRY SLESSER
Trade union law, like commercial law, has rested for the last hundred years on the assumption that the persons concerned are free contracting parties.
(*Agenda for a Free Society — The Legal Status of Trade Unions*)

Freedom and Peace

WINSTON S. CHURCHILL

If we look to our responsibility to the generations yet unborn who will come after us, how can we fail to recognise that peace and freedom are inextricably bound up one with another and that the threat to one is a threat to both.

(*Address at a National Association for Freedom meeting, 1976*)

It might be said of east-west détente that never has so much been written about so little.

(*The Economist, January 8, 1977*)

DOUGLAS WILLIAM JERROLD

We love peace, as we abhor pusillanimity; but not peace at any price. There is a peace more destructive of the manhood of living man than war is destructive of his material body. Chains are worse than bayonets.

(*Wit and Opinions of D. J. Peace*)

VLADIMIR ILYITCH LENIN

As an ultimate objective "peace" simply means communist world control.

(*Treatise on the Tasks of the Young League*)

FATHER PETER LEVI

What is mankind? What is justice? I say it is liberty and peace.

(*Christmas Sermon from Death is a Pulpit*)

BERTRAND RUSSELL

If men were actuated by self interest, which they are not, except in the case of a few saints, the whole human race would co-operate. There would be no more wars, no more armies, no more navies, no more atom bombs.

(*Human Society in Ethics and Politics*)

MASSIMO SALVADORI
Who works for liberty, at home or abroad, works also for peace.
(*Liberal Democracy*)

SOLZHENITSYN
The most important aspect of detente today is that there is no ideological détente.
(*Warning to the Western World*)

Freedom and Animal Life

ANON
'Tis bad enough in man or woman
To steal a goose from off a common;
But surely he's without excuse
Who steals the common from the goose.
(*On Enclosures; The Oxford Book of Light Verse*)

BOETHIUS
And spurns the seed with tiny desperate claws.
Naught but the woods despairing pleads,
The woods, the woods again, it grieves, it grieves.
(*Trans. Helen Waddell; More Latin Lyrics, from Virgil to Milton*)

GERARD MANLEY HOPKINS
But his own nest, wild nest, no prison.
(*The Caged Skylark*)

As a dare-gale skylark scanted in a dull cage . . .
That bird beyond the remembering his free fells;
This in drudgery, day-labouring-out life's age.
(*The Caged Skylark*)

JOHAN HUIZINGA
Play is older than culture, for culture, however inadequately defined,
always presupposes human society, and animals have not waited for
man to teach them their playing.
(*Homo Ludens*)

GEORGE ORWELL
All animals are equal, but some animals are more equal than others.
(*Animal Farm*)

HERBERT READ
Freedom is not an essence only available to the sensibility of men; it is
germinatively at work in all living beings as spontaneity and auto-
plasticity.
(*Anarchy and Order*)

147

VICTORIA SACKVILLE-WEST

The greater cats with golden eyes
Stare out between the bars . . .
They prowl the aromatic hill,
And mate as fiercely as they kill,
And hold the freedom of their will.
(*The Greater Cats*)

MARK TWAIN

If you pick up a starving dog and make him prosperous, he will not bite
you. This is the principal difference between a dog and a man.
(*Pudd'nhead Wilson's Calendar*)

One of the most striking differences between a cat and a lie is that a cat
has only nine lives.
(*Pudd'nhead Wilson's Calendar*)

There is no character, howsoever good and fine, but it can be
destroyed by ridicule, howsoever poor and witless. Observe the ass, for
instance; his character is about perfect, he is the choicest spirit among
all the humbler animals, yet see what ridicule has brought him to.
Instead of being complimented when we are called an ass, we are left in
doubt.
(*Pudd'nhead Wilson's Calendar*)

Freedom and the Media and the Arts

DAVID ASTOR
A newspaper hostile to the government can — on rare occasions — bring it down; the Washington Post and President Nixon is the most striking example. Now is it conceivable that any Government in its right mind would deliberately set up and maintain by licence a body (such as a newspaper or broadcasting station) that was free and capable of destroying the government.
(*How the British Press Censors Itself*)

A newspaper might easily commit suicide by challenging the censorship of the print unions.
(*How the British Press Censors Itself*)

The fact is that uncensored books and newspapers exist only in the liberal democracies and, what is more, only when private enterprise is permitted.
(*How the British Press Censors Itself*)

The idea of qualifying tests to engage in politics or writing is nonsense in a free society and journalism belongs to both politics and literature . . . But as with actors and musicians (the union) should not control admission.
(*How the British Press Censors Itself*)

The whole merit of the present BBC is that its Governors are, normally, chosen just because they are not politicians or the representatives of interests: the independent Governments protect the independence of broadcasters.
(*How the British Press Censors Itself*)

WILLIAM BLAKE
Poetry Fetter'd Fetters the Human Race.
(*To the Public from Jerusalem*)

THOMAS CARLYLE

Burke said there were Three Estates in Parliament; but, in the Reporters' Gallery yonder, there sat a *Fourth Estate* more important far than them all.

(*The Hero as Man of Letters from Heroes and Hero-Worship*)

MR JUSTICE CAULFIELD

The warning bark of the press is necessary to help in maintaining a free society. If the press is the watchdog of freedom and its fangs are drawn all that will ensue is a whimper, possibly a whine, but no bite.

(*In Sunday Telegraph, secrets case, January 2, 1971*)

CHARTER 77

The freedom of speech is suppressed through a central management of all mass media, including the publishing and cultural institutions.

JOHN DONNE

Forbids not books, but Authors.

(*Infinitati Sacrum from Poetry and Prose of Donne*)

ANDRÉ GIDE

Every morning Pravda teaches them just what they should know and think and believe. So that every time you talk to one Russian you feel as if you were talking to them all.

(*Back from the USSR*)

LORD GOODMAN

I can think of no greater enormity in a civilised society than that a man who has something to write is prevented from doing it because of industrial organisation.

(*TV, June 7, 1976*)

DAVID HUME

Those who employ their pens on political subjects, free from party-rage, and party-prejudices, cultivate a science, which, of all others, contributes most to public utility, and even to the private satisfaction of those who addict themselves to the study of it . . .

(*Essay XV — of Civil Liberty Essay, 1758*)

The spirit of the people must frequently be roused in order to curb the ambition of the court; and the dread of rousing the spirit, must be employed to prevent that ambition. Nothing so effectual to this purpose

as the liberty of the press, by which of the learning wit and genius of the nation may be employed on the side of liberty, and everyone be animated to its defence.
(*Essays and Treaties on several subjects, 1758*)

THOMAS JEFFERSON
Were it left to me to decide whether we should have a government without newspapers, or newspapers without a government, I should not hesitate to prefer the latter.
(*Letter to Edward Carrington, 1787*)

No government ought to be without censors; and where the press is free, no one ever will. If virtuous, it need not fear fair operation of attack and defence. Nature has given to man no other means of sifting out the truth, either in religion, law, or politics.
(*Writings of Thomas Jefferson, ed. Andrew A. Lipscomb*)

JUNIUS
The liberty of the press is the Palladium of all the civil, political, and religious rights of an Englishman.
(*Letters, dedication*)

ARTHUR KOESTLER
The state monopoly in publishing (in Russia) is in the long run a more decisive feature of the communist regime than the concentration camps or even the one-party system.
(*The Invisible Writing*)

MELVIN LASKY
Revolution was born in metaphor, and the literary marks of its birth have been ineradicable.
(*Utopia and Revolution*)

ALFONSO MARIA DE LIGOURI
In the choice of opinions it was always a matter of great concern to me to put reason before authority.
(*Moral Theology*)

JOHN LILBURNE
That you will open the Press, whereby all treacherous and tyranical designers may be the easier discovered, and so prevented, which is a liberty of greatest concern to the Commonwealth, and which such only as intend a tyrannie are engaged to prohibit.
(*Pamphlet; Englands New Chains Discovered, presented as petition to Parliament, February, 1649*)

THOMAS MACAULAY
The gallery in which the reporters sit has become a fourth estate of the realm.
(*Historical Essays Contributed to the Edinburgh Review*)

JOHN STUART MILL
If the employees of all different enterprises were appointed and paid by government, and looked to the government for every rise in life; not all the freedom of the press and popular constitution of the legislatures would ¬ake this or any other country free otherwise than in name.
(*On Liu rty*)

ARTHUR MILLER
If American and Soviet astronauts can transfer from one space ship to another applause comes hard when, as Ludvik Vaculik has recently written, he and other Czech writers cannot transfer a thought from the right to the left sides of their brains without fear of retribution.
(*Statement before US Senate subcommittee, 1975*)

JOHN MILTON
As good almost kill a man as kill a good book. Who kills a man kills a reasonable creature; but he who destroys a good book, kills reason itself, kills the image of God, as it were in the eye.
(*Areopagitica*)

If we think to regulate printing, thereby to rectify manners, we must regulate all recreations and pastimes, all that is delightful to man . . . and who shall silence all the airs and madrigals that whisper softness in chambers.
(*Areopagitica*)

The State shall be my governors but not my critics: they may be mistaken in the choice of a licenser, as easily as this licenser may be mistaken in an author.
(*Areopagitica*)

For what Magistrate may not be misinformed, and much the sooner, if Liberty of Printing be reduced into the power of a few?
(*Areopagitica*)

Is it a fair course to assert truth, by arrogating to himself the only freedom of speech, and stopping the mouths of others equally gifted.
(*Of True Religion, Heresy, Schism and Toleration*)

LUDWIG von MISES

Every attempt to restrict the freedom of the decadent, troublesome literate, pseudo artists would vest in the authorities the power to determine what is good and bad.
(*The Anti-Capitalist Mentality*)

A free press can only exist where there is private control over the means of production.
(*The Anti-Capitalist Mentality*)

Freedom of the press is a mere blind if the authority controls all printing offices and paper plants.
(*Human Action*)

The apostles of violence wrote their books under the sheltering roof of "bourgeois security" which they derided and disparaged. They were free to publish their incendiary sermons because the liberalism they served guaranteed freedom of the press.
(*Human Action*)

MALCOLM MUGGERIDGE

In the Leftist legend of the thirties it is usually assumed that attacking the Soviet Regime was made temptingly lucrative, whereas supporting it involved penury and perhaps martyrdom. For the most part, precisely the opposite was the case; most of the best-selling writers about the USSR were strongly favourable.
(*Chronicles of Wasted Time: The Green Stick*)

BORIS PASTERNAK

Hot pointless in the day of the Great Soviet,
Where strongest passions are assigned a place,
To have a vacancy left over for the poet:
It's dangerous if not an empty space.
(*To a Friend; trans. Lydia Pasternak Slater; from Fifty Poems*)

PLATO

The inspired poet is like a fountain which gives free course to the rush of its waters.
(*Laws*)

ALEXANDER POPE
A little learning is a dang'rous thing;
Drink deep, or taste not the Pierian spring:
There shallow draughts intoxicate the brain,
And drinking largely sobers us again.
(*Essay on Criticism*)

HERBERT READ
It was not always understood that having cast off tyranny's obsolete laws, the poet was under the necessity of originating his own.
(*The True Voice of Feeling*)

FRIEDRICH von SCHILLER
The word is free.
(*Wallenstein's Lager*)

CHARLES SCOTT
Comment is free, facts are sacred.

L. C. B. SEAMAN
For those who wanted to be journalists the freedom of the press was something more than a lofty idea. It was an economic necessity.
(*1815-1848: The Age of Frustration in From Vienna to Versailles*)

GEORGE BERNARD SHAW
Assassination is the extreme form of censorship.
(*The Rejected Statement*)

BRIAN TESLER
Any attempt by business interests outside TV to influence what you see on your screens has not succeeded and it never will succeed.
(*Observer Sayings of the Week December, 1976*)

ALEXIS de TOCQUEVILLE
The influence of the liberty of the press does not affect political opinions alone, but it extends to all the opinions of men, and it modifies customs as well as laws.
(*Democracy in America, Part 1*)

The liberty of writing, like all other liberties, is most formidable when it is a novelty. A people who have never been accustomed to hearing state affairs discussed in front of them place implicit confidence in the first tribune who presents himself.

The nations among which this liberty (of the press) exists are as apt to cling to their opinions from pride as from conviction. They cherish them because they hold them to be just, and because they exercised their own free will in choosing them; and they maintain them not only because they are true, but because they are their own.
(*Democracy in America, Part 1*)

LIONEL TRILLING
If I had the job of instructing anybody in democracy, I would send him first to the generous pages of these poets and say, "There is the hardest basic political democratic fact."
(*On Walt Whitman, Marianne More and E. E. Cummings in Walt Whitman; ed. Francis Murphy*)

A. N. WHITEHEAD
Fertilisation of the soul is the reason for the necessity of art. A static value, however serious and important, becomes unendurable by its appalling monotony of endurance. The soul cries aloud for release into change. It suffers the agonies of claustrophobia. The transitions of humour, wit, irreverence, play, sleep, and — above all — of art are necessary for it.
(*Science and the Modern World*)

E. ZAMIATIN
There can be a real literature only when it is produced by madmen, hermits, heretics, dreamers and sceptics and not by patient and well-meaning officials.

Freedom and Religion

AUGUSTINE

A man who is afraid of sinning because of Hell-fire, is afraid, not of sinning, but of burning.

Some men try hard to discover in our will what good is particularly due to themselves, that owes nothing to God: how they can find this out, I just do not know.

KARL BARTH

Even though man as he is here and now does not see or understand himself as a child of God, the God-given freedom breaks through in a new dimension, in a decisive and definitive way. Man is free to call God "Our Father," here and now. Man is free to see things from the standpoint of the beginning, the revealed act of the free God in the here and now.
(*The Humanity of God*)

Man is free to bring his plea before God. In so doing he is free to hope for the great light, the great vision that will illumine the world, the Church, his fellow man, and himself.
(*The Humanity of God*)

This is freedom of conscience. Such freedom is dependent on the Kingdom. "Where is the kingdom," says Christ, "there is true conscience."
(*The Faith of the Church*)

Man's freedom as the directive and criterion for his actions is the gift bestowed upon him in a historical event of the free God's encounter with him.
(*The Humanity of God*)

A free theologian starts steadily and happily with the *Bible* . . . He starts with the Bible because in the Bible he learns about the free God and free man, and as a disciple of the Bible he may himself become a witness to the divine and human freedom.
(*The Humanity of God*)

FREDERIC BASTIAT
And now that the legislators and do-gooders have so futilely inflicted so many systems on society, may they finally end where they should have begun. May they reject all systems, and try liberty, for liberty is an acknowledgement of faith in God and his works.
(*The Law*)

ERNEST BECKER
Unrepression has become the only religion after Freud.
(*The Denial of Death*)

The ideal of the knight of faith is surely one of the most beautiful and challenging ideals ever put forth by man.
(*The Denial of Death*)

WILLIAM BLAKE
And Priests in black gowns were walking their rounds,
And binding with briars my joys and desires.
(*The Garden of Love*)

NORMAN O. BROWN
The perfect body, promised by Christian theology, enjoying that perfect felicity promised by Christian theology, is a body reconciled with death.
(*Life Against Death*)

MARTIN BUBER
Something indigenously Jewish rose in me, blossoming in the darkness of exile, to a new conscious expression. I perceived the very resemblance of man to God, as deed, as an act of becoming, as a duty.
(*Memoirs of My People*)

In the centre of our conversation stood the problem that has even laid claim to me in the course of my life: the failure of the spiritual man in his historical undertakings.
(*A Believing Humanism: conversation with Dag Hammarskjöld*)

RUDOLF BULTMANN
The bondage, to which the world has surrendered itself, consists in this: that by disavowing God the creator as its origin it falls into the hands of Nothing. And freedom is this, that, by acknowledging the truth the world opens itself to the reality from which alone it can live.
(*The Theology of the New Testament*)

In God, freedom, righteousness and life have their cause, and it is in them that the glory of God as ultimate meaning and ultimate goal comes to its own.
(*Theology of the New Testament*)

ALBERT CAMUS

For in the presence of God there is less a problem of freedom than a problem of evil. You know the alternative: either we are not free and God the all-powerful is responsible for evil. Or we are free and responsible but God is not all-powerful. All the scholastic subtleties have neither added anything to nor subtracted anything from the acuteness of this paradox.
(*The Myth of Sisyphus*)

AUSTIN CLARKE

. . .this land, where every woman's son
Must carry his own coffin and believe,
In dread, all that the clergy teach the young.
(*The Straying Student; Collected Poems*)

FYODOR DOSTOYEVSKY

Man, so long as he remains free, has no more constant and agonising anxiety than to find as quickly as possible someone to worship.
(*Ivan Karamazov's Grand Inquisitor in The Brothers Karamazov*)

If you were to destroy in mankind the belief in immortality, not only love but every force maintaining the life of the world would at once be dried up. Moreover, nothing then would be immortal, everything would be permissible, even cannibalism.
(*Brothers Karamazov*)

JOHN S. DUNNE

Faith for him (Kierkegaard) consisted of facing this dreadful thing, his own individuality, and accepting it, like St Francis of Assisi kissing the leper.
(*A Search for God in Time and Memory*)

If faith is the opposite of doubt, then the doubt of doubt looks like it might be faith, and if faith is the opposite of despair, then the despair of despair looks like it too might be faith.
(*A Search for God in Time and Memory*)

In the modern period when life is conceived as a story of appropriation, the quest, for instance the quest that carried Kierkegaard from Hegelianism to Christianity, tends to involve a man in the problem of alienation and autonomy.
(*A Search for God in Time and Memory*)

If there is a lesson in the history of religious experience in modern times, it is that the quest for certainty is self-defeating . . . It may well be that certainty and unambiguous existence can be attained only if they are not sought.
(*A Search for God in Time and Memory*)

The search for the outward heaven runs through the great political revolutions of modern times; the search for the inward heaven runs through the great religious revolutions. A Divine comedy is being acted out in life after life, but it seldom comes to its happy ending.
(*A Search for God in Time and Memory*)

JULIAN GREEN
The starting point of almost all heresies is a truth misunderstood.
(*Diary 1928-1957*)

I formerly taxed psychoanalysis with suppressing the freedom of the individual by making him the tool of circumstance and, above all, of heredity; now I understand suddenly that circumstances and, in particular, those caused by heredity are like a sphere of action chosen by God, where our freedom is exercised in a measure known to Him only.
(*Diary 1928-1957*)

JOHN HICK
Man is not compelled to be conscious of God. He has an innate tendency to interpret his experience religiously, and if he gives rein to this tendency his resulting awareness of the divine is the kind of partially free awareness that we call faith. Thus man's existence as part of the natural order ensures his status as a relatively free being over against the infinite Creator.
(*Death and Eternal Life*)

JULIA WARD HOWE

In the beauty of the lilies Christ was born across the sea,
With a glory in his bosom that transfigures you and me:
As he died to make men holy, let us die to make men free,
While God is marching on.
(*Battle Hymn of the American Republic*)

JOSHUA

Have not I commanded thee: Be strong and of good courage, be not
affrighted, neither be thou dismayed: for the Lord thy God is with thee
withersoever thou goest.
(*The Bible*)

C. G. JUNG

In order to free the fiction of the sovereign State — in other words, the
whims of those who manipulate it — from every wholesome restriction,
all socio-political movements tending in this direction invariably try to
cut the ground from under the religions.
(*The Undiscovered Self*)

SÖREN KIERKEGAARD

By relating itself to its own self, and by willing to be itself, the self is
grounded transparently in the Power which constituted it.
(*Sickness unto Death*)

HUGH KINGSMILL

The attempt to externalise the kingdom of heaven in a temporal shape
must end in disaster.

JOHN CARDINAL KROL, ARCHBISHOP OF
PHILADELPHIA

Governments that are dedicated to the principles of Karl Marx's
atheistic materialism are by that very fact committed to the goal of
making society godless. As members of a free society, we know the
Marxian ideology and we know the laws of the books, but we also
know that the atheistic ideology does prevail.
(*Message to Religion in Communist Dominated Areas, Nov. 16,
1976*)

VLADIMIR ILYITCH LENIN

Every religious idea, every idea of God, even flirting with the idea of
God, is unutterable vileness.
(*Letter to M. Gorki*)

J. LOCKE
The toleration of those that differ from others in matters of religion is so agreeable to the Gospel and to the genuine reason of mankind, that it seems monstrous for men to be so blind as not to see the necessity and advantage of it in so clear a light.
(*Letters Concerning Toleration*)

ROLLO MAY
One has only to look carefully at the New England churches built by the Puritans and in the Puritan heritage to see the great refinement and dignity of form which surely implies a passionate attitude towards life. They had the dignity of controlled passion, which made possible an actual living with passion in contrast to our present pattern of expressing and dispersing all passion. The deterioration of Puritanism into our modern secular attitudes was caused by the confluence of three trends; industrialism, Victorian emotional compartmentalisation, and the secularisation of all religious attitudes.
(*Love and Will*)

Van Gogh was maimed; Nietzsche was maimed; Kierkegaard was maimed. It is the danger of the razor-blade edge of heightened consciousness on which the creative person lives. No man shall see God and live; but Jacob did see God — and had to — and, though he lived, he was maimed. This is the paradox of consciousness.
(*Love and Will*)

WILLIAM LAMB, VISCOUNT MELBOURNE
Things have come to a pretty pass when religion is allowed to invade the sphere of private life.
(*Remark on hearing an Evangelical Sermon*)

JOHN STUART MILL
The only ground on which restrictions on Sunday amusements can be defended, must be that they are religiously wrong . . . It remains to be proved that society or any of its officers holds a commission from on high to avenge any supposed offence to Omnipotence.
(*On Liberty*)

JOHN MILTON
Surely it is not for nothing that tyrants, by a kind of natural instinct, both hate and fear none more than the true church and saints of God, as the most dangerous enemies and subverters of monarchy, though indeed of tyranny.
(*The Tenure of Kings and Magistrates*)

God's glory in the whole administrations of the gospel according to his own will and counsel ought to be fulfilled by weakness, at least so refuted, not by force; and if by force, inward and spiritual, not outward and corporeal.
(*Treatise of Civil Power in Ecclesiastical Causes*)

For belief or practice in religion . . . no man ought to be punished or molested by any outwards force on earth whatsoever.
(*Treatise of Civil Power in Ecclesiastical Causes*)

Our whole practical in religion is contained in charity, or the love of God and our neighbour, no way to be forced.
(*Treatise of Civil Power in Ecclesiastical Causes*)

JÜRGEN MOLTMANN
From first to last, and not merely in the epilogue, Christianity is eschatology, is hope, forward looking and forward moving, and therefore also revolutionizing and transforming the present.
(*Theology of Hope*)

In the past two centuries, a Christian faith in God without hope for the future of the world has called forth a secular hope for the future of the world without faith in God . . . The messianic hopes emigrated from the church and became invested in progress, evolution and revolutions.
(*Hope and History, in Theology Today, October 1968, Princeton, NJ*)

MALCOLM MUGGERIDGE
I've spent a number of years in India and Africa, where I found much righteous endeavour undertaken by Christians of all denominations; but I never, as it happens, came across a hospital or orphanage run by the Fabian Society or a Humanist leper colony.
(*Jesus Rediscovered*)

RABBI NACHMAN
As the hand held before the eye conceals the greatest mountain, so the little earthly life hides from the glance and enormous lights and mysteries of which the world is full, and he who can draw it away from before his eyes, as one draws away a hand, beholds the great shining of the inner worlds.
(*Sayings of Rabbi Nachman, from The Tales of Rabbi Nachman, by Martin Buber*)

NICODIM OF LENINGRAD AND NOVGOROD, RUSSIAN ORTHODOX METROPOLITAN
How can there be a dialogue of Christians and Marxists when between them there is an insuperable abyss, and when the basic beliefs of the one are denied by the other?
(*At World Council of Churches, Uppsala*)

WILLIAM PENN
If men will not be governed by God, then they must be governed by tyrants.

WILLIAM PITT, EARL OF CHATHAM
We have a Calvinistic creed, a Popish liturgy, and an Armenian clergy.
(*Speech in House of Lords, 19 May 1772*)

PROVERBS
The Lord possessed me in the beginning of his ways, before he made any thing from the beginning. I was set up from eternity, and of old before the earth was made . . . I was with him forming all things: and was delighted every day, playing before him at all times; playing in the world. And my delights were to be with the children of men.
(*Douai translation, based on Vulgate*)

KARL RAHNER
In an age of totalitarian states, when individuality is suppressed and "ideology" supplied, the Church has to delimit her position more clearly . . . She will now have to come down more firmly on the side of the individual's responsibility and freedom both in his secular and religious life.
(*Free Speech in the Church*)

BERTRAND RUSSELL
Only . . . on the firm foundation of unyielding despair, can the soul's habitation henceforth be safely built.
(*A Free Man's Worship*)

ST JOHN
The Son shall make you free.
(*The Bible*)

ST MATTHEW
You have forced the conscience, which was not to be forced; but judgment and mercy you have not executed; this you should have done, and the other let alone.
(*The Bible*)

ST PAUL
Am I not free to do as I will? Am I not an apostle, have I not seen our Lord Jesus Christ?
(*Corinthians; The Bible*)

Now the Lord is the Spirit, and where the Spirit of the Lord is, there is freedom.
(*Corinthians; The Bible*)

Where the Spirit of the Lord is, there is liberty.
(*Corinthians; The Bible*)

If a slave is called to enter Christ's service he is a freed man, just as the free man, when he is called, becomes the slave of Christ.
(*Corinthians; The Bible*)

. . . and (you), having been set *free* from sin, have become slaves of righteousness . . . When you were slaves of sin, you were *free* in regard to righteousness.)
(*Romans; The Bible*)

For the law of the spirit of life in Christ Jesus has set me *free* from the law of sin and death.
(*Romans; The Bible*)

. . . because creation itself will be set *free* from its bondage to decay and obtain the glorious liberty of the children of God.
(*Romans; The Bible*)

Created nature has been condemned to frustration, not for some deliberate fault of its own, but for the sake of him who condemned it, namely that nature in its turn will be set free from the tyranny of corruption, to share in the glorious freedom of God's sons.
(*Romans; The Bible*)

Here there cannot be . . . barbarian, Scythian, slave, free men, but Christ is all and in all.
(*Colossians; The Bible*)

There is neither Jew nor Greek, there is neither *slave* nor *free* . . . for you are all one in Christ.
(*Galatians; The Bible*)

ADAM SMITH
Benevolence may, perhaps, be the sole principle of action in the Deity . . . but so imperfect a creature as man . . . must often act from many other motives.
(*The Theory of Moral Sentiments*)

JAMES STEPHENS
. . . I think that whatever passes understanding, which is imagination, is terrible, standing aloof from humanity and from kindness, and that this is the sin against the Holy Ghost, the great Artist.
(*The Crock of Gold*)

ALEXIS de TOCQUEVILLE
Liberty regards religion as its companion in all its battles and its triumphs — as the cradle of its infancy and the divine source of its claims.
(*Democracy in America*)

MARINA TSVETAYEVA
. . . what a black mountain
has blocked the world from the light.
It's time — It's time — It's time
to give back to God his ticket.
(*Poems to the Czech Lands*)

UPANISHADS
He who attains to knowledge of Brahman, being freed from all evils, finds the Eternal, the Supreme.
(*The Upanishads: Breath of the Eternal. Translated by Swami Prabhavananda and Frederick Manchester*)

JOHN WESLEY
If anyone asks, "How is God's foreknowledge consistent with freedom?" I must plainly answer, "I cannot tell".

VICTOR WHITE

The Christian idea of unity and fellowship . . . is based not on numbers, mechanical efficiency, co-ordination of productive forces, the loss of the personality in the mass by regimentation and blind obedience, but on that which totalitarianism precisely destroys: free personal relationship.

(*God the Unknown*)

If ever Christendom becomes sufficiently organised and powerful to meet the modern mass movement of secularism in such a way on their own ground, the issue of the struggle would be unimportant. For Christendom would have ceased to be Christian, and would have already surrendered to the enemy.

(*God the Unknown*)

A. N. WHITEHEAD

The death of religion comes with the repression of the high hope of adventure.

(*Science and the Modern World*)

CHARLES WILLIAMS

Gamaliel was the first, in Christian times, to utter a maxim too often forgotten by Christians — that there is no need to be too ardent against other people on behalf of the Omnipotence.

(*The Descent of the Dove*)

Freedom and Equality

WILLIAM BLAKE
One Law for the lion and ox is Oppression.

OLIVER WENDELL HOLMES, Jun.
I have no respect for the passion for equality, which seems to me merely idealising envy.
(*Holmes-Laski letters*)

PRINCE PHILIP
Some people obviously do think you can have a totally egalitarian system. But no one has achieved one yet above the level of a tribal society.

WILLAM PICKLES
It is historically untrue to say that ''Socialism is about equality'' . . . Socialism in this country has always been about freedoms . . . and the road to it has required a steady and cautious diminution of inequalities . . . but the pursuit of equality *for its own sake* is not only pointless, because literally nobody wants it, but also dangerous, because it provokes envy.
(*Daily Telegraph*, *December 14*, *1976*)

BERTRAND RUSSELL
If a more just economic system were only attainable by closing men's minds against free enquiry, and plunging them back into the intellectual prison of the middle ages, I should consider the price too high.
(*Bolshevism: Practice and Theory*)

WILLIAM SHAKESPEARE
The oppressor's wrong, the proud man's contumely,
. . . the law's delay,
The insolence of office, and the spurns
That patient merit of the unworthy takes.
(*Hamlet*)

ALEXIS de TOCQUEVILLE

There exists in the human heart a depraved taste for equality which impels the weak to attempt to lower the powerful down to their own level, and reduce men to prefer equality in slavery to inequality with freedom.
(*Democracy in America*)

The nations of our time cannot prevent the condition of man from becoming equal: but it depends on themselves whether the principle of equality is to lead them to servitude or freedom, to knowledge or barbarism, to prosperity or wretchedness.
(*Democracy in America*)

Democracy and socialism have nothing in common but one word: equality. But notice the difference. While democracy seeks equality in liberty, socialism seeks equality in restraint and servitude.
(*Complete Works, Vol. IX*)

MARK TWAIN

It were not best that we should all think alike; it is difference of opinion that makes horse races.
(*Pudd'nhead Wilson's Calendar*)

The Free Will

ALCUIN

Nor king, not judge, yea, not thy dearest friend
Muzzle thy lips from righteousness.
(*To Adelhard, Archbishop of Canterbury; trans. Helen Waddell:
More Latin Lyrics, from Virgil to Milton*)

AUGUSTINE

I could say with absolute truth and conviction (that men were not
sinless) because they did not want to be sinless. But if you were to ask
me *why* they did not want to be so, then we are getting out of our
depth — *imus in longum.*

ERNEST BECKER

All men are here to use themselves up, and the problem of ideal
illusion doesn't spare any man from that. It only addresses the question
of the best quality of work and life that men can achieve, depending on
the beliefs they have and the powers they lean on.
(*The Denial of Death*)

ERNST BENZ

Our life remains a struggle between life and death, and as long as this
struggle lasts, anxiety lasts also.
(*Der Vollkommene Mensch nach Jacob Boehme*)

MARTIN BUBER

All real living is meeting.
(*Encounter with Martin Buber, Aubrey Hodes*)

These men will not be bound by the aims of the hour, they are gifted
with the free far-sightedness of those called by the unborn; they will be
independent persons with no authority save that of the spirit.
(*Pointing the Way*)

169

RUDOLF BULTMANN

Only in action as the free expression of a person — or rather in the free act in which a lone person really exists — can persons come into a relationship with persons. Such relationship is totally destroyed if the action is brought under the category of conformity to law.
(*Faith and Understanding*)

JAMES BRANCH CABELL

I am willing to taste any drink once.
(*Jurgen*)

ALBERT CAMUS

Ah, mon cher, for anyone who is alone, without God and without a master, the weight of days is dreadful. Hence one must choose a master, God being out of style.
(*The Fall*)

THOMAS CARLYLE

The true liberty of a man, you would say, consisted in his finding out, or being forced to find out, the right path, and to walk thereon.
(*Past and Present*)

ANGELA CARTER

"Yet his performance was remarkable. In bed, one could almost have believed the Count was galvanised by an external dynamo. This galvanic mover was his will. And, indeed, his fatal error was to mistake his will for his desire . . ."
I interrupted her with a certain irritation.
"But how is one to distinguish between the will and a desire?"
"Desire can never be coerced," said Albertina with the crispness of a pedagogue even though, at that moment, she was coercing mine. She immediately resumed her discourse.
". . . and so he willed his own desires."
(*The Infernal Desire Machines of Doctor Hoffman*)

G. K. CHESTERTON

For there is good news yet to hear and fine things to be seen,
Before we go to Paradise by way of Kensal Green.
(*The Rolling English Road*)

FYODOR DOSTOYEVSKY
You did not come down (from the cross) because you did not want to enslave man by a miracle and because you hungered for a faith built on free will and not miracles.
(*Ivan Karamazov's Grand Inquisitor in The Brothers Karamazov*)

JOHN S. DUNNE
The immediate man was restricted in his awareness and concern to the here and now; the existential man's consciousness was expanded to his past and future; the historic man's was extended beyond the confines of his lifetime to the past and future of mankind.
(*A Search for God in Time and Memory*)

A. S. EDDINGTON
Science . . . withdraws its moral opposition to freewill. Those who maintain a deterministic theory of mental activity must do so as the outcome of their study of the mind itself and not with the idea that they are thereby making it more conformable with our experimental knowledge of the laws of inorganic nature.
(*The Nature of the Physical World*)

RALPH WALDO EMERSON
Nothing is at last raised but the integrity of your mind.

SIGMUND FREUD
It is out of the question that part of the analytic treatment should consist of advice to "live freely".
(*A General Introduction to Psychoanalysis*)

OLIVER ST JOHN GOGARTY
Hard is the stone, but harder still
The delicate performing will.
(*The Image-Maker*)

JULIAN GREEN
As long as something inside us protects against ourselves, there is room for hope. It is when one accepts oneself as one is, and gives up, that the game is in danger of being lost. In other words (if I wanted to be funny), one can set one's mind at rest so long as one feels uneasy!
(*Diary 1928-1957*)

That is one of the greatest mistakes I will have to answer for some day, a far more serious mistake, to my mind, than everyday covetousness. I have held my tongue when I should have spoken out. And I could have spoken; I had the means, I still have them.
(*Diary 1928-1957*)

JORGE GUILLÉN
O grace of that recondite calm!
The animal soars,
Pure spirit, at last,
Over effortless meadows.
Past all impediments there
Over the floor of the darkness!
(*Horses in the Air*)

F. A. HAYEK
The importance of our being free to do a particular thing has nothing to do with one question of whether we, or the majority, are ever likely to make use of that particular possibility.
(*The Constitution of Liberty*)

Independence of mind of strength of character are rarely found among those who cannot be confident that they will make their way by their own effort.
(*The Road to Serfdom*)

HERMAN HESSE
"Look," said God, "I wanted you the way you are and no different. You were a wanderer in my name and wherever you went you brought the settled folk a little homesickness for freedom."
(*Knulp*)

JOHN HICK
The basic moral and spiritual dispositions which are said to inhere in the soul presumably actualise themselves in our fundamental choices as free beings.
(*Death and Eternal Life*)

We have to presume our own freedom, as minds and wills, because any claim to have rational grounds for believing that we are totally determined is necessarily self-refuting.
(*Death and Eternal Life*)

AUBREY HODES
"There was a Dutch professor" (I knew he was thinking of Johan Huizinga) "who wrote a book about the natural playing man — someone who enjoys play as an expression of freedom. Well," Buber said, "perhaps we can also recognise what I would call the natural studying man — someone for whom learning and study are equally an expression of human freedom."
(*Encounter with Martin Buber*)

HENRIK IBSEN
No, it is the Will that matters,
Makes the freedom or the fall!
Firm, while all around it shatters
Firm, in sunshine or in squall.
(*Brand*)

SAMUEL JOHNSON
Sir, we *know* our will is free, and *there's* an end on't.
(*"Sir"*, *said Dr Johnson; arranged by H. C. Biron*)

BRIAN KEEBLE
For the poet the coterminous nature of humility and free-will are the precondition of the creative act itself.
(*Time's Glass Breaks. The Metaphysics of Vision in the Poetry of Vernon Watkins — article in Thames Poetry*)

SÖREN KIERKEGAARD
The spirit cannot do away with itself . . . Neither can man sink down into the vegetative life . . . He cannot flee from dread.
(*The Concept of Dread*)

RONALD KNOX
I cannot agree . . . that God's foreknowledge robs human life of its adventure and reduces it to the level of private theatricals, because I do believe in the real freedom of my will and in the power of my actions to affect the course of events . . . I only feel I am God's puppet in the sense that God could, if he liked have picked on somebody else to do any job I have ever done or am ever likely to do.
(*Difficulties*)

D. H. LAWRENCE
I wish that I could go . . .
. . . And leave my flesh discarded lying
Like luggage of some departed traveller
Gone one knows not whither.
(*In Trouble and Shame*)

GOTTFRIED WILHELM LEIBNIZ
There are two labyrinths of the human mind: one concerns the
composition of the continuum, and the other the nature of freedom,
and both spring from the same source — the infinite.
(*Philosophical Writings*)

For God sees from all time that there will be a certain Judas, whose
notion or idea, which God has, contains this future free action.
(*Philosophical Writings*)

ANTHONY LEJEUNE
Countries cannot become free. Countries cannot be oppressed. Only
men can be free or not free.
(*Freedom and the Politicians*)

C. D. LEWIS
Come up, Methuselah,
You doddering superman!
Give me an instant realized
And I'll outdo your span.
(*Come up, Methuselah*)

LOUIS MACNEICE
Here is no mass-production of neat thoughts
No canvas shrouds for the mind.
(*Turf-stacks*)

MARBOD OF RENNES
You gape in vain for wealth, you plough in vain
If your own mind lies untilled.
(*Meditation among Trees; trans. Helen Waddell; More Latin Lyrics,
from Virgil to Milton*)

ROLLO MAY

In every act of love and will — and in the long run they are both present in each genuine act — we mould ourselves and our world simultaneously. This is what it means to embrace the future.
(*Love and Will*)

After the five years in his late twenties and early thirties, when he was paralysed with his own depression and scarcely able to will the simplest thing, he decided one day that he could make an act of will to believe in freedom. He *willed* freedom, made it his fiat. "The first act of freedom," he writes, "is to choose it."
(*On William James — Love and Will*)

Freedom and will consist not in the abnegation of determination but in our *relationship* to it.
(*Love and Will*)

Human will, in its specific form, always brings in a ''no''. We must stand against the environment, be able to give a negative.
(*Love and Will*)

JOHN STUART MILL

No great improvements in the lot of mankind are possible, until a great change takes place in the fundamental constitution of their modes of thought.
(*Autobiography*)

Judgement is given to men that they may use it. Because it may be used erroneously, are men to be told that they ought not to use it at all?
(*On Liberty*)

JOHN MILTON

Truth and understanding are not such wares as to be monopolized and traded in by tickets and statutes and standards.
(*Areopagitica*)

Give me the liberty to know, to utter, and to argue freely according to conscience, above all liberties.
(*Areopagitica*)

For he who freely magnifies what hath been nobly done, and fears not to declare as freely what might be done better, gives ye the best covenant of his fidelity.
(*Areopagitica*)

Our belief and practice, which comprehend our whole religion, flow from faculties of the inward man, free and unconstrainable of themselves in nature, and our practice not only from faculties endued with freedom but from love and charity besides, incapable of force and all these things by transgression lost.
(*Areopagitica*)

LUDWIG von MISES
What distinguishes man from other animals is precisely that he does not yield without any will of his own to an instinctive urge.
(*Human Action*)

What impels every man to the utmost exertion in the service of his fellow man . . . is, in the market not compulsion on the part of gendarmes, hangmen and penal courts it is self interest. The member of a contractual society is free because he serves others only in serving himself.
(*Human Action*)

SIR THOMAS MORE
I die the King's good servant, but God's first.
(*On scaffold*)

EMMANUEL MOURNIER
Abstract purity always tends to the general, the fabricated principle, the dream situation, to those incorporeal goods which are nothing, belong to no one. Personal initiative, however, is affirmation, concrete insertion, accepted responsibility in a world of happenings.
(*Be Not Afraid: The Personalism of Purity*)

MALCOLM MUGGERIDGE
When Pastor Bonhoeffer was taken off by his Nazi guards to be executed, as I have read, his face was shining with happiness, to the point that even those poor clowns noted it. In that place of darkest evil, he was the happiest man — the executed. I find this an image of supreme happiness.
(*BBC broadcast*)

FRIEDRICH NIETZSCHE
My death I commend to you, the free death which comes to me because I *will*.
(*Thus Spake Zarathustra*)

A man passes through three metamorphoses: First he is a beast of burden, loaded down with the beliefs and values and prescriptions of other men, then he is a roaring lion who has thrown off all these burdens, and finally he is a child who is at one with all reality and says *Yes* to life.
(*Thus Spake Zarathustra*)

RAINER MARIA RILKE
Whoever rightly understands and celebrates death, at the same time magnifies life.
(*Rehm, Orpheus: Der Dichter und die Toten*)

JEAN-JACQUES ROUSSEAU
Who ever refuses to obey the General Will, shall be compelled to do so by the whole body; and this means only that he will be *compelled to be free*.

BERTRAND RUSSELL
The discovery that man can be successfully manipulated and that governments can turn large masses this way or that as they choose, is one of the causes of our misfortunes.
(*Unpopular Essays — An Outline of Intellectual Rubbish*)

ST PAUL
There is no reason why I should let my freedom be called into question by another man's conscience.
(*Corinthians; The Bible*)

GEORGE SANTAYANA
If a man were a wild spirit without a body or a habitat his philosophy might harmlessly change at every moment, and he might well pride himself on changing it often and radically, so as to display fertility of spirit and enjoy an inexhaustibly rich experience. Being absolutely free and unfettered by circumstances, why should he stick to any particular principles or ideas and waste his time repeating himself like an idiot or a cuckoo?
(*My Host the World*)

A truly free spirit will never repent; he cannot revert to his true self, since he has no particular self to revert to.
(*My Host the World*)

JEAN-PAUL SARTRE
Man is condemned to be free.
(*Being and Nothingness*)

FRIEDRICH von SCHILLER
Alas! I did not choose my lot.
(*Die Jungfrau von Orleans*)

PERCY BYSSHE SHELLEY
. . . Freemen never
Dream that God will damn for ever . . .
(*The Mask of Anarchy*)

STEPHEN SPENDER
Born of the sun, they travelled a short while toward the sun
And left the vivid air signed with their honour.
(*The Truly Great; Collected Poems*)

Never allow gradually the traffic to smother
With noise and fog, the flowering of the Spirit.
(*The Truly Great; Collected Poems*)

BENEDICT SPINOZA
A free man thinks of death least of all things; and his wisdom is a meditation not of death but of life.
(*Ethics*)

The virtue of a free man is seen to be as great, when it declines dangers, as when it overcomes them.
(*Ethics*)

The free man is as courageous in timely retreat as in combat; or, a free man shows equal courage or presence of mind whether he elect to give battle or to retreat.
(*Ethics*)

Only free men are thoroughly grateful one to another.
(*Ethics*)

The free man who lives among the ignorant, strives, as far as he can, to avoid receiving favours from them.
(*Ethics*)

The free man never acts fraudulently, but always in good faith.

JAMES STEPHENS
... the chief business of the gods is to give protection and assistance to such of their people as require it; but (and this is their limitation) they cannot give any help until it is demanded, the free-will of mankind being the most jealously guarded and holy principle in life.
(*The Crock of Gold*)

MARGARET THATCHER
Let our children grow tall — and some grow taller than others, if they have it in them to do so.
(*Institute of Socioeconomic Studies, New York, 1975*)

When people are free to make their own mistakes they learn from them and then get things right. Only people can save themselves, according to their own lights.
(*National Press Club, Washington, 1975*)

PAUL TILLICH
Man's vitality is as great as his intentionality: they are interdependent. This makes man the most vital of all beings. He can transcend any given situation in any direction and this possibility drives him to create beyond himself. Vitality is the power of creating beyond oneself without losing oneself.
(*The Courage to Be*)

UNKNOWN LATIN POET
Death, the last pain,
Is not for men to fear.
(*trans. Helen Waddell; More Latin Lyrics, from Virgil to Milton*)

WALTON
His mind was liberal and unwearied in the search of knowledge.
(**On Donne; quoted by Helen Waddell in More Latin Lyrics**, *from Virgil to Milton*)

CHARLES WILLIAMS
... the freedom of all that is beyond necessity.
(*The Descent of the Dove*)

WILLIAM WORDSWORTH
Joyous, not scar'd with a heart at its own liberty.
(*The Prelude — Introduction*)

Enough that I am free.
(*The Prelude — Introduction*)

Now I am free, enfranchis'd and at large,
My fix my habitation where I will.
(*The Prelude — Introduction*)

Fair seed-time had my soul.
(*The Prelude — Childhood and school-time*)

I was a Freeman; in the purest sense
Was free, and to majestic ends was strong.
(*The Prelude — Residence at Cambridge*)

WILLIAM BUTLER YEATS
An aged man is but a paltry thing,
A tattered coat upon a stick, unless
Soul clap its hands and sing.
(*Sailing to Byzantium*)

RABBI ZUSYA
In the world to come I shall not be asked: "Why were you not Moses?" I shall be asked: "Why were you not Zusya?"

The Individual

APPIUS CAECUS
Each man the architect of his own fate.

AUGUSTINE
For no one is known to another so intimately as he is known to himself, and yet no one is so well known even to himself that he can be sure as to his conduct on the morrow.

I know, O Lord, that the way of a man is not in his power; nor is it for him to walk and direct his own steps.

ERNEST BECKER
In this world each organism lives to be consumed by its own energies; and those that are consumed with the most relentlessness, and burn with the brightest flame, seem to serve the purposes of nature best, so far as accomplishing anything on this planet is concerned.
(*The Denial of Death*)

MIRON BIALOSZEWSKI
The elect are few
Everybody in the last resort
Elects only himself.

MARTIN BUBER
If I stood before the prospect of finding myself in a minority of *one* voice, I humbly believe that I would have the courage to remain in a such a hopeless minority. This is for me the only truthful position.
(*On Gandhi; quoted by Aubrey Hodes, encounter with Martin Buber*)

The process of transforming our inner lives must be expressed in the transformation of our outer life, of the life of the individual as well as that of the community.
(*Israel and the World*)

VLADIMIR BUKOVSKY
The frontiers of freedom and lack of freedom lie inside each one of us.
. . . A man can retain freedom of choice, can he not, even in prison? He
can leave prison if he pays the price of betrayal . . . He can demean
himself to obtain some small favour, or he can fight . . . A man who is
not free within himself can find a mass of self-justifying arguments.
Tomorrow you may refuse to defend your own workers, and the day
after tomorrow no one will defend you.
(*Speech to the Free German Association, Berlin, May 9, 1977*)

RUDOLF BULTMANN
The man of faith is freed from the care of one who relies upon himself,
has the world (supposedly) at his disposal.
(*Theology of the New Testament*)

Only in action as the free expression of a person — or rather in the free
act in which alone a person really exists — can persons come into
relationship with persons. Such relationship is totally destroyed if the
action is brought under the category of conformity to law.

There is only one possible way to become free from the past, free for a
true hearing of the claim which comes to us in the present moment;
that freedom is given to us through forgiveness.

SAMUEL BUTLER
He that complies against his will
Is of his own opinion still.
(*Haelibras*)

ALBERT CAMUS
. . . death and the absurd are here the principles of the only reasonable
freedom: that which a human heart can experience and live.
(*The Myth of Sisyphus*)

ELIAS CANETTI
Seldom does his obduracy allow him to speak, but here, in the
apparent disguise of a character, it suddenly bestows upon him the
freedom of speech.
(*Kafka's Other Trial — the Letters to Felice*)

DESCARTES
To conquer himself rather than the world.
(*Discourse on Method*)

KEITH DIXON
Marxist philosophy pays scant attention to actual social conditions, preferring to concentrate upon the integrity of theory rather than upon integrity of the individual.
(*Letter, The Guardian, December 21, 1976*)

JOHN S. DUNNE
Youth is the time when the immediate man becomes an existential man, when the person who in childhood had been concerned primarily about the immediate here and now begins to bring his whole lifetime to mind and become concerned about his past and future.
(*A Search for God in Time and Memory*)

Consider again our image of all men standing around the circumference of an immense circle. There are an infinity of points on the circle, and each man stands at a different point, but there is only one centre . . . What locates a man on the circumference is the partiality of his actual self; what lies at the centre is the integral self . . . The radical line he must follow to reach the centre from his particular point on the circumference is a line no other man can take.
(*A Search for God in Time and Memory*)

To discover his character, a man has had to recollect his past behaviour in immediate situations, particularly, as Aristotle would have it, the balance of passion and caution his behaviour has exhibited.
(*A Search for God in Time and Memory*)

The feeling of being thrown upon one's own resources has become commoner and stronger with the disappearance of the hierarchical structure of society in which each person was given a determinate place.
(*A Search for God in Time and Memory*)

The method of existentialism is based on Kierkegaard's principle that "truth is subjectivity", according to which a man will arrive at the truth about himself only if he abandons the attempt to treat himself as though he were another person and takes instead the standpoint he alone can occupy with regard to himself. The method of psychoanalysis, by contrast, is based on Freud's ideal of freedom from illusion and delusion, according to which a man will arrive at the truth about himself, whether these by "delusions" actually contrary to objective fact or simply "illusions" unsupported by any objective evidence.
(*A Search for God in Time and Memory*)

The Socratic wisdom, the knowledge of ignorance, is one of the most central of all human insights.
(*A Search for God in Time and Memory*)

A transformation of the self occurs . . . as a man goes from living on time borrowed from the encompassing time to living on time given him for his own.
(*A Search for God in Time and Memory*)

Man is to some extent an actor and an inventor of himself.
(*A Search for God in Time and Memory*)

WILSON van DUSEN
The inner life obtrudes very little into the freedom of the individual's will. For the most part it stands in the wings, waiting to be summoned.
(*The Natural Depth in Man*)

ALBERT EINSTEIN
Everything that is really great and inspiring is created by the individual who can labour in freedom.
(*Out of My Later Years*)

JOHN KENNETH GALBRAITH
In accordance with an old but not outworn tradition, it might now be wise for all to conclude that crime, or even misbehaviour, is the act of an individual, not the predisposition of a class.
(*The Great Crash 1929*)

GALILEO
You cannot teach a man anything; you can only help him to find it within himself.

DAVID GASCOYNE
We are always free
To turn away. Our hearts can always harden to refuse
To suffer mortal anguish.
(*Night Thoughts*)

F. A. HAYEK
The guiding principle, that a policy of freedom for the individual is the only truly progressive policy, remains as true today as it was in the nineteenth century.
(*The Road to Serfdom*)

WILLIAM ERNEST HENLEY
I am the master of my fate;
I am the captain of my soul.
(*Invictus*)

HERMANN HESSE
There is one virtue that I love, and only one.
I call it self-will.
(*Self-will, 1919; If the War Goes On*)

The obedient well-behaved citizen who does his duty is not a "hero". Only an *individual* who has fashioned his "self-will", his noble, natural inner law, into his destiny can be a hero.
(*Self-will, 1919; If the War Goes On*)

I had incurred the first of those attacks, threats, insults which in so-called heroic times conformists never fail to heap upon a man who walks alone.
(*Foreword to 1946 edition, If the War Goes On*)

JOHN HICK
The first emergence of the idea of a blessed hereafter as a privilege of kings and other outstanding leaders may well reflect the fact that they were, in our modern sense of the word, the first individuals . . . as individuals perished and went down to the underworld others were born and the life of the tribe went on.
(*Death and Eternal Life*)

Whilst the self as ego is essentially finite because bounded, the self as personal is in principle infinite, or virtually infinite, as a part of the totality of interpersonal life.
(*Death and Eternal Life*)

It is commonly supposed that it was in Jaspers' "axial period", between about 800 and 200 BC, that the idea of the autonomous, responsible human individual was born (1) — and hence, in due course, the question of his personal destiny after death.
(1) *Karl Jaspers, The origin and Goal of History.*
(*Death and Eternal Life*)

GRAHAM HUTTON
Whatever one's race, colour or creed, one must admit the necessity of "freedom" as the environment within which the ultimate social atom, the individual, develops to the fullest extent his or her potentialities.
(*Agenda for a Free Society, the Individual and Society*)

JEWISH PROVERB
Only he is worthy of respect who is grateful for the good and knows how to bear evil.

BENJAMIN JONSON
If he were
To be made honest by an act of parliament,
I should not alter in my faith of him.
(*The Devil Is An Ass*)

BERTRAND de JOUVENEL
There would be no need for laws at all if each separate ego could be trusted to live by the inspiration of love, or at least by the authority of custom.

The free man is in essence the voluntary executive of his own moral judgment.

C. G. JUNG
The communal ideal reckons without its host, overlooking the individual human being, who in the end will assert his claims.
(*The Undiscovered Self*)

Resistance to the organised mass can be effected only by the man who is as well organised in his individuality as the mass itself.
(*The Undiscovered Self*)

ALEXANDER KERENSKY
Man's life is not determined by the law of causality of the material world, but rather by the free intuitive choice of his "ego", which expresses itself in deliberate acts of the will.
(*The Kerensky Memoirs*)

JOHN MAYNARD KEYNES
Above all, individualism, if it can be purged of its defects and its abuses, is the best safeguard of personal liberty in the sense that, compared with any other system, it greatly widens the field for the exercise of personal choice.
(*The General Theory of Employment, Interest and Money, 1936-1947 edition*)

SÖREN KIERKEGAARD
Everyone in whom the animal disposition is preponderant believes firmly that millions are more than one; whereas spirit is just the opposite, that one is more than millions, and that every man can be the one.
(*Journals*)

For the self is a synthesis in which the finite is the limiting factor, and the infinite is the expanding factor. Infinitude's despair is therefore the fantastical, the limitless.
(*Sickness*)

D. H. LAWRENCE
For every man has a mob-self and an individual self, in varying proportions. Some men are almost all mob-self.
(*Obscenity and Pornography*)

FRAY LUIS de LÉON
Fearing nothing, man sets for his labours
Appointed hours.

J. LOCKE
The care of every man's soul belongs to himself, and is to be left unto himself. Men cannot be forced to be saved whether they will or no.
(*Letters Concerning Toleration*)

JOHN MACMURRAY
Personality is mutual in its very being. The self is one term in a relation between two selves. It cannot be prior to that relation and equally, of course, the relation cannot be prior to it. "I" exist only as one member of the "you and I". The self only exists in the communion of selves.
(*Interpreting the Universe*)

WALTER de LA MARE
Now each man's mind all Europe is.
(*Happy England*)

JOHN STUART MILL
The only freedom which deserves the name is that of pursuing our own good in our own way, so long as we do not attempt to deprive others of theirs, or impede their efforts to obtain it.

He who knows only his own side of the case knows little of that.
(*On Liberty*)

The liberty of the individual must be thus far limited: he must not make himself a nuisance to other people.
(*On Liberty*)

Liberty consists in doing what one desires.
(*On Liberty*)

No society in which eccentricity is a matter of reproach, can be in a wholesome state.
(*On Liberty*)

If a person possesses a tolerable amount of common sense and experience, his own mode of laying out his existence is the best, not because it is the best in itself, but because it is his own mode.
(*On Liberty*)

We have a right in various ways to act upon our unfavourable opinion of any one, not to the oppression of his individuality, but in the exercise of ours.
(*On Liberty*)

Individuality . . . will stand its ground with increasing difficulty, unless the intelligent part of the public can be made to feel its value — to see that it is good there shall be differences.
(*On Liberty*)

A people, it appears, may be progressive for a certain length of time, and then stop: when does it stop? When it ceases to possess individuality.
(*On Liberty*)

I hold that it is allowable in all, and in the more thoughtful and cultivated often a duty, to assert and promulgate, with all the force they are capable of, their opinion of what is good or bad, admirable or contemptible, but not to compel others to conform to that opinion.

JOHN MILTON
You therefore who wish to remain free, either instantly be wise, or, as soon as possible, cease to be fools; if you think slavery an intolerable evil, learn obedience to reason and the government of yourselves.

LUDWIG von MISES
"Rugged" individualism is the signature of our civilization.
(*Human Action*)

MICHEL de MONTAIGNE
The greatest thing in the world is to know how to be self-sufficient.
(*Essays*)

Baron de MONTESQUIEU
Each individual advances the public good, while he only thinks of promoting his own self interest.
(*The Spirit of the Laws*)

EMMANUEL MOURNIER
We do not believe that the free man must needs be solitary.
(*Be Not Afraid: To the Heart of Materialism*)

RABBI NACHMAN
Man is afraid of things that cannot harm him, and he knows it, and he craves things that cannot be of help to him, and knows it; but in truth the one thing man is afraid of is within himself, and the one thing he craves is within himself.
(*Sayings of Rabbi Nachman, from The Tales of Rabbi Nachman by Martin Buber*)

CARDINAL NEWMAN
Real assent, then as the experience which it presupposes, is an act of the individual, as such, and thwarts rather than promotes the intercourse of man with man.
(*Grammar of Assent*)

FRIEDRICH NIETZSCHE
You are young and desire marriage and children but I ask you: are you a man who *ought* to desire a child? . . . I would have your victory and your freedom long for a child. You should build living memorials to your victory and your liberation.
You should build beyond yourself. But first you must be built yourself, square-built in body and soul.
(*Thus Spoke Zarathustra*)

JOSÉ ORTEGA Y GASSET

Take stock of those around you and you will . . . hear them talk in precise terms about themselves and their surroundings, which would seem to point to them having ideas on the matter. But start to analyse those ideas and you will find that they hardly reflect in any way the reality to which they appear to refer . . . Quite the contrary; through these notions the individual is trying to cut off any personal vision of reality, of his own very life . . . It does not worry him that his ''ideas'' are not true, he uses them as trenches for the defence of his existence, as scarecrows to frighten away reality.

(*The Revolt of the Masses*)

RICHARD OVERTON

No man hath power over my rights and liberties, and I over no man's; I may be but an Individual . . . an may write my selfe no more than my selfe, or presume any further.

(*An Arrow Against all Tyrants*, 1646)

JOHN PASSMORE

A man is dehumanised . . . when he is robbed of his freedom or when he is treated as a thing, rather than as a person.

PELAGIUS

In the beginning God set man and left him in his own counsel . . . He placed before you water and fire, to what you wish, stretch out your hand.

(*Eccles.*, 15, 14 sq., *cited by Caelestius*)

PRINCE PHILIP

It is all very well to say that (. . . it is possible to control human morality and behaviour by legislation and) this is justified because it is in the interests of the common good. The fact is that the liberty of the individual is a vital part of the common good also.

(*A Place for the Individual — Royal Society of Arts Lecture*, 1976)

Governments are obviously required to maintain a balance between the various factions in society, not for the benefit of the Governments or of the factions, but for the protection of the individual's freedom, security and rights before the law.

(*A Place for the Individual — Royal Society of Arts Lecture*, 1976)

It is patently impossible to achieve the public good by coercion or by discrimination against law abiding individuals, whatever minority group they happen to belong to.
(*A Place for the Individual — Royal Society of Arts Lecture, 1976*)

It is patently a denial of liberty to withold from the individual the opportunity of becoming a responsible member of the community.
(*A Place for the Individual — Royal Society of Arts Lecture, 1976*)

It may be that more controls give the individual greater freedom from want; but there is a very great difference between freedom from something and freedom to do something.
(*A Place for the Individual — Royal Society of Arts Lecture, 1976*)

PLATO

Beloved Pan, and all ye other gods who haunt this place, give me beauty in the inward soul; and may the outward and inward man be at one. May I reckon the wise to be the wealthy, and may I have such a quantity of gold as none but the temperate can carry.
(*Socrates — in Phaedo*)

DENIS de ROUGEMONT

If a man does not recognise in himself any vocation, his claim of liberty is meaningless; the Devil will take a hand in it in a thousand different guises, of which the commonest is Public Opinion. But if a man does recognise in himself a vocation, he demands no other right than to obey it.
(*Talk of the Devil*)

Man *is* free, which means that at any time he is confronted with two possibilities: to do the good that God wills, which will give him freedom; or to do the good as his own consciousness conceives it, which will forthwith put him in chains.
(*Talk of the Devil*)

JEAN-JACQUES ROUSSEAU

I am like no one in the whole world. I may be no better, but at least I am different.
(*Confessions*)

JOHN RUSKIN

Note finally that all effectual advancement towards this true felicity of the human race must be individual, not public effort.
(*Unto this Last*)

ST PAUL
Let every man prove his own work, and then shall he have rejoicing in himself alone, and not in another: for every man shall bear his own burden.
(*Galatians: The Bible*)

GEORGE SANTAYANA
In the midst of his shabby adventures, which whatever he may have been reaching towards brought him nothing but ''expense of spirit in a waste of shame'', this heroic spirit remained alive, as in all romantic prodigals; it was proud and brave enough not to be overwhelmed by any folly or any mischance. For this I admired him to the end, as I do Byron, not for what he did or thought, but for what he was.
(*On Lord Russell; My Host the World*)

Yet this compulsive and self-tormenting creature called ''Me'' was more odious and cruel to the ''I'' within than were the sea and sky, the woods and mountains, or the very cities and crowds of people that this animal ''M'' moved among: for the spirit in me was happy and free, ranging through that world, but troubled and captive in its close biological integument.
(*My Host the World*)

VERNON SCANNELL
I understand
And, understanding, I rejoice in my condition:
This sweet accident of being here and human.
(*Here and Human, anthology compiled by F. E. S. Finn, 1976*)

WILLIAM SHAKESPEARE
Luciana: A man is master of his liberty.
(*Comedy of Errors*)

PERCY BYSSHE SHELLEY
That heart which had grown old, but had corrupted not.
(*The Revolt of Islam*)

Good, great and joyous, beautiful and free;
This is alone Life, Joy, Empire, and Victory.
(*Prometheus Unbound*)

ADAM SMITH
It is not from the benevolence of the butcher, the brewer, or the baker that we expect our dinner, but from their regard to their own interests . . .
(*The Wealth of Nations*)

. . . we are all naturally disposed to overrate the excellencies of our own character.
(*The Theory of Moral Sentiments*)

. . . he is a bold person who does not hesitate to pull off the mysterious veil of self-delusion which covers from his view the deformities of his own conduct . . .
(*The Theory of Moral Sentiments*)

The uniform, constant, and uninterrupted effort of every man to better his condition, the principle from which public and national, as well as private opulence is originally derived, is frequently powerful enough to maintain the natural progress of things towards improvement, in spite of both the extravagance of government and of the greatest errors of administration.

ALEXANDER SOLZHENITSYN
Each person has his special moment in life when he unfolded himself to the fullest, felt to the deepest, and expressed himself to the utmost, to himself and to others.

FRANCIS THOMPSON
And all man's Babylons strive but to impart
The grandeurs of his Babylonian heart.
(*The Heart(ii)*)

KURT VONNEGUT Jr
We are what we pretend to be, so we must be careful about what we pretend to be.
(*Mother Night*)

ALFRED NORTH WHITEHEAD
In modern states there is a complex problem. There are many types of character. Freedom means that within each type the requisite co-ordination should be possible without the destruction of the general ends of the whole community.

The great Harmony is the harmony of enduring individualities, connected in the unity of a background. It is for this reason that the notion of freedom haunts the higher civilisations. For freedom, in any one of its many senses, is the claim for vigorous self-assertion.

WALT WHITMAN
One's-self I sing, a simple separate person,
Yet utter the word Democratic, the word En-Masse.
(*One's-self I sing: in Leaves of Grass*)

WILLIAM WORDSWORTH
I still retain'd
My first creative sensibility.
(*The Prelude — School-time*)

WILLIAM BUTLER YEATS
. . . which is in every man and called by every man his freedom. Doubtless, for it can do all things and knows all things, it knows what it will do with its own freedom but it has kept the secret.

Liberty and the Free Society

H. B. ACTON
Free Societies . . . by their variety and inventiveness, actively prevent the possibility of anything approaching social omniscience. Omniscient men are only conceivable, if at all, in societies where routine prevails, in the sort of society favoured by Mr Khruschev in which "every minute is calculated, a life built on calculation".
(*Agenda for a Free Society*)

C. C. ALLEN
It is to the free and multifarious movements of human activity that civilisation owes its most noteable achievements.
(*Economic Fact and Fantasy*)

WILLIAM BLAKE
. . . at liberty from the Doubts of other Mortals.

WILLY BRANDT
Our great political trump is that large areas of our society are free of political control or influence. Freedom is strength.
(*The Ordeal of Co-existence; Harvard University Press*)

MARTIN BUBER
I do not think that the victims should also be the judges.
(*Encounter with Martin Buber, Aubrey Hodes*)

In the beginning Liberty, Equality and Fraternity went hand in hand. Then their paths divided. Liberty turned towards the West, but changed its nature on the way. Equality turned towards the East: but it also changed during this journey. No one knows what happened to Fraternity. It seems to have been lost.
(*Encounter with Martin Buber, Aubrey Hodes*)

EDMUND BURKE
The only liberty I mean, is a liberty connected with order; that not only exists along with order and virtue, but which cannot exist at all without them.
(*Speech at Bristol*)

Abstract liberty, like other mere abstractions, is not to be found.
(*Conciliation with America*)

The people never give up their liberties but under some delusion.
(*Speech at Bucks County Meeting*)

Whenever our neighbour's house is on fire, it cannot be amiss for the engines to play a little on our own.
(*Reflections on the Revolution in France*)

A good parson once said, that where mystery begins, religion ends. Cannot I say, as truly at least, of human laws, that where mystery begins, justice ends?
(*A Vindication of Natural Society*)

THOMAS CARLYLE
Brothers, I am sorry I have got no Morrison's Pill for curing the maladies of Society. It were infinitely handier if we had a Morrison's Pill, Act of Parliament, or remedial measure, which men could swallow, one good time, and then go on in their old courses, cleared from all miseries and mischiefs! Unluckily we have none such; unluckily the Heavens themselves in their rich pharmacopoeia, contain none such.
(*Past and Present*)

SIR WINSTON S. CHURCHILL
I doubt whether any of the Dictators had as much effective power throughout his whole nation as the British War Cabinet. When we expressed our desires we were sustained by the people's representatives and cheerfully obeyed by all.
(*Their Finest Hour*)

The people of any country have the right . . . to choose or change the character or form of government under which they dwell; that freedom of speech and thought should reign; that courts of justice, independent of the executive, unbiased by any party, should administer laws which have the broad assent of large majorities or are consecrated by time and custom.
(*Sinews of Peace — Postwar Speeches*)

CALVIN COOLIDGE
One with the law is a majority.
(*Speech of Acceptance, July 27, 1920*)

BRIAN CROZIER
Democratic countries under military threat may face the need to surrender or suspend certain long-held liberties, basic to their way of life; this was the case of United Kingdom during World War II. In a democracy, these liberties are restored when the threat is removed.
(*Security and the Myth of "Peace"*)

BENJAMIN DISRAELI
I was told that the Privileged and the People formed Two Nations.
(*Sybil*)

JOHN DRYDEN
For who can be secure of private right,
If sovereign sway may be dissolv'd by might?
Nor is the people's judgment always true:
The most may err as grossly as the few.
(*Absalom and Achitophel*)

Either be wholly slaves or wholly free.
(*The Hind and the Panther*)

DAVID FRIEDMAN
Ask not what the government can do for you. Ask what the government is doing to you.
(*The Machinery of Freedom*)

MILTON FRIEDMAN
In a free society, it is hard for ''good'' people to do ''good'', but that is a small price to pay for making it hard for ''evil'' people to do ''evil'', especially since one man's good is another's evil.
(*Social Responsibility of Business, New York Times Magazine, September 13, 1970*)

The free society badly needs, and certainly deserves, the support not the hostility of intellectuals.
(*An Economist's Protest 1972*)

A free and orderly society is a complex structure. We understand but dimly its many sources of strength and weakness. The growing resort to political solutions is not the only and may not be the main source of the resort to violence that threatens the foundations of freedom. But it is one that we can do something about.
(*Politics and Violence — on the assassination of Senator Robert Kennedy, Newsweek, June 24, 1968*)

LORD HALIFAX
If none were to have liberty but those who understand what it is, there would not be many free men in the world.

GRAHAM HALLETT
. . . free trade in people is easiest when the disparities between the countries are not too wide: in levels of income, economic development and unemployment, and in race and culture.
(*Economic Issues in Immigration*)

F. A. HAYEK
Liberty . . . that condition of man in which coercion of some by others is reduced as much as possible in society.
(*The Constitution of Liberty*)

There is only one such principle that can preserve a free society: namely, the strict prevention of all coercion except in the enforcement of general abstract rules equally applicable to all.
(*The Constitution of Liberty*)

We can of course in a free society provide a floor below which nobody need fall, by providing outside the market for all some insurance against misfortune.
(*Economic Freedom and Representative Government*)

There is no reason why in a free society government should not assure to all protection against severe deprivation in the form of an assured minimum income.
(*Law Legislation and Liberty*)

THOMAS JEFFERSON
The tree of liberty must be refreshed from time to time with the blood of patriots and tyrants. It is its natural manure.
(*Letter to W. S. Smith, 1787*)

BERTRAND de JOUVENEL

It is an obvious mistake to regard majority decis⁘ as the criterion of the regimes which we call "democratic". So far from massive majorities in favour of a government and its policy giving us a feeling of the excellence of a regime, they render it suspect to us; we get the suspicion that so much unanimity is the result of hindrances placed in the way of the expression and propagation of adverse opinions . . . For this reason majority decision derives its virtue in our eyes from the liberty of opinion which precedes it.

C. G. JUNG

The free society needs a bond of an effective nature, a principle of a kind like *caritas*, the Christian love of your neighbour.
(*The Undiscovered Self*)

In the democracies, too, the distance between man and man is much greater than in conducive to public welfare or beneficial to our psychic needs.

LORD KAGAN of ELLAND

The free way of life which Britain enjoys is indeed not an optional extra: it is a condition for wishing to be alive. But sometimes I fear that the fortunate inhabitants of these islands are not always sufficiently aware of the blessings of freedom or of the horror of losing it.
(*House of Lords, November 25, 1976*) (*He had experience of a German concentration camp*)

ANTHONY LEJEUNE

The perfectly Good State, a perfectly free and just society, is not to be found in this world; but unless we keep in front of us a true image, against which policies and proposals can be tested, "progress" will be not just meaningless but as dangerous as a will-o'-the-wisp hanging over a marsh.
(*Freedom and the Politician*)

ABRAHAM LINCOLN

A new nation, conceived in liberty, and dedicated to the proposition that all men are created equal.
(*Gettysberg Address*)

TIBOR MACHAN

It is only within a free society that the crucial moral features of human life can be protected and preserved.

MACMILLAN COMMITTEE

Parliament finds itself increasingly engaged in legislation which has for its conscious aim the regulation of the day-to-day affairs of the community and now intervenes in matters formerly thought to be entirely outside its scope.
(*Report, 1931*)

JOHN STUART MILL

Mankind are greater gainers by suffering each other to live as seems good to themselves, than by compelling each to live as seems good to the rest.
(*On Liberty*)

Genius can only breathe freely in an atmosphere of freedom.
(*On Liberty*)

There is a limit to the legitimate interference of collective opinion with individual independence, and to find that limit, and maintain it against encroachment, is as indispensable to a good condition of human affairs, as protesters against political despotism.
(*On Liberty*)

Disinterested benevolence can find other instruments to persuade people to their good than whips and scourges, either of the literal or metaphorical sort.
(*On Liberty*)

It is a truism to assert, that labour exorted by fear of punishment is inefficient and unproductive.
(*Principles of Political Economy*)

A people may prefer a free government, but if, from indolence, or carelessness, or cowardice, or want of public spirit, they are unequal to the exertions necessary for preserving it . . . they are more or less unfit for liberty; and although it may be for their good to have had it even for a short time, they are unlikely long to enjoy it.

JOHN MILTON

When complaints are freely heard, deeply considered and speedily reformed, then is the utmost bound of civil liberty attained that wise men look for.
(*Areopagitica*)

If it be true that a wise man, like a good refiner, can father gold out of the drossiest volume, and a fool will be a fool with the best book . . . there is no reason that we should deprive any wise men of such advantage.
(*Areopagitica*)

If every action which is good or evil in a man of ripe years were under pittance and prescription and compulsion, what were virtue but a name, what praise should then be due to well-being, what gramercy to be sober, just or continent?

FRIEDRICH NIETZSCHE
He who is of the mob wants to live gratis; we others, however, to whom life has given itself — we are always considering what we can best give *in return*!
(*Thus Spake Zarathustra*)

JOSÉ ORTEGA Y GASSET
Order is not a pressure imposed upon society from without, but an equilibrium which is set up from within.
(*Mirabeau ó el politico*)

GEORGE ORWELL
It cannot be said too often — at any rate, it is not being said nearly often enough — that collectivism is not inherently democratic, but, on the contrary, gives to a tyrannical minority such powers as the Spanish Inquisition never dreamed of.
(*Tribute to The Road to Serfdom, by F. A. Hayek*)

KARL POPPER
If we wish to remain human, there is only one way, the way into the open society.
(*The Open Society and its Enemies*)

HERBERT READ
This new world would never have been discovered but for the invention of new vessels of exploration — new forms of literature like the novel and the short story, new techniques like free verse and the interior monologue. Even now further progress awaits new inventions.

Stability, which we foolishly yearn for, is but another name for stagnation, and stagnation is death. The ideal condition of society is the same as the ideal condition of any living body — a state of dynamic tension.

MURRAY N. ROTHBARD
Liberty has never been fully tried in the modern world.
(*For a New Liberty*)

For the libertarian, the main task of the present epoch is to cast off his needless and debilitating pessimism.

A flourishing libertarian movement, a lifelong dedication to liberty, can only be grounded on a passion for justice.

DENIS de ROUGEMENT
A democratic society must protect itself like any other.
(*Talk of the Devil*)

LOUIS ROUGIER
The worker would still be a proletarian if the emancipating machine had not transformed him into a true citizen. In three generations, the labourer has gained more wellbeing and liberty than during the 24 centuries which separated him from Aristotle at the start of this ascent.
(*Les Mystiques Economiques*)

RUSSIAN PROVERB
Life is not a walk across a field.
(*Quoted by Boris Pasternak in Hamlet; trans. Lydia Pasternak Slater*)

ST. PAUL
For though I am free from all men, I have made myself a slave to all.
(*Corinthians: The Bible*)

3rd MARQUESS OF SALISBURY
Municipal liberties, if you come to count them, are not the things for which people get themselves and their neighbours shot . . . The liberties (the Paris Commune) claimed, like many of the liberties for which men cry loudest, meant the liberty of doing as it liked with the lives and property of other people . . .
(*The Commune and the Internationale, Quarterly Review, October, 1871*)

GEORGE SAVILE, MARQUESS OF HALIFAX
Power and liberty are respectively managed in the world in a manner not suitable to their value and dignity.
(*The Political, Moral and Miscellaneous Reflections*)

WILLIAM SHAKESPEARE
True,
The people are the city.
(*Coriolanus*)

Vincentio, the Duke: So our decrees,
Dead to infliction, to themselves are dead,
And liberty plucks justice by the nose.
(*Measure for Measure*)

GEORGE BERNARD SHAW
Liberty means responsibility. That is why most men dread it.
(*Man and Superman*)

PERCY BYSSHE SHELLEY
Let there be light! said Liberty,
And like sunrise from the sea,
Athens arose!
(*Hellas*)

Let all be free and equal!
(*The Revolt of Islam*)

ARTHUR A. SHENFIELD
The brave but doomed attempt of Mr Dubcek to give Communism ''a human face'' suggests more than anything else that a human face will simply not fit.
(*Right Turn — Trial by Taxation*)

In a federation no single government is competent to act over the whole field of executive responsibility and so there are always likely to be havens for minorities to have concurrent power with majorities, and not merely to have the hope of some day becoming majorities.
(*Agenda for a Free Society — Law*)

ADAM SMITH
In the great chess-board of human society, every single piece has a principle of motion of its own, altogether different from that which the legislature might choose to impress upon it.

HENRY SMITH
The free society requires the existence of a free labour market in which no man is forced to accept employment on terms less favourable than those of alternative occupations open to him and in which no employer is forced to employ labour above the level at which he could do without it.
(*Freedom or Free For All — The Wage Fixers*)

HERBERT SPENCER
No one can be perfectly free till all are free; no one can be perfectly moral till all are moral; no one can be perfectly happy till all are happy.
(*Social Statics*)

ADLAI STEVENSON
My definition of a free society is a society where it is safe to be unpopular.
(*Speech in Detroit, October 1952*)

MARGARET THATCHER
If your only opportunity is to be equal, then it is not opportunity.
(*November 1976*)

ALEXIS de TOCQUEVILLE
The only nations which deny the utility of provincial liberties are those which have fewest of them; in other words, those only censure the institution who do not know it.
(*Democracy in America*)

Liberty is generally established with difficulty in the midst of storms; it is perfected by civil discord; and its benefits cannot be appreciated until it is already old.

MAX WEBER
Freedom and democracy are only possible where the resolute will of a nation not to allow itself to be ruled like sheep is permanently alive. We are "individualists" and partisans of "democratic" institutions "against the stream" of material constellations.
(*From Max Weber — Essays in Sociology*)

WILLIAM WORDSWORTH
From yon City's walls set free.
(*The Prelude — Introduction*)

Licence and Liberty

AESCHYLUS
From anarchy
And slavish masterdom alike . . .
Preserve my people! Cast not from your walls
All high authority; for where no fear
Awful remains, what mortal will be just?
(*Oresteia*)

KARL BARTH
Human freedom is the God-given freedom to obey.
(*The Humanity of God*)

. . . human freedom to respond with thanksgiving.
(*The Humanity of God*)

ERNEST BECKER
Yet we see the books by the mind-healers with garish titles:
"Joy!", "Awakening", and the like . . . I have never seen or heard
them communicate the dangers of the total liberation that they claim
to offer; say, to put up a small sign next to the one advertising joy,
carrying some inscription like "Danger: real probability of the
awakening of terror and dread, from which there is no turning back."
(*The Denial of Death*)

ISIAH BERLIN
Freedom is not the mere absence of frustration of whatever kind; this
would inflate the meaning of the word until it meant too much or too
little.
(*Two Concepts of Liberty*)

JOHN BIGGS-DAVIDSON
. . . Without civil order there can be no civil liberty. This they know
full well in those parts of Northern Ireland terrorized by private armies
and their protection rackets. Anarchy is the enemy of freedom.
(*Address to Loughton Conservatives, March 14, 1976*)

Man is a mystery. To trivialise that mystery, to treat human life as of little consequence, is to make human society inhuman. Some may call it freedom to resolve personal and social problems without giving human life at every stage of its existence the absolute respect that is its due. But freedom is emptied of all value if it degrades and brutalises.
(*Address to a rally organised by Society for the Protection of Unborn Children, Chelmsford, November 7, 1976*)

W. J. BROWN
Freedom has not one right, to give others the freedom to kill it.

SIR ARTHUR BRYANT
The multiplication of administrative offences punishable by imprisonment is such a deplorable feature of modern legislation in England. Those who frame such laws forget the supreme importance of liberty and the obligation which free men, who value their own freedom, lie under not to deprive other men of freedom without the clearest necessity.
(*The Ultimate Evil; Illustrated London News, March 27, 1948*)

RUDOLF BULTMANN
Only if we could forget our own work, should we be free; only if we were acting solely from obedience.
(*Faith and Understanding*)

ALBERT CAMUS
Absolute freedom mocks at justice. Absolute justice denies freedom.
(*The Rebel*)

THOMAS CARLYLE
You do not allow a palpable madman to leap over precipices; you violate his liberty, you that are wise.
(*Past and Present*)

LORD CHALFONT
The balance between freedom and order is a delicate one, and to maintain it there may often have to be encroachments upon the absolute freedom of action of the individual — especially if it threatens to restrict or erode the freedom of others.
(*The Times, May 9, 1977*)

HAVELOCK ELLIS
The particular twist of our culture has on one side impeded the manifestations of obscenity and on the other side, when that impulse has burst its bonds, subjected it to our British tendency to what Coleridge called *nimiety*, too-muchness, with the inevitable result that a natural reaction of disgust has been set up to fortify the artificial reaction of moral propriety.
(*Impressions and Comments*)

JAMES FERMAN
The essential question is: if we have freedom of expression, should we not also be free to abuse that freedom?
Society is nowadays freer for artists to talk frankly as adults to other adults about the kind of problems that concern us. It's also free for exploiters to take the seamier side of life and turn it into entertainment.
(*British film censor; Evening News, London, January 18, 1977*)

MAHATMA GANDHI
Freedom is not worth having unless it connotes the right to err.

EDWARD GIBBON
Corruption, the most infallible symptom of constitutional liberty.
(*Decline and Fall of the Roman Empire*)

JORGE GUILLÉN
In disorder, evil is always at work, and therefore the world's vision must be ethical.
(*Cántico*)

JOHN HICK
If human beings were not free to be cruel, they would never *be* cruel, but they would also not be free or, therefore, moral beings. Thus the question is whether a good human fulfilment, the realisation of which requires man's freedom, can render worthwhile the whole process of freely interacting human lives which ultimately leads to this fulfilment but which includes on the way the fearful misuse of freedom in acts of wickedness and cruelty.
(*Death and Eternal Life*)

THOMAS HOBBES
They that approve a private opinion, call it opinion; but they that dislike it, heresy: and yet heresy signifies no more than private opinion.
(*Leviathan*)

IVOR JENNINGS

It has always been true that there could be no liberty without law; for if everybody is free to do as he pleased there is no liberty for anybody to do as he pleases . . . On the other hand every law is a restriction of liberty . . . The problem has been to find out where law should end and liberty begin.
(*The Queen's Government*)

ROLLO MAY

Duke Ellington recounts that when he writes music, he must keep in mind that his trumpeter cannot hit the very high notes securely, whereas the trombonist is very good at them; and writing under these impediments, he remarks, "It's good to have limits."
(*Love and Will*)

JOHN STUART MILL

The State, while it respects the liberty of each in what specially regards himself, is bound to maintain a vigilant control over his exercise of any power which it allows him to possess over others.
(*On Liberty*)

The acts of an individual may be hurtful to others, or wanting in due consideration to their welfare, without going to the length of violating any of their constitutional rights. The offender then may be justly punished by opinion, though not by law.
(*On Liberty*)

Human liberty requires liberty of tastes and pursuits; of framing the plan of our life to suit our own character; of doing as we like, subject to such consequences as may follow; without impediment from our fellow creatures, so long as what we do does not harm them, even though they should think our conduct foolish, perverse, or wrong.
(*On Liberty*)

JOHN MILTON

Licence they mean when they cry Liberty;
For who loves that, must first be wise and good.
(*On the Same*)

None can love freedom heartily, but good men; the rest love not freedom, but licence.
(*Tenure of Kings and Magistrates*)

EZRA POUND
It is quite possible that we have already attained the maximum liberty compatible with civilisation.
(*Freedom de Facto*)

AYN RAND
The right of free speech means that a man has the right to express his ideas without danger of suppression, interference or punitive action by the government. It does not mean that others must provide him with a lecture hall, a radio station or a printing press through which to express his ideas.
(*The Virtue of Selfishness, a New Concept of Egoism*)

HERBERT READ
And so with the individual and the community: complete freedom means inevitable decadence. The mind must feel an opposition — must be tamped with hard realities if it is to have any blasting power.
(*Politics of the Unpolitical*)

There are many manifestations in the art of today which are vulgar and moronic, and there is no reason why, in the sacred name of liberty, we should condone them.
(*The Limits of Permissiveness in Art*)

JEAN-JACQUES ROUSSEAU
Each man alienates, I admit, by the social compact, only such part of his powers, goods and liberty as it is important for the community to control; but it must also be granted that the sovereign is sole judge of what is important.
(*The Social Contract, II*)

JOHN RUSKIN
Government and co-operation are in all things the laws of life; anarchy and competition the laws of death.
(*Unto this Last*)

ST. PAUL
I am free to do what I will, but I must not abdicate my own liberty.
(*Corinthians; The Bible*)

I am free to do what I will; yes, but not everything can be done without harm. I am free to do what I will, but some things disedify.
(*Corinthians; The Bible*)

Yes, brethren, freedom claimed you when you were called. Only do not let this freedom give a foothold to corrupt nature; you must be servants still, serving one another in a spirit of charity.
(*Galatians; The Bible*)

ST. PETER
As free, and not using your liberty as a cloak for maliciousness, but as the servants of God.
(*The Bible*)

Free men, but the liberty you enjoy is not to be made a pretext for wrong doing; it is to be used in God's service. Give all men their due; to the brethren, you love; to God, your reverence; to the king, due honour.
(*The Bible*)

GEORGE SAVILE, MARQUESS OF HALIFAX (1633-95)
If none were to have liberty but those who understand what it is, there would not be many freed men in the world.
(*The Political, Moral and Miscellaneous Reflections*)

WILLIAM SHAKESPEARE
Luciana: Headstrong liberty is lash'd with woe.
(*Comedy of Errors*)

GEORGE BERNARD SHAW
Children, if they are to grow up as citizens, must learn a good deal that their parents could not teach them even if they had the necessary time. The statesman must make provision for this teaching or he will presently find himself faced with the impossible task of maintaining civilization with savages instead of citizens.
(*Everybody's Political What's What*)

The statesman who imagines that a formula of Liberty, Equality, Fraternity, will solve all his problems will discover, if he is capable of learning from experience, that liberty must give way to equality and that fraternity may mean either the fraternity of Cain and Abel or the friendship of David and Jonathan.

BENEDICT SPINOZA
Free is, not he who acts upon his individual pleasure, but he who can wholeheartedly live in accordance with the precepts of reason.

Freedom is the recognition of necessity.

ADLAI STEVENSON
We have confused the free with the free and easy.
(*Putting First Things First*)

WILLIAM BUTLER YEATS
After us the savage god.
(*After seeing the first performance of Jarry's Ubu Roi; quoted by Kathleen Raine in Herbert Read: A Memorial Symposium, edited by Robin Skelton*)

The Other

ALCUIN
No time, there is no time for private sorrow:
So vast the evil,
So universal through the whole wide world,
A man's own grief seems lighter.
(*On the Killing at Lindisfarne; trans. Helen Waddell; More Latin Lyrics, from Virgil to Milton*)

Think upon your fathers. Be not degenerate sons.
(*trans. Helen Waddell*)

WILLIAM R. ALLEN (with A. A. ALCHIAN)
The postulates of economic theory do not say that man is concerned only about himself. He can also be concerned about other people's situations.
(*The Economics of Charity*)

ATHANASIUS
Your life and your death are with your neighbour.

BAAL SHEM TOV
No encounter with a being or a thing in the course of our life lacks a hidden significance . . . The highest culture of the soul remains basically arid and barren unless, day by day, waters of life pour forth into the soul from those little encounters to which we give their due.

MARTIN BUBER
Love is responsibility of an I for a Thou.
(*I and Thou*)

Every particular Thou is a glimpse through to the Eternal Thou.
(*I and Thou*)

I often hear men prizing their solitude, but that is only because there are still men somewhere on earth, even though in the far distance.
(*Pointing the Way*)

JAMES CALLAGHAN
. . . the whole essence of democracy as I understand it is that you can listen to other people's views even though you dislike them — but sit and listen to them and not just prevent them from being heard.
(Speech to the Boilermakers' Union at Largs, May 28, 1976)

SEBASTIAN CASTELLIO
To burn a man alive does not defend a doctrine, but slays a man. When the Genevese executed Servetus, they were not defending a doctrine, but sacrificing a man. We do not testify our own faith by burning another, but only by our readiness to be burned on behalf of our faith.

PIERRE TEILHARD de CHARDIN
At what moment do lovers come into the most complete possession of *themselves*, if not when they are *lost* in each other?
(The Phenomenon of Man)

WILLIAM GERHARDIE
The terrific power that, like a screen of fire, leaps up from within us and prevents our speaking freely to another being who has through unrequited love intimidated us, assailed her.
(Of Mortal Love)

MARTIN HEIDEGGER
No one can take the Other's dying away from him. Of course someone can ''go to his death for another'' . . . Such ''dying for'' can never signify that the Other has thus had his death taken away in even the slightest degree . . . By its very essence, death is in every case mine, in so far as it ''is'' at all.
(Being and Time)

This evasive concealment in the face of death dominates everydayness so stubbornly that, in Being with one another the ''neighbours'' often still keep talking the ''dying person'' into the belief that he will escape death and soon return to the tranquillized everydayness of the world of his concern. Such ''solicitude'' is meant to ''console'' him . . . Indeed the dying of Others is seen often enough as a social inconvenience, if not even a downright tactlessness, against which the public is to be guarded.
(Being and Time)

HUBERT H. HUMPHREY
We cannot seek democracy and social justice at home and abandon these principles abroad.

ROLLO MAY
Sometimes a woman patient will report to me, in the course of describing how a man tried to seduce her, that he cites as part of his seduction line how efficient a lover he is, and he promises to perform the act eminently satisfactorily for her. (Imagine Mozart's Don Giovanni offering such an argument!).
(*Love and Will*)

The vast need of our society for touch and the revolt against its prohibition are shown in the growth of all the forms of touch therapy, from Esalen on down to the group therapy in the next room. These rightly reflect the need, but they are in error in their anti-intellectual bias and in the grandiose aims which they assert for what is essentially a corrective measure. They are also in error in their failure to see that this is an aspect of the whole society which must be changed, and changed on a deep level involving the whole man.
(*Love and Will*)

The new puritanism brings with it a depersonalisation of our whole language. Instead of making love, we "have sex"; in contrast to intercourse, we "screw"; instead of going to bed, we "lay" someone or (heaven help the English language as well as ourselves!) we "are laid" . . . Everyone seems so intent on sweeping away the last vestiges of Victorian prudishness that we entirely forget that these different words refer to different kinds of human experience.
(*Love and Will*)

JOHN RUSKIN
The goodness of a man is a question of his sensibility; it is the goodness of his heart, not of his brain . . . the ennobling difference between one man and another . . . is precisely in this, that one feels more than another . . . We are only human in so far as we are sensitive, and our honour is precisely in proportion to our passion.

Physical Freedom

ALCUIN
He lies bedridden now, who coursed with stags
Over the ploughed lands.
(*On the Killing at Lindisfarne; trans. Helen Waddell; More Latin Lyrics, from Virgil to Milton*)

When you sit happy in your own fair house
Remember all poor men that are abroad.
(*trans. Helen Waddell; More Latin Lyrics, from Virgil to Milton*)

THE ECOLOGIST
While most people receive the bare minimum of calories necessary for survival a large proportion are deprived of the nutrients (especially protein) essential for intellectual development. They are alive, but unable to realise their full potential.
(*A Blueprint for Survival, vol. 2 no. 1*)

JOHN HICK
A package of genetic information has programmed the growth of a living organism in continuous interaction with its environment — the developing self exercising throughout a measure of free creativity within the narrow limits of an inherited nature and of a given world.
(*Death and Eternal Life*)

C. D. LEWIS
Come, live with me and be my love,
And we will all the pleasures prove
Of Peace and plenty, bed and board,
That chance employment may afford.
(*Come live with me and be my Love*)

ANDREI D. SAKHAROV
The freedom to emigrate, which only a small number of people would in fact use, is an essential condition of spiritual freedom. A free country cannot resemble a cage, even if it is gilded . . .
(*Religion in Communist Dominated Areas, USA, No. 7/9, 1976*)

GEORGE SANTAYANA
There is a wonderful sense of freedom in standing on one's two legs.
(*My Host the World*)

JAMES STEPHENS
The human body is an aggregation of flesh and sinew, around a central bony structure. The use of clothing is primarily to protect this organism from rain and cold, and it may not be regarded as the banner of morality without danger to this fundamental premise. If a person does not desire to be so protected who will quarrel with an honourable liberty?
(*The Crock of Gold*)

WILLIAM BUTLER YEATS
Nor public men, nor cheering crowds,
A lonely impulse of delight
Drove to this tumult in the clouds;
(*An Irish Airman foresees his Death*)

Power — as Friend and Enemy

LORD ACTON
Power tends to corrupt and absolute power corrupts absolutely.
(*Historical Essays and Studies*)

ARMEN A. ALCHIAN
The man who enters political life to restrain the growth of public ownership, publicly-operated agencies and services, will find that he must dismantle his major sources of power and wealth once he is in office. His survival chances in political office will diminish compared to those of another man taking the opposite position.
(*Pricing and Society*)

ANON
There are two pursuits, love and power, but no man can have both.
(*Inscription by Roman centurion found in Libyan desert*)

CHARLES d'AVENANT
Custom, that unwritten law,
By which the people keep even kings in awe.
(*Circe*)

FRANCIS BACON
It is a strange desire to seek power and to lose liberty.
(*Of Great Place*)

WALTER BAGEHOT
The best reason why Monarchy is a strong government is, that it is an intelligible government. The mass of mankind understand it, and they hardly anywhere in the world understand any other.
(*The English Constitution: The Monarchy*)

EDVARD BENES
The philosophy of power is barbaric, inhuman and absurd philosophy.

WILLIAM BILDERDIJK
The cheering subjects of a king,
That is where liberty flourishes

JOHN BRADSHAW
Rebellion to tyrants is obedience to God.
(*Supposititious epitaph, Randall's Life of Jefferson*)

JOHN BRIGHT
Force is not a remedy.
(*Speech, Birmingham, November 16, 1880*)

EDMUND BURKE
The greater the power, the more dangerous the abuse.
(*Middlesex Election, 1771*)

Tyrants seldom want pretexts.
(*Letter to a Member of the National Assembly*)

Those who have been once intoxicated with power, and have derived
any kind of emolument from it, even though but for one year, can
never willingly abandon it.
(*Letter to a Member of the National Assembly*)

JIMMY CARTER
We have already found a high degree of personal liberty, and we are
now struggling to enhance equality of opportunity. Our commitments
to human rights much be absolute, our laws fair, our natural beauty
preserved, the powerful must not persecute the weak and the human
dignity must be enhanced.
(*Inaugural speech, January 20, 1977*)

SIR WINSTON S. CHURCHILL
Dictators ride to and fro upon tigers which they dare not dismount.
And the tigers are getting hungry.
(*While England Slept*)

BENJAMIN DISRAELI
I repeat . . . that all power is a trust — that we are accountable for its
exercise — that, from the people, and for the people, all springs, and
all must exist.
(*Vivian Grey*)

E. M. FORSTER
As soon as people have power, they go crooked and sometimes dotty as well because the possession of power lifts them into regions where normal honesty never pays . . . the more highly public life is organised, the lower does its morality sink.
(*Two Cheers for Democracy*)

MILTON FRIEDMAN
I must say I object to being ruled either by the natural-born aristocracy or by a meritocracy but, if I have to be ruled by either, it seems to me that artistocracy of birth is much the lesser evil if only because those who are born to be aristocrats are less likely to be arrogant.
(*Talk: The Conventional Wisdom of J. K. Galbraith; 1976*)

JOHN KENNETH GALBRAITH
I believe that almost everyone enjoys testifying before a friendly Congressional Committee or even a moderately censorious one. For the moment you are an oracle, a minor oracle to be sure, but possessed of knowledge important for the future of the Republic.
(*The Great Crash 1929*)

CHARLES DE GAULLE
Power is impotence.

JOHANN WOLFGANG von GOETHE
It is in in self-limitation that a master first shows himself.
(*Sonnet: Natur und Kunst*)

WALTER GOETZ
That is the great lesson of our time: the improvable republic is better than the unimprovable monarchy.
(*Republik und Monarchie*)

ROLAND GRIBBEN
It has become an all-pervading organisation of power without responsibility — a dangerous development which threatens the foundations of our society.
(*The Civil Service*)

F. A. HAYEK
It is a curious consequence of giving the representative assembly unlimited power that it has largely ceased to be chief determining agent in shaping the law proper, but has left this task more and more to the bureaucracy.
(*Economic Freedom and Representative Government*)

In any society freedom of thought will probably be of direct significance for a small minority. But this does not mean that anyone is competent, or ought to have power, to select those to whom this freedom is to be reserved.
(*The Road to Serfdom*)

Although the professed aims of planning would be that man should cease to be a mere means, in fact . . . the individual would more than ever become a mere means, to be used by the authority in the service of such abstractions as "social welfare" or "the good of the community".
(*The Road to Serfdom*)

HENRY HAZLITT
One would think that the horrible examples of Mussolini, Hitler, Mossadegh, Peron, etc., would give pause to our own advocates of more and more executive power . . . It is the only illusion that "it can't happen here".
(*On Freedom and Free Enterprise — The Road to Totalitarianism*)

WILLIAM HAZLITT
The love of liberty is the love of others; the love of power is the love of ourselves.
(*Political Essays. The Times Newspaper*)

GRAHAM HUTTON
There is little purely economic difference between what are vulgarly (and wrongly) called Communism and Capitalism. The big differences are in control over human beings.
(*All Capitalists Now*)

W. R. INGE
A man may build himself a throne of bayonets, but he cannot sit on it.
(*Marchant: Wit and Wisdom of Dean Inge, No. 108*)

JOHN OF SALISBURY
When all the affairs of the subjects are disposed at one strong man's nod.
(*Letters*)

SAMUEL JOHNSON
In every government though terrors reign,
Though tyrant Kings or tyrant laws restrain,
How small, of all that human hearts endure,
That part which laws or Kings can cause or cure.
(*Inserted end of Goldsmith's Traveller*)

For righteous monarchs,
Justly to judge, with their own eyes should see;
To rule o'er freemen, should themselves be free.
(*Earl of Essex (parodied by Dr Johnson)*)

JOHN MAYNARD KEYNES
There are valuable human activities which require the motive of money-making and the environment of private wealth-ownership for their full fruition . . . It is better that a man should tyrannise over his bank balance than over his fellow-citizens.
(*The General Theory of Employment, Interest and Money, 1936-1947 edition*)

F. H. KNIGHT
The authorities of a collectivist state "would have to do these things whether they wanted to or not: and the probability of the people in power being individuals who would dislike the possession and exercise of power is on a level with the probability that an extremely tender-hearted person would get the job of whipping-master in a slave plantation."
(*The Journal of Political Economy, December, 1938*)

VLADIMIR ILYITCH LENIN
There is absolutely no contradiction in principle between Soviet democratism and the use of dictatorial power by single individuals.

The purpose of "liquidate illiteracy" is only that every peasant should be able to read by himself, without help, our decrees, orders and proclamations. The aim is completely practical.

WALTER LIPPMANN

In an economy which is directed according to a plan, and for definite national objectives, the official must be superior to the citizen. The citizen is a conscript; in principle his life is dedicated to the State, in practice it is dedicated to the officers who issue his orders to him.
(*The Method of Freedom*)

ANTHONY LEJEUNE

There is a popular fallacy that people want to be free . . . Very few people would choose to be absolutely free. Many do not really want to be free at all, but would prefer to live comfortably secure "like battery hens".
(*Freedom and the Politicians*)

ABRAHAM LINCOLN

With some the word liberty may mean for each man to do as he pleases with himself and the produce of his labour; while with others the same word may mean for some men to do as they please with other men, and the product of other men's labour. Here are two, not only different, but incompatible things, called by the same name, liberty.
(*Internal Message to Congress, 1862*)

JOHN STUART MILL

The only purpose for which power can be rightfully exercised over any member of a civilised community, against his will, is to prevent harm to others.
(*On Liberty*)

The "people" who exercise the power are not always the same people over whom it is exercised.
(*On Liberty*)

HENRY MILLER

Man will be forced to realise that power must be kept open, fluid and free. His aim will be not to possess power but to radiate it.
(*Sunday After the War*)

MALCOLM MUGGERIDGE

It was true, as she explained at many subsequent lectures, that Soviet officials sometimes disappeared; and naturally she deplored such goings-on, just as she deplored the press censorship and the suppression of all opposition opinion. At the same time she had to admit that, given the peculiar conditions prevailing in Russia, administrative disappearances carried with them certain advantages which she for one was not going to overlook. How agreeable, she thought, if Alderman Butterfield, who had publicly called her an incompetent, sentimental busybody, could be made to disappear!
(*Winter in Moscow* — *by Beatrice Webb*)

MICHAEL OAKESHOTT

To some people ''Government'' appears as a vast reservoir of power. They have favourite projects, of various dimensions, which they sincerely believe are for the benefit of mankind, and to capture this source of power, if necessary to increase it, and to use it for imposing their favourite projects upon their fellows, is what they understand as the adventure of governing men.

JOSE ORTEGA Y GASSET

Liberalism is the supreme form of generosity: it is the right the majority concedes to minorities. It announces the determination to share existence with the enemy.
(*The Revolt of the Masses*)

GEORGE ORWELL

A ruling group is a ruling group so long as it can nominate its successors. The Party is not concerned with perpetuating its blood but with perpetuating itself. Who wields power is not important, provided that the hierarchical structure remains always the same.
(*1984*)

Power is not a means, it is an end. One does not establish a dictatorship in order to safeguard a revolution; one makes the revolution in order to establish the dictatorship.
(*1984*)

KARL POPPER

The dogma that economic power is the root of all evil must be discarded. Its place must be taken by an understanding of the dangers of any form of uncontrolled power.

HERBERT READ
Power corrupts even the intellect.

ST. JAMES
There is only one law giver, only one Judge, he who has power to destroy and to set free. Who art thou, to sit in judgment on thy neighbour?
(*Epistle: The Bible*)

ST. PAUL
For power comes in weakness to perfection.
(*Corinthians: The Bible*)

PERCY BYSSHE SHELLEY
To defy Power, which seems omnipotent.
(*Prometheus Unbound*)

ADAM SMITH
(People engaged in the administration of government) are generally disposed to reward both themselves and their immediate dependents rather more than enough.
(*The Theory of Moral Sentiments*)

BENEDICT SPINOZA
Insofar as men are influenced by envy or any kind of hatred, one towards another, they are at variance, and are therefore to be feared in proportion, as they are more powerful than their fellows.
(*Ethics*)

ADLAI STEVENSON
Power corrupts, but lack of power corrupts absolutely.

W. M. THACKERAY
Whenever he met a great man he grovelled before him, and my-lorded him as only a free-born Briton can do.
(*Vanity Fair*)

HENRY C. WALLICH
Power is the great enemy of freedom.

WILLIAM WALWYN

Very good men there be, who affirme, that a Parliament being once chosen, have power over all our lives estates and liberties, to dispose of them at their pleasure whether for our good or hurt . . . they are accountable unto none, they are above MAGNA CARTA and all Lawes whatsoever, and there is no pleading of any thing against them.

Others are (as good wise and judicious men) who affirme, that a Parliamentary authority is a power intrusted by the people (that chose them) for their good, safetie, and freedom; and therefore that a Parliament cannot justlie doe any thing, to make the people lesse safe or lesse free, then they found them: MAGNA CARTA (you must observe) is but a part of the peoples rights and liberties, being no more but what with much striving and fighting, was by the blood of our Ancestors, wrestled out of the pawes of those Kings, who by force had conquered the Nation, changed the lawes and by strong hand held them in bondage.

(*Englands Lamentable Slaverie, 1645*)

K. W. WATKINS

All experience shows that the centralisation of economic power leads to the centralisation of political power . . . Disagreement with the élite becomes heresy or deviation, since by definition the élite, armed with the true ideology, know what is best for the people.

MAX WEBER

In a democracy, the people choose a leader whom they trust; the leader who is chosen then says, "Now shut up and do what I say".

(*Gesammelte politische Schriften*)

TOM WILSON

It is hard to explain in rational terms why any western rebels should believe that the libertarian society they want is to be obtained by transferring more and more power to central authority. The ultimate absurdity in the west is surely the communist beatnik.

(*The Contradiction in our Attitudes to Freedom, New Society, February 15, 1968*)

Prisons

BROTHER ALEXEI
Each day in prison as I went to work I buried my little book in the soil
or the snow — at night I would rush to see if it was still safe, then
press it to my heart.
(*Challenge, October 2, 1976*)

VENERABLE BEDE
Where there is no voice unless of bitter weeping,
No face, unless the face of the tormentors.
(*Quoted by Helen Waddell in More Latin Lyrics, from Virgil to
Milton*)

LORD BYRON
Eternal Spirit of the chainless Mind!
Brightest in dungeons, Liberty! thou art.
(*Sonnet on Chillon*)

T. S. ELIOT
Liberty is a different kind of pain from prison.
(*The Family Reunion*)

IVOR GURNEY
And who loves joy as he
That dwells in shadows?
(*Song; Poems of Ivor Gurney*)

ISAIAH
To bind up the broken-hearted, to proclaim liberty to the captives, and
the opening of the prison to them that are bound.
(*The Bible*)

MICHAEL IVENS
. . . the best way to appreciate freedom is to lose it. Prisoners are likely
to be more aware of its attractions than happy and free men.
(*Pressures for Conformity, article in Patterns of Prejudice, Jan/Feb
1977*)

FRANZ KAFKA

I have often thought that the best mode of life for me would be to sit in the innermost room of a spacious locked cellar with my writing things and a lamp. Food would be brought and always put down far away from my room, in my dressing gown, through the vaulted cellars, would be my only exercise.

(*Letter*)

FATHER PETER LEVI

I am always climbing back into prison.

(*Christmas Sermon from Death is a Pulpit*)

PERCY WYNDHAM LEWIS

I . . . believe . . . that people should be compelled to be freer and more "individualistic" than they naturally desire to be . . . I believe they could with advantage be compelled to remain absolutely alone for several hours every day; and a week's solitary confinement . . . every two months, would be an excellent provision.

(*Time and the Western Man*)

RICHARD LOVELACE

Stone walls do not a prison make
Nor iron bars a cage;
Minds innocent and quiet take
That for an heritage.

(*To Althea, From Prison*)

If I have freedom in my love
And in my soul am free,
Angels alone, that soar above,
Enjoy such liberty.

(*To Althea from Prison*)

MICAH

For I . . . *redeemed* you from the house of *bondage*; . . .

(*The Bible*)

MALCOLM MUGGERIDGE

There is a remarkable passage in Pasternak's *Dr Zhivago* in which the hero reflects that in a Communist society freedom only exists in concentration camps — in other words, that the only way to be free is to be imprisoned.

(*Jesus Rediscovered*)

PAUL THE DEACON

For seven years one man has lived a captive
Within your frontiers: that man is my brother,
Naked and penniless and broken-hearted.
(*He intercedes with Charlemagne for his brother in exile; trans. Helen Waddell: More Latin Lyrics from Virgil to Milton*)

PAULINUS OF AQUILEIA

Hands bound behind their backs, the living go
Captive to slavery.
(*Lament for Aquileia destroyed, and never to be built again; trans. Helen Waddell; More Latin Lyrics, from Virgil to Milton*)

SIR WALTER RALEIGH

The world itself is but a large prison, out of which some are daily led to execution.

CARL SANDBURG

And when he was most in jail
Crummy among the crazy in the dark
Then he was most of all out of jail
Shambling, dark, and strong.
Always asking: Where did that blood come from?
(*John Brown's Body from Smoke and Steel*)

GEORGE BERNARD SHAW

You cannot have the argument both ways. If the prisoner is happy, why lock him in? If he is not why pretend that he is?
(*Man and Superman*)

PERCY BYSSHE SHELLEY

The Tyrant peoples dungeons with his prey.
(*The Revolt of Islam*)

STEPHEN SPENDER

When have their lives been free from walls and dark
And airs that choke?
(*The Prisoners; Collected Poems*)

Belsen, Theresenstadt, Buchenwald, where
Faces were a clenched despair
Knocking at the bird-song-fretted air.
(*Memento; Collected Poems*)

MARINA TSVETAYEVA
I am a convict. You won't fall behind.
You are my guard. Our fate is therefore one.
And in that emptiness that we both share
the same command to ride again is given.
(*Poems for Akhmatova*)

DOROTHY WELLESLEY
Barabbas disorderly,
Bawdy Barabbas,
Drank, stole, and swore;
Next day was back in the prison!
By word of a whore.
(*The Morning After*)

OSCAR WILDE
I know not whether Laws be right,
Or whether Laws be wrong;
All that we know who lie in gaol
Is that the wall is strong.
(*The Ballad of Reading Gaol*)

There is no chapel on the day
On which they hang a man:
The Chaplain's heart is far too sick,
Or his face is far too wan.
(*The Ballad of Reading Gaol*)

I never saw a man who looked
With such a wistful eye
Upon that little tent of blue
Which prisoners call the sky.
(*The Ballad of Reading Gaol*)

WILLIAM BUTLER YEATS
She that but little patience knew,
From childhood on, had not so much
A grey gull lost its fear and flew
Down to her cell and there alit,
And there endured her fingers' touch
And from her fingers ate its bit.
(*On a Political Prisoner*)

Minorities and Discrimination

WILLIAM COWPER
Slaves cannot breathe in England; if their lungs
Receive our air, that moment they are free;
They touch our country, and their shackles fall.
(*The Timepiece*)

Freedom has a thousand charms to show,
That slaves, howe'er contented, never know.
(*Table Talk*)

ANTHONY HOPE (ANTHONY HOPE HAWKINS)
"*Bourgeois*," I observed, "is an epithet which the riff-raff apply to
what is respectable, and the aristocracy to what is decent."
(*Dolly Dialogues*)

A. KOLNAI
The principle of Race is meant to embody and express the utter
negation of human freedom, the denial of equal rights, a challenge in
the face of mankind.
(*The War Against the West*)

JAMES RUSSELL LOWELL
I do believe in Freedom's cause,
Ez fur away es Payris is;
I love to see her stick her claws
In them infarnal Phayrisees;
It's wall enough agin a king
To dror resolves an' triggers —
But libbaty's a kind o'thing
(*The Pious Editor's Creed*)

JOHN STUART MILL
I am not aware that any community has a right to force another to be
civilised.
(*On Liberty*)

MOLOTOV
We are entering into the period of decolonization which will be followed by a general independence. Then, on those territories that were yesterday slaves, will fall a period of unbelievable disorder. There will be political and economic anarchy. Afterwards, and then only, the dawn of communism will rise.

JEAN-FRANÇOIS REVEL
Paradoxically, the United States is one of the least racist countries in the world today.
(*Without Marx or Jesus*)

WILLIAM SHAKESPEARE
I am a Jew. Hath not a Jew eyes? hath not a Jew hands, organs, dimensions, senses, affections, passions?
Fed with the same food, hurt with the same weapons, subject to the same diseases, healed by the same means, warmed and cooled by the same winter and summer as a Christian is?
(*Shylock; The Merchant of Venice*)

A. N. WHITEHEAD
The differences between the nations and races of mankind are required to preserve the conditions under which higher development is possible.
(*Science and the Modern World*)

Resistance Movements

ERNEST BECKER
When at the time of the Nazi invasion his daughter wondered why
they did not all just kill themselves, Freud characteristically remarked,
"Because that is exactly what they want us to do."
(*The Denial of Death*)

ARTHUR BRYANT
All over the world backs bowed to slavery stiffened instinctively at the
sight of the British mongoose poised to spring, with every hair taut
and bristling as it faced the giant Teuton cobra. That was the rallying
hour of freedom . . .
(*The Summer of Dunkirk, Daily Sketch, June 4, 1943*)

MARTIN BUBER
There appears before me, from reliable reports, some who have
become as familiar to me by sight, action and voice as if they were
friends, those who refused to carry out the orders and suffered death or
put themselves to death, and those who learned what was taking place
and opposed it and were put to death, or those who learned what was
taking place and because they could do nothing to stop it killed
themselves.
(*Pointing the Way*)

ANGELA CARTER
A man constructs his own fate out of his sense of the world. You
engaged in conspiracies because you believed the humblest objects
were engaged in a conspiracy against you.
(*Fireworks*)

MAHATMA GANDHI
Have I not repeatedly said that I would rather India became free even
by violence rather than she should remain in bondage?
(*March, 1922*)

YVAN GOLL
But as things go
Since one must eat
In the lower intestine
Your vengeance can flow.
(*Jean Sans Terre Fills His Belly; trans. Eric Sellin*)

C. D. LEWIS
Bayonets are closing round.
I shrink; yet I must wring
A living from despair
And of steel a song.
(*Tempt me no more*)

CARLOS MARIGHELLA
It is necessary to turn political crisis (always at hand in some countries)
into armed conflict by performing violent actions that will force those
in power to transform the political situation in the country into a
military (or police) situation. That will alienate the masses who from
then on will revolt against the army and police and blame them for this
state of things.

KARL MARX
Communism disdains to conceal its views and aims. It openly declares
that its ends can be attained only by the forcible overthrow of the
existing social conditions.
(*Manifesto*)

MALCOLM MUGGERIDGE
Tourism today is a more dynamic force than revolution, swaying, as it
does, crowns and thrones; Thomas Cook and the American Express,
not the *Internationale*, unite the human race.
(*Jesus Rediscovered*)

CHRIS MYANT
Revolution in Britain can never be achieved if British workers are not
taking part in it.
(*Morning Star, November 1, 1976*)

EWALD OSERS
. . . the human torch,
that exclamation mark after
the passage of tanks.
(*Prague 1971*)

GEORGE SAVILE, MARQUESS OF HALIFAX (1633-95)
When the People contend for their liberty they seldom get anything by
their victory but new masters.
(*Political, Moral and Miscellaneous Reflections*)

GEORGE SOREL
The class struggle is the Alpha and Omega of Socialism.
(*Matériaux d'une Théorie du Proletariat*)

MARINA TSVETAYEVA
Bullets they took from us, they took our rifles
Minerals they took, and comrades too:
But while our mouths have spittle in them
The whole country is still armed.
(*Poems to the Czech Lands*)

CHARLES WILLIAMS
Something general and very deep in man awoke to revolt, of which
Elizabeth and Catherine and Henry of Navarre were the political signs.
It may have been mere exhaustion, or perhaps mere humanitarianism
(which at such times is seen to have a beauty all its own), which gave
it an opportunity. But it rose. It was a quality of spirit, not clarity
(though charity). It is a rare thing, and it may be called the quality of
disbelief.
(*The Descent of the Dove*)

WILLIAM BUTLER YEATS
Bred to a harder thing
Than Triumph, turn away . . .
. . . Be secret and exult,
Because of all things known
That is most difficult.
(*To A Friend whose Work has come to Nothing*)

Rights of Man

ERNEST BARKER

Liberty is always also responsibility, and to be free to act is also to be responsible for action.

(*Principles of Social and Political Theory*)

EDMUND BURKE

The moment you abate anything from the full rights of men each to govern himself, and suffer any artificial, positive limitations upon those rights, from that moment the whole organisation of government becomes a consideration of convenience.

THOMAS CARLYLE

Surely of all ''rights of man'', the right of the ignorant man to be guided by the wiser, to be, gently or forcibly, held in the true course by him, is the indisputablest.

(*Chartism from Critical and Miscellaneous Essays*)

JIMMY CARTER

Because we are free we can never be indifferent to the fate of freedom elsewhere. Our moral sense dictates a clear-cut preference for those societies which share with us an abiding respect for individual human rights.

(*Inaugural speech, January 20, 1977*)

CHARTER 77

The responsibility for the preservation of civil rights naturally rests with the political and state power in the country. But not on it alone. Each individual bears a share of responsibility for the general conditions and thus also for the compliance with the enacted pacts which are binding, for the government as for the people.

G. K. CHESTERTON

I did not really understand what I meant by Liberty, until I heard it called by the new name of Human Dignity. It was a new name to me; though it was part of a creed nearly two thousand years old.

(*Autobiography*)

SIR WINSTON S. CHURCHILL

We must never cease to proclaim in fearless tones the great principles of freedom and the rights of man which are the joint inheritance of the English speaking world and which through Magna Carta, the Bill of Rights, the Habeas Corpus, trial by jury, and the English common law find their most famous expression in the American Declaration of Independence.

(*The Sinews of Peace and Postwar Speeches*)

BRIAN CROZIER

That rule by Communists would involve the total expropriation of private enterprise has never been disguised . . . More fundamental still would be the disappearance of the fundamental liberties: of freedom of speech and expression, of the press and other media, of freedom from arbitrary arrest and the right to a fair trial if arrested; the freedom to form political parties and independent trade unions; the right to dissent and opposition . . .

(*A Theory of Conflict*)

LORD DENNING

A man's right to work is just as important to him as, if not more important than, his rights of property. The courts intervene every day to protect rights of property. They must also intervene to protect the right to work.

(*Lee vs Showmen's Guild*)

MILTON FRIEDMAN

I propose simply that we add an eleventh amendment to the Bill of Rights. Every person shall be free to do good — at his own expense.

(*Talk at University of Rochester*)

HENRY M. JACKSON

If the United States in its diplomacy and international negotiations does not stand up for human rights, there is little prospect that nations whose governments are based on the denial of fundamental rights will make up even a minimal effort to comply with their human rights commitments.

(*Introduction to International Human Rights, published by the US Senate, September1976*)

THOMAS JEFFERSON
We hold these truths to be sacred and undeniable; that all men are created equal and independent, that from that equal creation they derive rights inherent and inalienable, among which are the preservation of life, and liberty, and the pursuit of happiness.
(*Original draft for the American Declaration of Independence*)

DAVID LANE
In collectivist Bolshevik social theory . . . claims for the assertion of individual rights are claims against society.
(*The Socialist Industrial State*)

HAROLD J. LASKI
By liberty I mean the eager maintenance of that atmosphere in which men have the opportunity to be their best selves. Liberty, therefore, is a product of rights.
(*A Grammar of Politics*)

B. C. ROBERTS
In democratic societies the right to strike is regarded as one of the basic freedoms enjoyed by employees.
(*Trade Unions in a Free Society*)

Trade unions in a free society are an expression of the fundamental right of men and women to organise themselves in order to protect and promote their interests by collective action.
(*Trade Unions in a Free Society*)

3rd MARQUESS OF SALISBURY
The protection of each individual human being from more interference than is indispensably necessary to protect the freedom of his neighbours, is what we used to understand as the meaning of freedom.

ALEXIS de TOCQUEVILLE
To the European, a public officer represents a superior force, to an American, he represents a right.
(*Democracy in America*)

The first characteristic of judicial power in all nations is the duty of arbitration. But rights must be contested in order to warrant the interference of a tribunal.
(*Democracy in America*)

ARNOLD TOYNBEE
No annihilation without representation.

Speaking of Freedom

AITZEMA
Liberty, and more such specious terms.

WOODY ALLEN
Freedom is a wonderful thing. But if you're dead it's a tremendous loss to your sex life.
(*Bananas*)

L. D. AMERY
A true policy of social reform must aim, not at fitting our citizens into mechanical schemes of State education or State employment, but at so planning its educational or employment policy that within its framework every incentive is given to initiative, to originality, to variety.

ANON
It's a cock-and-bull story, gentlemen!
It is well known to the whole world that the Soviet Union has not threatened anybody, and does not threaten anyone at present.
(*Pravda, October 27, 1976*)

JULIEN BENDA
It is to be noted that the dogma that history is obedient to scientific laws is preached especially by partisans of arbitrary authority. This is quite natural, since it eliminates the two realities they most hate, i.e. human liberty and the historical action of the individual.
(*Trahison des Clercs*)

A. C. BENSON
Land of Hope and Glory, Mother of the Free,
How shall we extol thee, who are born of thee?
Wider still and wider shall thy bounds be set;
God who made the mighty, make thee mightier yet.
(*Song from Pomp and Circumstance, set by Sir Edward Elgar*)

WILLIAN BLAKE
And by came an Angel who had a bright key.
And he open'd the coffins and set them all free.
(*Songs of Innocence: The Chimney Sweeper*)

HENRY BROOKE
Righteous monarchs,
Justly to judge, with their own eyes should see;
To rule o'er freemen, should themselves be free.
(*Earl of Essex*)

EDMUND BURKE
The only liberty I mean, is a liberty connected with order; that not only exists along with order and virtue, but which cannot exist at all without them.
(*Speech at Bristol, 1774*)

Govern two millions of men, impatient of servitude, on the principles of freedom.
(*Speech on Conciliation with America, 1775*)

ROBERT BURNS
Liberty's in every blow!
Let us do or die!
(*Scots, Wha Hae*)

R. A. BUTLER
Land of Hope and Glory,
Country of the Free,
Go on voting Tory
Till eternity
(*Parody written at Cambridge, quoted in Observer, May 31, 1964*)

LORD BYRON
Yet, Freedom! yet thy banner, torn, but flying
Streams like the thunder-storm *against* the wind.
(*Childe Harold*)

THOMAS CAMPBELL
Again to the battle, Achaians!
Our hearts bid the tyrants defiance;
Our land, the first garden of Liberty's tree —
It has been, and shall yet be, the land of the free!
(*Song of the Greeks*)

LEWIS CARROLL
"A cat may look at a king," said Alice.
(*Alice in Wonderland*)

ANGELA CARTER
"He set up a new slogan, 'If the name is right, you see the light'."
(*The Infernal Desire Machines of Doctor Hoffman*)

G. K. CHESTERTON
A reeling road, a rolling road, that rambles round the shire,
And after him the parson ran, the sexton and the squire;
A merry road, a mazy road, and such as we did tread
The night we went to Birmingham by way of Beachy Head.
(*The Rolling English Road*)

NEVILL COGHILL
The most untranslatable of all are words which were in common use in Chaucer's day and still are so but with a partially changed meaning. Two outstanding examples are the words "gentle" and "free". Each of these has a variety of shades of meaning in Chaucer . . . "Freedom" is one of the highest qualities of being a gentleman . . . It is one of the first things loved and followed by the Knight in the *Prologue*. The nearest equivalent I can think of is "generous thought". Basically it is the opposite of a crabbed meanness or villein-like behaviour. It means doing the fine thing, being open-hearted, having the impulse to give rather than to get. It is the ideal shown in the actions of Arveragus, Aurelius, and the magician at the end of the *Franklin's Tale*.
(*The Canterbury Tales translated into modern English*)

LORD COLERAINE
A spontaneous economic order is more efficient than an imposed order . . . A spontaneous order is inconceivable without personal freedom and, in particular, without freedom of choice.

CONFUCIUS
Only the truly kind man knows how to love and how to hate.

JULIAN CRITCHLEY
The issue that divides East from West is not capitalism versus socialism but liberty.
(*The Daily Telegraph, January 12, 1977*)

OLIVER CROMWELL
Man never mounts higher than when he knows not where he is going.
(*Memoires du Cardinal de Retz*)

E. E. CUMMINGS
... "then shall the voices of liberty be mute?"
He spoke. And drank rapidly a glass of water.
(*Collected Poems, 1938*)

DAILY MAIL
Perhaps the real reason why we have always been able to champion free speech in this country is that we know perfectly well that hardly anybody has got anything to say, and that no one will listen to anyone that has.
(*Editorial*)

DECLARATION OF INDEPENDENCE
We hold these truths to be self-evident, that all men are created equal, that they are endowed by their Creator with certain unalienable Rights, that among these are Life, Liberty and the pursuit of happiness.

CHARLES DICKENS
I only ask to be free. The butterflies are free.
Mankind will surely not deny to Harold Skimpole
what it concedes to the butterflies!
(*Bleak House*)

THE ECONOMIST
In the defence of liberty it is no crime to call a spade a spade, inefficiency, inefficiency, and murder, murder. It is necessary to realise that Lenin was not Marx and Stalin not Lenin, that the Russian revolution was neither inevitable nor justified by success, and that revolution is not often the nurse of virtue or freedom.
(*January 8, 1977*)

DWIGHT D. EISENHOWER
Neither London nor Abilene, sisters under the skin, will sell her birthright for physical safety, her liberty for mere existence.

PHILIP VAN DER ELST
Socialism contains a fundamentally unresolvable contradiction in that its egalitarianism is combined with an adherence to a State controlled society that can be managed with the remotest hope of efficiency only by a managerial élite which develops its own caste identity and privileges.
(*The Unsocial Socialist*)

EDWARD FITZGERALD
Better a live sparrow than a stuffed eagle.

MILTON FRIEDMAN
Freedom and order are very fragile things.
(*Daily Express, November 30, 1976*)

JOHN KENNETH GALBTRAITH
I am not particular about freedom.

BALTASAR GIRACIAN
Freedom is more precious than any gifts for which you may be tempted to give it up.

GREEK MYTH
Eros, the god of love, emerged to create the earth. Before, all was silent, bare and motionless. Now all was life, joy and motion.

T. H. GREEN
We content ourselves with enacting that no man shall be used by other men as a means against his will, but we leave it to be pretty much a matter of chance whether or no he shall be qualified to fulfil any social function, to contribute anything to the common good, and to do so freely.
(*Political Obligation*)

IVOR GURNEY
Courage and wisdom that made good
Each tiny freedom.
(*The Old City (Gloucester; Poems of)*)

JUDGE LEARNED HAND
The spirit of liberty is the spirit which is not too sure that it is right.

F. A. HAYEK
Today it is rarely understood that the limitation of all coercion to the enforcement of general rules of just conduct was the fundamental principles of classless liberalism, or I would almost say, its definition of liberty.
(*Economic and Representative Government*)

GEORG WILHELM FRIEDRICH HEGEL
Freedom begins with the recommendation of necessity.

VICTOR HUGO
Liberty has its roots in the hearts of the people, as the tree in the heart of the earth; like the tree it raises and spread its branches to heaven; like the tree it is ceaseless in its growth, and it covers generations with its shade.
(*At planting of Liberty Tree, Place des Vosges, Paris 1848*)

DAVID HUME
It is seldom that liberty of any kind is lost all at once.

THOMAS JEFFERSON
Error of opinion may be tolerated where reason is left free to combat it.
(*First inaugural address, 1801*)

The people are the only true censors of their governors: and even their errors will tend to keep these to the true principles of their institution. To punish these errors too severely would be to suppress the only safeguard of the public liberty.
(*Letter to Edward Carrington, 1787*)

SAMUEL JOHNSON
A decent provision for the poor is the true test of civilisation.

RUDYARD KIPLING
What stands if Freedom fall?
Who dies if England live?
(*For All We Have and Are*)

GOTTFRIED WILHELM LEIBNIZ
It is a very old doubt of mankind, how freedom and contingency can be reconciled with the series of causes and with providence.
(*Philosophical Writings, trans. Mary Morris and G. H. R. Parkinson*)

FATHER PETER LEVI
And the words for Freedom are prophecies.
(*Christmas Sermon from Death is a Pulpit*)

ABRAHAM LINCOLN
In giving to the slave, we assure freedom to the free.
(*Annual Message to Congress*)

ROB LYLE
We're martyrs for the glory that has been,
And we're impassioned where the World is randy,
Against their Dullness set a jewelled spleen,
Against their Uniformity — a Dandy.
(*The Splenetic Dandy, from Halcyon Poems 1943-53*)

ROGER L. MACBRIDE
America is the only country ever built on the truth of human freedom.
(*A New Dawn for America*)

WALTER DE LA MARE
When I go free,
I think 'twill be
A night of stars and snow.
(*The Little Salamander*)

ALFRED MARSHALL
Free human beings are not brought up to their work on the same principles as a machine, a horse, or a slave.
(*Principles of Economics*)

GEORGE MATHESON
Make me a captive, Lord, and then I shall be free.

METTERNICH
It is useless to close the gates against ideas; they overlap them.

JOHN STUART MILL
The habits and conduct which promote the advantage of each individual member of the community must be at least a part of those which contribute most in the end to the advancement of the community at a whole.
(*Representative Government*)

One of the benefits of freedom is that under it the ruler cannot pass by the people's minds, and amend their affairs for them without amending them.
(*Representative Government*)

In the present age of transition, everything must be subordinate to freedom of inquiry.

JOHN MILTON
The mountain nymph, sweet Liberty.
(*L'Allegro*)

Who ever know truth put to the worse, in a free and open encounter.
(*Areopagitica*)

We ourselves esteem not of that obedience, or love, or gift, which is of force: God therefore left him free, set before him a provoking object; herein consisted his merit, herein the sight of his reward, the promise of his abstention.
(*Areopagitica*)

LUDWIG von MISES
The fading of the critical sense is a serious menace to the preservation of our civilisation. It makes it easy for quacks to fool the people.

BARON de MONTESQUIEU
The inhabitants of islands have a higher relish for liberty than those of the continent . . . tyranny cannot so well dispose itself within a small compass; conquerors are stopped by the sea; and the islanders, being outside the reach of their arms, more easily preserve their own laws.
(*The Spirit of the Laws*)

FRANK O'CONNOR
Nor lords nor petty princes
Dispute the student's pleasure.
(*The Student*) (*from the Irish*)

GEORGE ORWELL
Freedom is the freedom to say that two plus two make four.
If that is granted, all else follows.
(*1984*)

BORIS PASTERNAK
And with their song of earth, entire
Freed territories add their mighty voice,
A booming octave in a choir.
(*Spring 1944; trans. Lydia Pasternak Slater; from: Fifty Poems*)

ENOCH POWELL
We offer freedom, and the risks, the dangers, the uncertainties, the untidiness, but also the responsibilities and the opportunities which are inseparable from it.

LORD ROBBINS
Liberty is a condition of any behaviour capable of being placed in a moral category. Unless it is present, human action is not susceptible to ethical judgment.
(*Liberty and Equality, 1977*)

BERTRAND RUSSELL
If freedom is to be secure, it is essential both that useful careers are open to energetic men, and the harmful careers should be closed to them.
(*Freedom and Government*)

ST PAUL
Free from the law of sin and death.
(*Romans: The Bible*)

GEORGE SANTAYANA
The truth is cruel, but it can be loved, and it makes free those who have loved it.
(*The Perpetual Pessimist*)

ROBERT L. SCHUETTINGER
Lord Acton, "the greatest historian of liberty", once wrote: "Liberalism is ultimately founded on the idea of conscience." Throughout his life, these were his two great concerns: freedom *and* morality. He was absolutely convinced one could not exist without the other and that both were required for the fulfilment of man's purpose on his earth.

PERCY BYSSHE SHELLEY
. . . the secret sound
Of hymns to truth and freedom.
(*The Revolt of Islam*)

ALEXANDER SOLZHENITSYN
The writer's tasks concern more general and eternal questions — the secrets of the human heart and conscience, the clash between life and death, and the overcoming of inner sorrow. They concern the laws of mankind in its uninterrupted course, conceived in the immemorial depths of time and ceasing only when the sun will be extinguished.

EDMUND SPENSER
What more felicity can fall to creature then to enjoy delight with liberty?

JAMES STEPHENS
The free winds are everywhere.
(*The Crock of Gold*)

SHIRLEY SUMMERSKILL
If the Government as a Government took action against organisations which they regarded as wrong-headed or even worse, we should be living in a rather different kind of society. The cost of such freedom is that some people will spend their money foolishly, be led astray by charlatans and even misunderstand the motives and feelings of their families and true friends.
(*House of Commons, February 23, 1977*)

TIBOR SZAMUELY
In Russia there is much official propaganda about the horrors of unemployment in Britain, the crowds of beggars in Leicester Square, and so on — but never once will you find an article in the Soviet press saying that there is no freedom in England. They will say this about America, they will say it about France — but never about England, because they know that this is the one thing that no one will believe.
(*Communism and Freedom*)

HENRY DAVID THOREAU
It takes two to speak the truth — one to speak, and another to hear.

ALEXIS de TOCQUEVILLE
Under a despotism communities give way at times to bursts of vehement joy; but they are generally gloomy and moody, because they are afraid. Under absolute monarchies tempered by the customs and manners of the country, their spirits are often cheerful and even, because as they have some freedom and a good deal of security, they are exempted from the most important cares of life; but all free peoples are serious, because their minds are habitually absorbed by the contemplation of some dangerous or difficult purpose. This is more especially the case among those free nations which form democratic communities.
(*Democracy in America, Part ii*)

HELEN WADDELL
They lie by the way in the shadow of death,
But they fell with their face to the morning.

It's wet, and the candle is blowing at the open window and there is a corncrake out in the dark, and I have felt human again for the first time. My mother died last Friday in her sleep. I found her, in the chair.
(*Letter*)

HENRY C. WALLICH
Freedom is like health, it is taken for granted while one has it. One becomes aware of it when it has gone.
(*Cost of Freedom*)

Every principle that wants to command strong allegiance must make a moral case. Men want to feel that what they are doing is useful, but they want also, and mainly, to feel that it is right. Freedom is one of these principles.

ALFRED NORTH WHITEHEAD
There is a freedom lying beyond circumstance, derived from the direct intuition that life can be grounded upon its absorption in what is changeless amid change.

CHARLES WILLIAMS
Since Alexandria there has hardly been such freedom of intellectual talk until today, and though our freedom is as great our intellect is no greater.
(*The Descent of the Dove*)

The Unfree

ALFRED ADLER
Neurosis and psychosis are modes of expression for human beings who have lost courage.

YURI ANDROPOV
Our Party stands firm on the stance of the People's struggle for freedom and social progress . . . The Soviet Union does not intend to interfere in the affairs of other countries . . . Every people decides its own destiny . . .
(*Head of KGB, April 22, 1976 — seven years after Soviet occupation of Czechoslovakia*)

ANON
Which country is the most neutral country in the world? The answer: It's Latvia, because here we don't even intervene in our own internal affairs.

What is the largest country in the world called? The answer is: Estonia. The boundaries run along the Baltic Sea, her capital city is Moscow and the population is in Siberia.

HANNAH ARENDT
It is far easier to act under conditions of tyranny than to think.

FRANCIS BACON
All colours will agree in the dark.
(*Essays: Of Unity in Religion*)

Why should man be in love with his fetters, though of gold?
(*An Essay on Death*)

PIERRE AUGUSTIN CARON de BEAUMARCHAIS
Slaves are as guilty as tyrants. It is hard to say if freedom can more justly reproach those who attack her than those who do not defend her.
(*Notes and Reflections*)

ERNEST BECKER
When therapies strip man down to his naked aloneness, to the real nature of experience and the problem of life, they slip into some kind of metaphysic of power and justification from beyond.
(*The Denial of Death*)

WILLIAM BLAKE
And the gates of this Chapel were shut,
And "Thou shalt not" writ over the door.
(*Songs of Experience: The Garden of Love*)

Prisons are built with stones of Law,
brothels with bricks of Religion.
(*The Marriage of Heaven and Hell,* "*Proverbs of Hell*")

In every voice, in every ban,
The mind-forg'd manacle I hear.

WILFRID SCAWEN BLUNT
On what poor stuff my manhood's dreams were fed
Till I too learned what dole of vanity
Will serve a human soul for daily bread.
(*Esther (ii)*)

JACOB BOEHME
No people understands any more the sensual language, and the birds in the air and the beasts in the forest do understand it according to their species. Therefore man may reflect what he has been robbed of, and what he is to recover in the second birth. For in the sensual language all spirits speak with each other, they need not other language, for it is the language of nature.
(*Yysterium Magnum*)

BOETHIUS
These were his poetry: he loved to rhyme
Earth's secret source and spring
But the light of his mind has dimmed,
He lies there, heavy chains about his neck.
(*Trans. Helen Waddell; More Latin Lyrics from Virgil to Milton*)

ERNEST BRAMAH (E. B. SMITH)
It is scarcely to be expected that one who has spent his life beneath an official umbrella should have at his command the finer analogies of light and shade.
(*Kai Lung's Golden Hours: The Inexorable Justice of Shan Tien*)

SAMUEL BRITTAN
Racial discrimination is a less important factor in Britain than the USA, but there is plenty of discrimination against the old, by compulsory retiring ages, and against the young, by forcing children to stay on at school for longer and longer periods.
(*Capitalism and the Permissive Society*)

ROBERT BROWNING
Love, we are in God's hand.
How strange now looks the life he makes us lead.
So free we seem, so fettered fast we are!
(*Andrea del Sarto, 49*)

ARTHUR BRYANT
Slavery is the ultimate and greatest evil. For it is based on a denial of the dignity of the human soul.
(*The Ultimate Evil; Illustrated London News, March 27, 1948*)

MARTIN BUBER
Modern collectivism is the last barrier raised by man against a meeting with himself.
(*Between Man and Man*)

EDMUND BURKE
Would twenty shillings have ruined Mr Hampden's fortune?
No! but the payment of half twenty shillings on the principle
it was demanded, would have made him a slave.
(*Speech on American Taxation, 1774*)

Slavery they can have anywhere. It is a weed that grows in every soil.
(*Speech on conciliation with America, 1775*)

LORD BYRON
And when we think we lead, we are most led.
(*The Two Foscari*)

There is no freedom, even for masters, in the midst of slaves.
(*Journals*)

ROY CAMPBELL
The curbed ferocity of beaten tribes,
The sullen dignity of their defeat.
(*The Zulu Girl*)

ALBERT CAMUS
To the extent to which he imagined a purpose to his life, he adapted himself to the demands of a purpose to be achieved, and became the slave of his liberty.
(*The Myth of Sisyphus*)

CHARTER 77
Tens of thousands of citizens have been prevented from working in the fields of their profession for the one reason alone that their views differ from the official ones.

G. K. CHESTERTON
Carlyle was the first who called in political inequality to remedy economic inequality, but he will not be the last.
(*Introduction to Carlyle's Past and Present*)

SIR WINSTON S. CHURCHILL
The vice of capitalism is its unequal sharing of blessings; the virtue of socialism is its equal sharing of misery.

CHARLES DICKENS
O let us love our occupations,
Bless the squire and his relations,
Live upon our daily rations,
And always know our proper stations.
(*The Chimes*)

BENJAMIN DISRAELI
Colonies do not cease to be colonies because they are independent.
(*House of Commons, 1838*)

MILOVAN DJILÁS
It is profoundly sickening to be compelled to remain silent when there is need for expression.
(*The New Class*)

Suicide, despair, alcoholism and debauchery, the loss of internal powers and integrity because the artist is forced to lie to himself and others — these are the most frequent phenomena in the Communist system among those who actually wish to, and could create.
(*The New Class*)

A work of art by its very nature, is usually a criticism of a given situation and of given relations. In Communist systems, therefore, artistic creation based on actual subjects is not possible.
(*The New Class*)

Communist systems stimulate technical progress but also hinder every research activity where undisturbed functioning of the mind is necessary.
(*The New Class*)

A citizen in the Communist system lives oppressed by the constant pangs of his conscience and the fear that he has transgressed. He is always fearful that he will have to demonstrate that he is not an enemy of socialism, just as in the Middle Ages a man had to constantly show his devotion to the Church.
(*The New Class*)

JOHN DONNE
That soule, which being borne free, is made a slave to this body, by comming to it.
(*Sermon XIX, March 28, 1624*)

Take me to you, imprison me, for I
Except you enthrall me, never shall be free,
Nor ever chaste, except your ravish me.
(*Holy Sonnets. Annunciation*)

FYODOR DOSTOYEVSKY
No one has a right to set me at liberty.
(*Shatov in The Devils*)

Every member of the society spies on the others, and it's his duty to inform against them. Every one belongs to all and all to every one. All are slaves and equal in their slavery. In extreme cases he advocates slander and murder but the great thing about it is equality. Slaves are bound to be equal. There has never been freedom or equality without despotism.
(*Stavrogin in The Devils*)

The world has proclaimed freedom, especially in recent times but what do we see in this freedom of theirs? Nothing but slavery and self destruction! For the world says ''You have needs and therefore satisfy them for you have the same rights as the rich and noble''.
(*Father Zossimov in The Brothers Karamazov*)

You hungered for freely given love and not for the servile raptures of the slave before the might that has terrified him for once and all. But here too your judgment was too high, for they are slaves though rebels by nature.
(*Ivan Karamazov's Grand Inquisitor in The Brothers Karamazov*)

Did you forget that a tranquil mind and even death is dearer to man than the free choice in the knowledge of good and evil?
(*Ivan Karamazov's Grand Inquisitor in The Brothers Karamazov*)

They will marvel at us and they will regard us as gods because, having become their masters, we consented to endure freedom and rule them — so dreadful will freedom become to them in the end.
(*Ivan Karamazov's Grand Inquisitor in The Brothers Karamozov*)

No science will give them bread so long as they (human race) remain free. But in the end they will lay their freedom at our feet and say to us ''We don't mind being slaves so long as you feed us.''
(*Ivan Karamazov's Grand Inquisitor in The Brothers Karamazov*)

JOHN S. DUNNE
The spirit of universal doubt or universal scepticism of universal despair pervaded the world in which Descartes and Pascal, Hegel and Kierkegaard lived and thought. This spirit has become in the twentieth century a sense of culture relativity and a sense of the relativity of all standpoints.
(*A Search for God in Time and Memory*)

EMILE DURKHEIM
Work is still for most men a punishment and a scourge.
(*Division of Labour*)

T. S. ELIOT
Where is the Life we have lost in living?
Where is the wisdom we have lost in knowledge?
Where is the knowledge we lost in information?
(*The Rock*)

EBENEZER ELLIOTT
Thou should'st have lived if they remain
Who fetter'd us and hated thee;
Oh Huskisson our friend in vain,
Where now are hope and liberty?
(*Anti-Corn Law writer and poet, on the death of William Huskisson,
former President of the Board of Trade and tariff reformer, 1830*)

E. M. FORSTER
Spoon feeding in the long run teaches us nothing but the shape of the
spoon.
(*Sayings of the Week, Observer, October 6, 1951*)

SIGMUND FREUD
The theory of repression is the pillar upon which the edifice of
psycho-analysis rests.
(*Basic Writings*)

ERICH FRIED
What did you do?
I let them
shout . . .
What did they shout?
They shouted
for help.
(*From Contemporary German Poetry; Obituary for those who shouted,
trans. Ewald Osers*)

ERICH FROMM
Living is a process of continuous birth. The tragedy in the life of most
of us is that we die before we are fully born.
(*Values, Psychology, and Human Existence, in New Knowledge in
Human Values*)

JOHN KENNETH GALBRAITH
It has always been imagined, especially by conservatives, that to
associate all, or a large part, of economic activity with the state is to
endanger freedom . . . But conservatives have looked in the wrong
direction for the danger. They have feared that the State might reach
out and destroy the vigorous, money-making entrepreneur. They have
not noticed that, all the while, the successors to the entrepreneur were
uniting themselves ever more closely with the State and rejoicing in the
result.

Business orators have spoken much about freedom in the past. But it can be lain down as a rule that those who speak most of liberty are least inclined to use it. The high executive who speaks fulsomely of personal freedom carefully submits his speeches on the subject for review and elimination of controversial words, phrases and ideas, as befits a good organisation man . . .

The danger to liberty lies in the subordination of belief to the needs of the industrial system. In this the state and the industrial system will be partners.
(*The New Industrial State*)

The bland leading the bland.

DAVID GASCOYNE
Now Man benighted huddles in his cave,
In mighty ignorance of what he is and what he's not.
(*Night Thoughts*)

OLIVER ST JOHN GOGARTY
But for your Terror
Where would be Valour?
(*To Death*)

YVAN GOLL
Dark names of towns where fear
Prowls in the market place
Speak to the ages
Of our hearts' disgrace.
(*Jean Sans Terre Is Landsick; trans. Clark Mills*)

JULIAN GREEN
I ask him (Gide) if he feels free, since his conversion to Communism . . .
He answers no and quotes what Barres said when asked what irked him most in his parliamentary career: ''To vote with my party!''
(*Diary 1928-1957*)

JO GRIMOND
We shall experience the final defeat of liberalism not when immigration but when emigration is forbidden.
(*The Bureaucratic Blight*)

F. A. HAYEK
There is no reason why the coalitions of organised interests on which the governing majorities rest should not discriminate against any widely disliked group . . . Once such discrimination is regarded as legitimate, all the safeguards of individual freedom and the liberal tradition are gone.
(*Economic Freedom and Representative Government*)

It is no accident that in the totalitarian countries, be it Russia or Germany or Italy, the question of how to organise the people's leisure should have become a problem of planning. The Germans have even invented for this problem the horrible and self-contradictory name of *Freizeitgestaltung* (literally: the shaping of the use made of the people's free time) as if it were still "free time" when it has to be spent in the way ordained by authority.
(*The Road to Serfdom*)

Wherever liberty as we understand it has been destroyed, this has almost always been done in the name of some new freedom promised to the people.
(*The Road to Serfdom*)

To make a totalitarian system function efficiently it is not enough that everybody should be forced to work for the same ends. It is essential that the people should come to regard them as their own ends.
(*The Road to Serfdom*)

OLIVER WENDELL HOLMES Jnr
The mind of a bigot is like the pupil of the eye; the more light you pour upon it, the more it will contract.

MIROSLAV HOLUB
You buy him
by weight, boneless,
a pound of wax flesh,
a pound of mousy philosophy,
a pound of jellied
flunkey.

DAVID HUME
It is evident, that if men were to regulate their conduct . . . by the view of a particular interest, either public or private, they would involve themselves in endless confusion, and would render all government, in a great measure ineffectual.
(*Treatise, Works*)

ALDOUS HUXLEY
Ninety-six identical twins working ninety-six identical machines! You really know where you are.

That is the secret of happiness and virtue, liking what you've *got* to do. All conditioning aims at that — making people like their unescapable social destiny.

MICHAEL IVENS
. . . there are pressures for conformity in organisations that must be resisted. The manager in particular can be exposed to pressures which make him neglect his family and those sides of his personality which cannot be satisfied by work alone.
(*Pressures for Conformity, article in Patterns of Prejudice, Jan/Feb 1977*)

But wryness is human. It is a small flower
That has to support the clinging weeds of hope.
It nods and allows wild thought of a clear, blue sky
And singing birds that fly for ever without hindrance.
(*To a Czech poet*)

THOMAS JEFFERSON
Timid men prefer despotism to the boisterous sea of liberty.

JOHN OF SALISBURY
That a man free-born shall spurn his liberty.
(*Letters*)

PAUL JOHNSON
Any political system which persecutes its middle class systematically is unlikely to remain either free or prosperous for long.
(*Enemies of Society*)

All mountebank dictators, from Napoleon III to Mussolini and Hitler, liked to be able to claim, with some plausibility, that they had been put in power by a ''free vote'', and that the people have, as it were, walked willingly into the dungeon before the portcullis slammed down for the last time.
(*New Statesman, February 11, 1977*)

C. G. JUNG

Freud never asked himself why he was compelled to talk continually of sex, why this idea has taken such possession of him . . . He remained the victim of the one aspect he could recognise, and for that reason I see him as a tragic figure; for he was a great man, and, what is more, a man in the grip of his daimon.
(*Memories*)

Anyone who had once learned to submit absolutely to a collective belief and to renounce his eternal right to freedom and the equally eternal duty of individual responsibility will persist in this attitude, and will be able to set out with the same credulity and the same lack of criticism in the reverse direction, if another and manifestly "better" belief is foisted upon his alleged idealism.
(*The Undiscovered Self*)

A million zeros joined together do not, unfortunately, add up to one.
(*The Undiscovered Self*)

FRANZ KAFKA

It's often safer to be in chains than to be free.
(*The Trial*)

SÖREN KIERKEGAARD

If one will compare the tendency to run wild in possibility with the efforts of a child to enunciate words, the lack of possibility is like being dumb . . . for without possibility a man cannot, as it were, draw breath.
(*Sickness*)

Philistinism tranquilises itself to the trivial.
(*Sickness*)

RUDYARD KIPLING

The Much Administered Man.
(*The Masque of Plenty*)

Man may hold all sorts of posts
If he'll only hold his tongue.
(*Pink Dominoes*)

IRVING KRISTOL
Dependency tends to corrupt and absolute dependency corrupts absolutely.

THOMAS KYD
Thus must we toil in other men's extremes,
That know not how to remedy our own.
(*The Spanish Tragedy*)

GOTTFRIED WILHELM LEIBNIZ
This is a vision favoured by some of our moderns, who seek the notion of freedom in indifference.
(*Philosophical Writings; trans. Mary Morris & G. H. R. Parkinson*)

ANTHONY LEJEUNE
If the majority wants to oppress them, the coming of democracy will mean, for the minority, not the beginning of freedom, but the permanent loss of it.
(*Freedom and the Politicians*)

FATHER PETER LEVI
The world's new age is slave society.
(*Death is a Pulpit*)

And all our working clothes are prison clothes.
(*Death is a Pulpit*)

Darkness is not a liberating thing.
(*Death is a Pulpit*)

Good God, I do not know how to be free.
(*Death is a Pulpit*)

WALTER LIPPMAN
The generation to which we belong is now learning from experience what happens when men retreat from freedom to a coercive organisation of their affairs. Though they promise themselves a more abundant life, they must in practice renounce it; as the organised direction increases, the variety of ends must give way to uniformity.
(*Atlantic Monthly, November, 1936*)

HENRY CABOT LODGE, Jr
It has been well said that a hungry man is more interested in four sandwiches than four freedoms.

ROSS MACDONALD
If you withdrew your spirit deep into yourself and out of sight, it couldn't be completely destroyed. But it might go blind in the internal darkness.
(*Sleeping Beauty*)

MARBOD OF RENNES
   . . . a perverse will
To death has finished many a feverish patient.
(*Meditation among Trees; trans. Helen Waddell; More Latin Lyrics, from Virgil to Milton*)

To be sunk so deep in the wreckage
That to pull out one's foot is cruel labour;
Or remain sunk for ever: this is the worse fate of all.
(*Meditation among Trees; trans. Helen Waddell; More Latin Lyrics, from Virgil to Milton*)

MASAS MARUYAMA
It is unreasonable to expect any genuine social science to thrive where there is no undergirding of civil liberty.
(*Thought and Behaviour in Modern Japanese Politics*)

KARL MARX
The Kingdom of freedom actually begins only when drudgery, enforced by hardship and by external purposes, ends; it thus lies, quite naturally, beyond the sphere of proper material production.
(*Das Kapital*)

ROLLO MAY
Playboy has indeed caught on to something significant in American society: Cox believes it to be "the repressed fear of involvement with women." I go further and hold that it, as an example of the new puritanism, gets its dynamic from a repressed anxiety in American men that underlies even the fear of involvement. This is the repressed anxiety about impotence.
(*Love and Will*)

One thing that is clear since Freud is that the ''first freedom'', the naive freedom of the Garden of Eden before the ''fall'' into consciousness or the infant before the struggle to achieve and enlarge consciousness, is a false freedom.
(*Love and Will*)

JOHN STUART MILL
There have been, and may again be, great individual thinkers in an atmosphere of mental slavery. But there never has been, nor ever will be, in that atmosphere an intellectually active people.
(*On Liberty*)

The despotism of custom is everywhere the standing hindrance to human advancement, being in unceasing antagonism to that disposition to aim at something better than customary.
(*On Liberty*)

Mankind speedily becomes unable to conceive diversity, when they for some time have been unaccustomed to see it.
(*On Liberty*)

JOHN MILTON
While we still affect by all means a rigid, external formality, we may as soon fall into a gross conforming stupidity, a stark and dead congealment of wood and hay and stubble, forced and frozen together.
(*Areopagitica*)

Revolutions of ages do not oft recover the loss of a rejected truth, for the want of which whole nations fare the worse.
(*Areopagitica*)

EMMANUEL MOURNIER
Organisation is progress towards order but not to the point at which man is reduced to a function. Collectivisation is a spiritual conquest, but not to the point at which initiative disappears in mechanism and the strong mind into the conformist mind.
(*Be Not Afraid: The Two Alienations*)

The greatest danger inherent in popular collectivism is the tendency to guide mass exaltation in the same direction as totalitarian passion . . . instead of laying hold of it in order to create an enthusiastic and diversified people.
(*Be Not Afraid: To the Heart of Materialism*)

MALCOLM MUGGERIDGE
Never forget that only dead fish swim with the stream.
(*Quoting remark made to him*)

BENITO MUSSOLINI
We were the first to assert that the more complicated the forms of civilisation, the more restricted the freedom of the individual must become.

FRIEDRICH NIETZSCHE
A thousand goals have existed thereto, for a thousand people existed. But the fetter for the thousand necks is still lacking, the one goal is still lacking. Humanity has no goal yet.
(*Thus Spake Zarathustra*)

This man set forth like a hero in quest of truth and at last he captured a little dressed-up lie. He calls it his marriage.
(*Thus Spake Zarathustra*)

This is (our) true predicament: together with the fear of man we have lost the love of man, the affirmation of man, *the will to man*.

LECOMTE du NOÜY
The negation of free will, the negation of moral responsibility; the individual considered merely as a physico-chemical unit, as a particle of living matter, hardly different from other animals, inevitably brings about the death of moral man, the suppression of all spirituality of all hope.
(*Human Destiny*)

JOSÉ ORTEGA Y GASSET
Many men . . . homesick for the herd . . . devote themselves passionately to whatever is left in them of the sheep. They want to march through life together, along the collective path, shoulder to shoulder, wool rubbing wool, and the head down.

GEORGE ORWELL
In every one of those little stucco boxes there's some poor bastard who's *never* free except when he's fast asleep and dreaming that he's got the boss down the bottom of a well and is bunging lumps of coal at him.
(*1984*)

In the end we shall make thoughtcrime literally impossible, because
there will be no words in which to express it.
(*1984*)

EWALD OSERS

. . . the criss-crossed tank traps obstructing escape from happiness or
the wilted flowers not commemorating
the ones who tried?
(*Berlin Wall*)

. . . A triumph of man's free spirit
and also, in a sense, of his ability
to close his eyes to all those unfree tears . . .
(*The Temples at Agrigento*)

N. A. PALKHIVALA

Liberty can die as surely, though not as swiftly, in a democracy as in a
totalitarian state. Only the husk of democracy — the one man one vote
rite — may survive after freedom has perished.
(*Our Constitution Defaced and Defiled*)

BORIS PASTERNAK

Does not the Five-Year Plan assess and score us,
And do I with it, too, not rise and fall?
(*To a Friend: trans. Lydia Pasternak Slater; from Fifty Poems*)

The sycophant toadies are used
To rule who should live and be lauded
And who should be dead and abused.
(*The Wind; trans. Lydia Pasternak Slater; from Fifty Poems*)

The world has too many people for us,
the sycophant, the spineless —
politely, like snakes in the grass, they sting.
(*Hamlet in Russia, a Soliloquy, rendered by Robert Lowell, "Imitations" by Robert Lowell*)

M. D. PETRE

The path of freedom is blocked much more by those who wish to obey
than by those who desire to command.

WILLIAM PITT, the Younger
Necessity is the plea for every infringement of human freedom. It is the argument of tyrants; it is the creed of slaves.
(*Speech, House of Commons, 1783*)

THE BIBLE: PROVERBS
The borrower is servant to the lender.

OTTO RANK
Every human being is . . . equally unfree, that is, we . . . *create* out of freedom, a prison . . .

LIONEL READ
If one cannot grow all the wheat he pleases on his own land, what matters if the taboo be called ''communism'' as in Russia or the ''farm program'' as in the USA?
(*To Free or Freeze*)

WILHELM REICH
You stand on your head and you believe yourself dancing into the realm of freedom. You will wake up from your nightmare, Little Man, finding yourself helplessly lying on the ground.
(*Listen, Little Man!*)

Slowly and gropingly, I found what makes you a slave:
You are your own slave-driver.
(*Listen, Little Man!*)

Instead, you asked yourself what your neighbour was going to say about it, or whether your honesty might cost you money.
(*Listen, Little Man!*)

You must come to realise that you made your little men your own oppressors.
(*Listen, Little Man!*)

PHILIP RIEFF
Repression is not falsification of the world, it is ''truth'' — the only truth that man can know, because he cannot experience anything.
(*Paraphrased by Ernest Becker in The Denial of Death*)

The heaviest crosses are internal and men make them so that, thus skeletally supported, they can bear the burden of their flesh. Under the sign of this inner cross, a certain inner distance is achieved from the infantile desire to be and have everything.
(*The Impossible Culture: Oscar Wilde and the Charisma of the Artist, Encounter, September, 1970*)

JEAN-JACQUES ROUSSEAU
Man is born free, and everywhere he is in chains.
(*Du contrat social*)

ST PAUL
You were bought with a price, do not become the slaves of men.
(*Corinthians; The Bible*)

Wherever you give a slave's consent, you prove yourselves the slave of that master.
(*Romans; The Bible*)

ST PETER
(the unrighteous) . . . they promise them innocent men freedom, but they themselves are slaves of corruption.
(*The Bible*)

WILLIAM SHAKESPEARE
Evermore in subjection.
(*All's Well That Ends Well*)

Juliet: To prison, eyes, n'er look on liberty.
(*Romeo and Juliet*)

Bondage is hoarse, and may not speak aloud.
(*Romeo and Juliet*)

LORD SHAWCROSS
I fear that we are leaving the age of freedom like the age of elegance behind us.
(*Speech to Wider Share Ownership Council, May 18, 1977*)

PERCY BYSSHE SHELLEY
. . . that inheritance of freedom
Which thou hast sold for thy despoiler's smile.
(*Charles the First*)

For they all pined in bondage.
(*The Revolt of Islam*)

The multitude of moving heartless things,
Whom slaves call men.
(*The Revolt of Islam*)

Until the subject of a tyrant's will
Became, worse fate, the abject of his own.
(*Prometheus Unbound*)

O Slavery; thou frost of the world's prime,
Killing its flowers and leaving its thorns bare!
(*Hellas*)

What are thou Freedom? O! could slaves
Answer from their living graves . . .
(*The Mask of Anarchy*)

ADAM SMITH
Slaves (have no motives to labour except the dread of punishment and) can never invent any machine for facilitating their business. Free men, who have a start of their own, can get anything accomplished which they think may be expedient for carrying on labour.

ALEXANDER SOLZHENITSYN
Ah, that first night of half freedom! . . . they weren't (yet) allowed into the village. But they were permitted to sleep on their own in a hay shelter in the yard of the security police building. They shared the shelter with horses who spent the night motionless, quietly munching hay. Impossible to imagine a sweeter sound!

JAMES STEPHENS
The dark people of the Fomor have ye in thrall; and upon your minds they have fastened a band of lead, your hearts are hung with iron, and about your loins a cincture of brass impressed, woeful!
(*The Crock of Gold*)

I saw a man and woman bound,
Middle to middle and knee to knee,
With a rusty iron chain.
(*Mount Derision from The Hill of Vision*)

KIM IL SUNG
For the people to become communist they should be brought up properly from childhood.
(*Supreme People's Assembly, April 29, 1976*)

TACITUS
They plunged into slavery.
(*Annals of Imperial Rome*)

ALEXIS de TOCQUEVILLE
Democracy extends the sphere of individual freedom, socialism restricts it.
(*Complete Works, Vol. IX*)

The only nations that deny the utility of provincial liberties are those which have fewest of them; in other words, those only censure the institution who do not know it.
(*Democracy in America*)

Centralization . . . provides skilfully for the details of the social police; represses small disorders and petty misdemeanours, maintains society in a status quo alike secure from improvement and decline and perpetuates a drowsy regularity in the conduct of affair which the heads of administration are wont to call good order and public tranquility.
(*Democracy in America*)

PIERRE VERGNIAUD
The Revolution, like Saturn, might devour in turn each one of its children.

VIRGIL
But God in wrath has taken it all from us,
And given it to the Greeks.
Troy's burnt.
And now they lord it in the gutted town.
(*The Aenid, trans. by Helen Waddell*)

HELEN WADDELL
I'll make the whole world one turnip-face,
Blind out the eyes,
Gash in a mouth,
To shout *Sieg Heil*!
(*Hitler Speaks*)

SIMONE WEIL
Nothing is worse than a mixture of monotony and the unpredictable. In the factory new work is sprung upon you in the form of an order which must be obeyed immediately. If only the boss would say a week in advance: "You're going to be put on crank-arms for two days, and then drilling", you would still have to obey, but at least it would be possible to hold the immediate future in your imagination, to possess it. But it's not like that. At any moment from clocking in to clocking out, a new order may come.
(*La condition ouvrière, from "Gateway to God"*)

CHARLES WILLIAMS
. . . those innocent sheep who by mere volume of imbecility have trampled over many delicate and attractive flowers in Christendom.
(*The Descent of the Dove*)

WILLIAM WORDSWORTH
Now and then
Forced labour; and, more frequently, forced hopes.
(*The Prelude — Residence at Cambridge*)

WILLIAM BUTLER YEATS
The unfinished man and his pain, brought face to face with his own nothingness.
(*A dialogue of Self and Soul; The Collected Poems*)

The finished man among his enemies?
How in the name of heaven can he escape
The defiling and disfiguring shape
The Mirror of malicious eyes
Casts upon his eyes until at last
He thinks that shape must be his shape?
(*A Dialogue of Self and Soul*)

Women's Freedom

APOCRYPHA
Neither (give) a wicked woman liberty to gad abroad.
(*Ecclesiasticus*)

SARAH M. GRIMKE
God created us equal; he created us free agents; he is our lawgiver, our king and our judge and to him alone is woman to be bound in subjection.
(*Letter to Mary Parker*)

H. L. MENCKEN
Women have broken many of their old chains, but they are still enmeshed in a formidable network of man-made taboos and sentimentalities.
(*In Defence of Women*)

Once women have the political power to obtain their just rights, they will begin to lose their old power to obtain special privileges by sentimental appeals.
(*In Defence of Women*)

. . . the grant of the ballot to women will mark the beginning of an improvement in our politics, and, in the end, in our whole theory of government.
(*In Defence of Women*)

In women of genius we see the opposite picture. They are commonly distinctly mannish, and shave as well as shine. Think of George Sand, Catherine the Great, Elizabeth, Rosa, Bonheur, Teresa Carreno or George Eliot.
(*In Defence of Women*)

The opposition to the extension of the suffrage, when it is not frankly sentimental and hence without any standing in logic whatsoever, is commonly based upon a mistaken fear of the woman voter. That fear arises out of confusing her with the suffragette. The two, in fact, are quite distinct, and even antagonistic.
(*In Defence of Women*)

That it should still be necessary, at this late date in the history of the human race, to argue that women are gifted with an acute and valuable form of intelligence is surely an eloquent proof of the defective observation, incurable superstitiousness and general dunderheadedness of man.
(*In Defence of Women*)

Find me an obviously intelligent man, a man free from sentimentality and illusion, a man hard to deceive, a man of the first class, and I'll show you a man with a wide streak of woman in him.
(*In Defence of Women*)

ALICE MEYNELL
The Lady Poverty was fair:
But she has lost her looks of late . . .
. . . Oh, is this she
Whom Francis met, whose step was free,
Who with Obedience carolled hymns,
In Umbria walked with Chastity?
(*The Lady Poverty*)

JOHN MILTON
Therefore God's universal law
Gave to the man despotic power
Over his female in due awe.
(*Samson Agonistes*)

MURRAY N. ROTHBARD
It was precisely capitalism and the "capitalist revolution" of the eighteenth and nineteenth centuries that freed women from male oppression and set each woman free to find her best level.

ST. PAUL
. . . so, brethren, we are not children of the slave but of the free woman.
(*Galatians; The Bible*)

For it is written (Genesis) that Abraham had two sons, one by a slave and one by a free woman . . . One is from Mount Sinai, bearing children for slavery, she is Hagar . . . but the Jerusalem above is free, and she is our mother.
(*Galatians; The Bible*)

MARGARET SANGER
There are no eight hour laws to protect the mother against overwork and toil in the home.
(*Women and the New Race*)

PERCY BYSSHE SHELLEY
But chiefly women, whom my voice did waken
From their cold, careless, willing slavery.
(*The Revolt of Islam*)

Woman! — she is his slave.
(*The Revolt of Islam*)

JAMES STEPHENS
. . . the Grey Woman and the Thin Woman, however, were not in the least softened by maternity — they said that they had not bargained for it, that the children were gotten under false pretences, that they were respectable married women, and that, as a protest against their wrongs, they would not cook any more food for the Philosophers.
(*The Crock of Gold*)

This is the price she has to pay,
For bread she gets no other way.
(*Light-O'-Love from The Hill of Vision*)

KIM IL SUNG
Rearing children collectively at state and social expense is also of importance for freeing women from the heavy housekeeping burdens and revolutionizing and working-classizing them.
(*People's Assembly of North Korea, April 29, 1976*)

THE TALMUD
God did not create woman from man's head, that he should command her, nor from his feet, that she should be his slave, but rather from his side, that she should be near his heart.

VIRGINIA WOOLF
Women have served all these centuries as looking glasses possessing the magic and delicious power of reflecting the figure of man at twice its natural size.
(*A Room of One's Own*)

The Utopians

ANON
Preserve us, good Heaven, from entrusting those
That ha' Much to get, and little to lose.
(*A Free Parliament Litany*)

CHARLES BAUDELAIRE
The watchmen think each isle that heaves in views
An Eldorado, shouting their belief;
Imagination riots in the crew
Who in the morning only find a reef.
(*The Flowers of Evil; trans. Roy Campbell*)

Those Utopians who by decree wish to make all Frenchmen rich and
virtuous at a single stroke.
(*Preface to The Flowers of Evil; trans. Jackson Mathews*)

ERNEST BECKER
Science betrays us when it is willing to absorb lived truth all into itself.
Here the criticism of all behaviorist psychology, all manipulations of
men, and all coercive utopianism comes to rest.
(*The Denial of Death*)

W. H. CHAMBERLIN
Socialism is certain to prove, in the beginning at least, the road NOT
to freedom, but to dictatorship and counter-dictatorships, to civil war
of the fiercest kind. Socialism achieved and maintained by democratic
means seems definitely to belong to the world of utopias.
(*A False Utopia*)

ERIC HEFFER
Socialism does not exist anywhere in the world.
(*The Times, 1976*)

EDUARD HEIMANN
Liberalism then has the distinction of being the doctrine most hated by Hitler.
(*The Rediscovery of Liberalism, Social Research (New York), vol. VIII, No. 4, November, 1941*)

HERMANN HESSE
Your speech shows a profound feeling of concern and responsibility for your people, its army and its honour. But it shows no feeling for mankind.
(*To a Cabinet Minister, August, 1917; If the War Goes On*)

PAUL JOHNSON
It is always a temptation to the *exalté* to hurry along whatever apocalypse he believes in. That is one of the many reasons why communist and fascist revolutionaries have so much in common; and why their differences, are, by comparison, of little importance.
(*New Statesman, February 11, 1977*)

SIR KEITH JOSEPH
Do not compare our shop-soiled reality . . . with some blueprint of a Utopia that doesn't exist. Compare like with like . . . compare our imperfect reality with the reality of a different system.
(*Stranded on the Middle Ground?*)

JOHN KEATS
Fanatics have their dreams, wherewith they weave
A paradise for a sect.
(*The Fall of Hyperion*)

JOHN STUART MILL
I am not countenancing the sort of "hero-worship" which applauds the strong man of genius for forcibly seizing on the government of the world and making it do his bidding in spite of itself. All he can claim is, freedom to point the way.
(*On Liberty*)

MALCOLM MUGGERIDGE
Utopianism, I am glad to see, is decidedly on the wane . . . Even the protesting young feel constrained to fix their hopes on Mao Tse-tung because he is a long way away and little is known about him, rather than to more vulnerable saviours nearer at hand.
(*Jesus Rediscovered*)

ROBERT NOZICK
The idea that there is . . . one best society for *everyone* to live in seems to me to be an incredible one . . . No one should attempt to describe a Utopia unless he's recently re-read, for example, the works of Shakespeare, Tolstoy, Jane Austen, Rabelais and Dostoyevsky to remind himself of how different people are.
(*Anarchy, State and Utopia*)

WILLIAM BUTLER YEATS
I know not what the younger dreams —
Some vague Utopia — and she seems,
When withered old and skeleton-gaunt,
An image of such politics.
(*In Memory of Eva Gore-Booth and Con Markiewicz*)

Acknowledgments

Ernest Barker, Principles of Social and Political Theory; *Oxford University Press*.
George Barker, The Leaping Laughers from Collected Poems; *Faber & Faber Ltd*.
Karl Barth, The Faith of the Church; *The New American Library*.
Karl Barth, The Humanity of God; *Collins Publishers*.
Ernest Becker, The Denial of Death; *Macmillan Publishing Co. Inc.*
Isaiah Berlin, Two Concepts of Liberty; *Oxford University Press*.
Jacob Boehme, Mysterium Magnum; *Watkins Publishing House*.
Ernest Bramah, Kai Lung's Golden Hours; *Garnstone Press*.
Willy Brandt, The Ordeal of Coexistence; *Harvard University Press*.
Samuel Brittan, Capitalism and the Permissive Society; *Macmillan London and Basingstoke*.
Norman O. Brown, Life Against Death; *Routledge & Kegan Paul Ltd*.
Martin Buber, Pointing the Way; *Routledge & Kegan Paul Ltd*.
    The Way of Man According to the Teaching of Hasidism; *Watkins Publishing House*.
    Israel and the World: Essays in a Time of Crisis; *Schocken Books Inc*.
    The Tales of Rabbi Nachman; *Souvenir Press Ltd*.
Rudolf Bultmann, Faith and Understanding; *SCM Press Ltd*.
    Theology of the New Testament; *SCM Press Ltd*.
Albert Camus, The Rebel; *Hamish Hamilton Ltd*.
    The Myth of Sisyphus; *Hamish Hamilton Ltd*.
Angela Carter, The Infernal Desire Machines of Doctor Hoffman; *Robert Hart-Davis Ltd./Granada Publishing Ltd*.
Austin Clarke, Straying Student from Collected Poems; *George Allen & Unwin (Publishers) ltd*.
Richard Crossman, Inside View; *Jonathan Cape Ltd*.
Brian Crozier, Power in a Free Society; *David Higham Associates Ltd*.
    Security and the Myth of Peace; *David Higham Associates Ltd*.
    A Theory of Conflict; *David Higham Associates Ltd*.
W. H. Davies, The Complete Poems; *Jonathan Cape Ltd*.
John S. Dunne, A Search for God in Time and Memory; *Sheldon Press*.
Emile Durkheim, Division of Labor in Society; *Macmillan Publishing Co. Inc*.
Wilson Van Dusen, Natural Depth in Man; *Harper & Row, Publishers, Inc*.
T. S. Eliot, The Family Reunion; *Faber & Faber Ltd*.
Erich Fried, Obituary for those who shouted from Contemporary German Poetry; *by courtesy of Ewald Osers and The Oleander Press*.
Milton Friedman, Capitalism and Freedom; *University of Chicago Press Ltd*.
Erich Fromm, New Knowledge in Human Values; *Harper & Row, Publishers, Inc*.
J. K. Galbraith, The New Industrial State; *Andre Deutsch Ltd*.
David Gascoyne, Night Thoughts; *Andre Deutsch Ltd*.
Ortega y Gasset, The Revolt of the Masses; *George Allen & Unwin (Publishers) Ltd*.
William Gerhardie, Of Mortal Love; *Macdonald & Jane's Publishers Ltd*.
Porter Grainger, T'ain't Nobody's Biz-ness If I Do; *Lawrence Wright Music Company ©1922*.
J. Green, Diary 1928-1957; *Harvill Press Ltd*.
F. A. Hayek, Law, Legislation and Liberty; *Routledge & Kegan Paul Ltd*.
    The Road to Serfdom; *Routledge & Kegan Paul Ltd*.
Martin Heidegger, Being and Time; *Basil Blackwell*.

Hermann Hesse, If the War Goes on; *Jonathan Cape Ltd.*
Knulp; *Jonathan Cape Ltd.*
Johan Huizinga, Homo Ludens; *Routledge & Kegan Paul Ltd.*
C. Jung, Psychology and Religion; *Routledge & Kegan Paul Ltd.*
Undiscovered Self; *Routledge & Kegan Paul Ltd.*
J. M Keynes, The Economic Consequences of the Peace; *Macmillan London and Basingstoke.*
General Theory of Employment; *Macmillan London & Basingstoke.*
Essays in Persuasion; *Macmillan London & Basingstoke.*
John Hick, Death and Eternal Life; *Collins Publishers.*
Sidney Hook, Revolution, Reform and Social Justice; *Basil Blackwell.*
Paul Johnson, Enemies of Society; *Weidenfeld & Nicolson Ltd.*
Franz Kafka, Kafka's Other Trial — the Letters to Felice; *Calder & Boyars Ltd.*
Kena, The Upanishads: Breath of the Eternal. Translated by Swami Prabhavananda and Frederick Manchester, *with permission of Vedanta Society of Southern California.*
Arthur Koestler, The Heel of Achilles; *A. D. Peters & Co. Ltd.*
The Invisible Writing; *A. D. Peters & Co. Ltd.*
David Lane, The Socialist Industrial State; *George Allen & Unwin (Publishers) Ltd.*
G. W. Leibniz, Philosophical Writings. Translated by Mary Morris and G. H. R. Parkinson; *Everyman's University Library; J. M. Dent & Sons Ltd.*
Peter Levi, Death is a Pulpit; *John Johnson (author's agent).*
John MacMurray, Interpreting the Universe; *Faber & Faber Ltd.*
Norman Mailer, Barbary Shore; *Jonathan Cape Ltd.*
Herbert Marcuse, Eros and Civilisation; *Beacon Press.*
Alfred Marshall, Principles of Economics; *Macmillan London and Basingstoke.*
Basil Mitchell, Law, Morality and Religion in a Secular Society; *Oxford University Press.*
Jürgen Moltmann, Theology of Hope; *SCM Press Ltd.*
Malcolm Muggeridge, Jesus Rediscovered; *Collins Publishers.*
F. Musgrove, The Family, Education and Society; *Routledge & Kegan Paul Ltd.*
Ewald Osers, The Temples at Agrigento and Berlin Wall; *Hub Publications Ltd.*
Boris Pasternak, Hamlet in Russia from Imitations by Robert Lowell; *Faber & Faber Ltd.*
Spring 1944, It is Not Seemly, The Wind, To a Friend, After the Storm, from Fifty Poems. Translated by Lydia Pasternak Slater; *George Allen & Unwin (Publishers) Ltd.*
Enoch Powell, Freedom and Reality; *Elliot Right Way Books.*
Herbert Read, Herbert Read: A Memorial Symposium by Robin Skelton; *David Higham Associates.*
Anarchy and Order; *David Higham Associates.*
The Tenth Muse; *David Higham Associates.*
The Limits of Permissiveness in Art; *David Higham Associates.*
Politics of the Unpolitical; *David Higham Associates.*
To a Conscript of 1940 from Collected Poems: *Faber & Faber Ltd.*
Wilhelm Reich, Listen, Little Man! *Souvenir Press Ltd.*
Jean-Francois Revel, Without Marx or Jesus; *Paladin Books Ltd/Granada Publishing Ltd.*
Rainer Maria Rilke, Pigeons from Imitations by Robert Lowell; *Faber & Faber Ltd.*

Everett Robbins, T'ain't Nobody's Biz-ness If I Do; *Lawrence Wright Music Company* ℗*1922.*

Bertrand Russell, Unpopular Essays; *George Allen & Unwin (Publishers) Ltd.*
    Human Society in Ethics and Politics; *George Allen & Unwin (Publishers) Ltd.*
    On Education; *George Allen & Unwin (Publishers) Ltd.*
    A Free Man's Worship; *Longman Group Ltd.*

Jean-Paul Sartre, Being and Nothingness; *Methuen & Co. Ltd. First Published in 1943 under the title of L'Etre et le Néant by Gallimard* ©*1943 by Jean-Paul Sartre. First published in English 1958 by Methuen & Co. English Translation* ℗*1958 Philosophical Library.*

J. A. Schumpeter, Capitalism, Socialism and Democracy; *George Allen & Unwin (Publishers) Ltd.*

L. C. B. Seaman, From Vienna to Versailles; *Methuen & Co. Ltd.*

G. B. Shaw, Man and Superman, Everybody's Political What's What, The Intelligent Woman's Guide to Socialism, Maxims for Revolutionists, The Rejected Statement, History of the English People; *The Society of Authors on behalf of the Bernard Shaw Estate.*

Stephen Spender, The Truly Great, Memento, The Prisoners from Collected Poems; *Faber & Faber Ltd.*

Tibor Szamuely, Communism and Freedom; *Conservative Political Centre.*

Paul Tillich, The Courage To Be; *James Nisbet & Co. Ltd.*

Arnold J. Toynbee, A Study of History; *Oxford University Press.*

Veblen Thorstein, Theory of the Leisure Class; *George Allen & Unwin (Publishers) Ltd.*

Kurt Vonnegut, Mother Night; *Jonathan Cape Ltd.*

Helen Waddell, More Latin Lyrics; *The Executor of the Estate of the Late Helen Waddell and Victor Gollancz Ltd.*

K. W. Watkins, The Practice of Politics; *Thomas Nelson & Sons Ltd.*

Vernon Watkins, The Interval from Affinities; *Faber & Faber Ltd.* ©*Gwen Watkins.*

Simone Weil, Gateway to God; *Collins Publishers.*

V. White, God the Unknown; *Harvill Press Ltd.*

A. N. Whitehead, Adventure of Ideas; *Macmillan Publishing Co. Inc.*
    Science and the Modern World; *Cambridge University Press.*

Clarence Williams, Florida Bound Blues; *B. Feldman & Co. Ltd.*

Virginia Woolf, A Room of One's Own; *the Author's Literary Estate and The Hogarth Press Ltd.*

We are also grateful to the Institute of Economic Affairs for permission to use several of the quotations which appeared in "Not From Benevolence", by Ralph Harris and Arthur Seldon, and for the help of their library staff.

Index of Authors